CIVIL RIGHTS

A current guide

A CBS NEWS REFERENCE BOOK

CIVIL RIGHTS

*A current guide
to the people,
organizations,
and events*

by A. JOHN ADAMS
& JOAN MARTIN BURKE

R. R. BOWKER COMPANY, NEW YORK & LONDON, 1970

Published by R. R. Bowker Co. (A XEROX COMPANY)
1180 Avenue of the Americas, New York, N. Y. 10036
Copyright © 1970 by Columbia Broadcasting System, Inc.

ISBN: 0-8352-0405-7
Library of Congress Catalog Card Number: 70-126010

Printed and bound in the United States of America

Cover photo from Magnum Photos Inc.

Contents

Foreword

This *Current Guide* was originally prepared as a quick reference for the correspondents, producers, and editors of CBS News.

In a time of kaleidoscopic and frequently confusing civil rights activity, when a whole new generation of leaders is jostling for national attention, it is virtually impossible for individual newsmen—or anyone, for that matter—to keep track of the interplay of events and personalities that today are shaping the society of tomorrow. This work was planned simply as a practical aid, to refresh memories on some of the principal persons, dates, and events of the struggle as it has developed over the last fifteen years and as it is happening now. It is intended to be a useful book, not a definitive one.

Nothing is more certain than that those closely involved in the civil rights movements will be able to think of names and events that are not included. There will also be those who feel that a disproportionate amount of attention has been accorded such figures as Stokely Carmichael and Eldridge Cleaver. And still others will wonder at the inclusion of Marlon Brando. Our criterion has been information that the well-informed newsman—and citizen—needs to know, not the specialist. Opinions have been included only where they seem helpful to understanding.

We believe, and most sincerely hope, that this compilation will also be of value to political officials, legislators, teachers, students, agencies, and all individuals who are in some degree concerned with the civil rights movement; and perhaps especially to the person who may have found himself an involuntary spectator, and might like to know more (without being preached to) about who's who and what's what in one of the most important and dramatic periods of social change in the nation's history.

Except where otherwise indicated, most persons in the alphabetical section of *Current Guide* are black. A case undoubtedly could be made for including more white notables, such as New York's Mayor John Lindsay and Senator Jacob Javits, Senator Fred Harris of Oklahoma, former Chief Justice Earl Warren, and others whose contributions can be documented. But a line has to be drawn, and as a guide to the performance of white politicians we have included, as an appendix, the voting record of all congressmen on the landmark civil rights bills of the sixties. Otherwise, the only concession in this direction has been the formal inclusion of former President Johnson, whose administration's contribution to civil rights legislation was of historic proportions.

A. John Adams & Joan Martin Burke
September, 1970

Acknowledgments

Acknowledgments are due particularly to the assistance and advice of
Peter Bailey, *Ebony* magazine; Ponchitta Pierce, CBS News Correspon-
dent; Daniel Watts, *Liberator* magazine; John Henrik Clarke,
Freedomways magazine; Fred Shuttlesworth, former aide to the late
Dr. Martin Luther King, Jr.; Henry Lee Moon, National Association
for the Advancement of Colored People; Ernest Kaiser, Schomburg
Collection of Negro Literature and History, New York Public Library;
Eleanor Farrar and Pauline Schneider, MARC (Metropolitan Applied
Research Center), Washington, D.C.; Howard Glickstein, Civil Rights
Commission, Washington, D.C.; the research staff of the American
Jewish Congress; William V. Shannon and Charlayne Hunter, *New York
Times;* Walter Eling, Esther Safran, and Frances Rademaekers,
Congressional Quarterly, Inc.; Albert Carter, Small Business
Administration; Elmo Roper; William Kunstler; Phyllis Bosworth,
Pamela Gray, Judy Hole, Virginia Huber, and Howard Stringer of the
CBS News Broadcast Research staff; Sherley Abrams and Elizabeth
Pedro, CBS News librarians; CBS News Archivist Samuel T. Suratt, and
Director of Resource Development and Production, Joseph P. Bellon,
without whom this volume would not have appeared; and not least
Richard S. Salant, president of CBS News, whose concern for civil
rights, as for the integrity of CBS News, provided the inspiration for the
original research.

Alphabetical Guide to Individuals & Organizations

". . . The whole gamut of Negro life is
an adventure if you can roll with the punches and
not let it get you into the valley of bitterness."
—*Roy Wilkins*

Alphabetical Guide to Individuals & Organizations

REV. RALPH D. ABERNATHY

President of Southern Christian Leadership Conference (SCLC) since August 1968. One of Martin Luther King's chief lieutenants and closest companions for more than a decade, he assumed leadership of the organization after King was assassinated in April 1968. Led the Poor People's March on Washington in May 1968, led a demonstration at Republican National Convention in Miami, July 1968. Arrested in September of the same year in Atlanta for blocking emergency garbage pickups in support of striking sanitation workers. Was jailed in June 1969, on charges of inciting Charleston, S.C. hospital workers to riot. Helped organize SCLC-sponsored march from Perry, Georgia to Atlanta in May 1970. After military service in World War II, graduated from Alabama State in 1950 and remained there as an instructor. In 1951, joined NAACP and became pastor of First Baptist Church in Montgomery. In 1955, worked with Martin Luther King to organize the famous 381-day Montgomery bus boycott. Then helped King establish the SCLC, and in 1961 became its secretary/treasurer. During the next four years went to jail 19 times with King. King named him his successor in 1965. Born Linden, Alabama, March 11, 1926. Married to the former Juanita O. Jones, 1952; 3 children.

ACT ASSOCIATES

A quasi-functional organization formed in 1965 by a dozen Negro activists dissatisfied with established leadership. Contended that civil rights bills were "not needed" and of little help to urban blacks. Most noted success was suit against Washington, D.C. school board which resulted in landmark decision by U.S. District Judge J. Skelly Wright, June 19, 1967, that "de facto" segregation in D.C. schools was unconstitutional. Currently has only one active group—based in Chicago, headed by Nahaz Rogers. ACT's members, including Jesse Gray, Milton Galamison, Julius Hobson (who filed the Washington suit), are now active with other groups (see individual entries).

ACTION FOR BOSTON COMMUNITY DEVELOPMENT (ABCD)

A long-established, federally-financed group supervising economic welfare projects in Boston's ghetto. Has broad grass-roots representation. Its goals have been described as: building a trade academy; reviewing job training and Head Start classes; initiating programs for the elderly; initiating programs for youth; and forming a consortium of the local universities to pool scholarship money to educate capable students from ghetto areas. Reportedly has helped place 17,000 in jobs since 1966 when its first neighborhood employment center opened. Director is Robert Coard. See also: ROBERT COARD.

ALASKA FEDERATION OF NATIVES

Federation of the native regional organizations in Alaska formed in 1966 to assert native claims to 90 percent of the state's land (340 million acres). The state's 60,000 Eskimos, Aleuts, and Indians contend they hold title to the land because, they argue, the United States did not buy Alaska from Russia in 1867, but only purchased the right to tax and govern the territory. Until Alaska became a state in 1958, ownership of the natives' land had not become an issue. In the eight years following statehood, the U.S. Bureau of Land Management ceded land to the state without consulting the native population. In 1966 a "land freeze" was imposed to halt the land transfers until the end of 1970 pending a congressional decision. A compromise proposal introduced in the Senate would require the natives to give up title to all land except 40 million acres (10 percent of the state) for the sum of $500 million plus 2 percent royalties on revenues from the surrendered land. The federation is supported by various church groups, labor organizations, and private grants. Officers: Emil Notti, founder, an Athapaskan Indian; John Bowbridge, member of the Tlingit and Haida tribe; Eben Hopson, an Eskimo. Headquarters: 1689 C. St., Anchorage, Alaska.

CLIFFORD ALEXANDER, JR.

Made headlines in April 1969 when he resigned as chairman of Equal Employment Opportunity Commission because he questioned the Nixon Administration's commitment to equal treatment for minorities. At that time, he said, "vigorous efforts to enforce laws on employment and discrimination are not among the goals of this administration." His term as a member of the commission ran until July 1972, but he resigned this membership in July 1969 to accept a partnership in Washington law firm of Arnold and Porter. Born 1934. Graduated from Yale Law School.

SAUL DAVID ALINSKY

By his own description a "professional radical" who has campaigned for the poor of all races for over 30 years. Works through Chicago-based Industrial Areas Foundation (IAF), which he formed in 1939, to organize slum-area residents into economic and political blocs. In 1960, helped Rev. Arthur Brazier form Woodlawn Organization to rehabilitate Chicago's South Side, later successfully resisted University of Chicago's efforts to displace a Negro neighborhood for an expansion program, and after Rochester riots of 1964 organized FIGHT (Freedom, Integration, God, Honor, Today) to force Kodak to hire and train 2,000 blacks. Led widespread boycott campaign before agreement with company finally reached June 23, 1967. A sociologist, Alinsky has lectured and written widely on community organization. Born Chicago, January 30, 1909. Graduated from University of Chicago, Ph.B., and St. Procopius College, LL.D. Married, two children. Office: 8 South Michigan Ave., Chicago, Illinois. *See also:* WOODLAWN ORGANIZATION.

AMERICAN CIVIL LIBERTIES UNION (ACLU)

Founded in 1920, ACLU claims to be "the nation's oldest civil liberties organization," and states as its aim "to champion the rights of man set forth in the Declaration of Independence and Constitution." Activities include test court cases, opposition to legislation considered in violation of the Constitution, and public protests. Its record includes numerous landmark cases, among them the Scopes anti-evolution trial, the right of the children of Jehovah's Witnesses not to salute the flag on grounds of their religious conscience, and a battle against official efforts to ban the importation of the James Joyce classic, *Ulysses*. In recent years it has been involved heavily in efforts to obtain full rights for Negroes, from open housing in Chicago to proper representation on juries in Mississippi. In 1964, ACLU opened a Southern Regional Office to expand its activities in the Southern states, where it has fought for proper Negro legal representation, against harassment of attorneys defending Negro clients, for Negro voting rights, and against bans on demonstrations. In the case of Cassius Clay (Muhammad Ali), it raised the issue of racial and religious discrimination in the Selective Service System. In its first five years of operation, the Southern Regional Office alone litigated more than 160 cases, winning 69, losing 34 (others still pending or on appeal). There are 47 affiliates in 45 states with a membership of 144,000. Annual budget (1969) $2 million. ACLU's executive director is John DeJ. Pemberton, Jr. Office: 156 Fifth Avenue, New York, New York. *See also:* CHARLES MORGAN.

AMERICAN G.I. FORUM

One of the oldest agencies aiding Mexican-Americans. Formed after World War II (1948) to help *chicano* veterans obtain their G.I. benefits. Later expanded into a family service organization. Currently is negotiating for funds to set up a series of low-cost housing projects to be based in 13 areas throughout the country. The forum has over 300 chapters in 25 states and the District of Columbia with a membership of more than 40,000. National chairman: Dr. Hector Garcia. National headquarters: 621 Gabaldon Road N.W., Albuquerque, New Mexico. Director of National Information Office: Dr. Andrew Yslas. National Information Office: 805 Fifteenth Street, N.W., Washington, D.C.

AMERICAN INDIANS MOVEMENT (AIM)

Organized in 1968 to mobilize Minneapolis' 9,000-member Indian community (one of the largest concentrations of urban Indians). Major effort to date has been the formation of an "Indian Patrol" (August 1968) in which AIM members, dressed in red jackets and carrying shortwave radios, patrolled the Indian community along with Minneapolis police. For 22 weeks after its inception no "indiscriminate" arrests of Indians were made. The group has also organized boycotts against discriminatory institutions and has been instrumental in establishing an all-Indian advisory board that counsels state and local education authorities. AIM also provides tutorial assistance and is planning to build an Indian center with a grant from the Model Cities program. Although not a national group, AIM units have been set up in Cleveland, Denver, Seattle, Rapid City, S.D., and St. Cloud, Minn. Financial support has been received from church groups and private donations. Claim overall membership of 1,200. Headquarters: 1337 East Franklin, Minneapolis, Minnesota. *See also:* CLYDE BELLECOURT.

AMERICANS FOR INDIAN OPPORTUNITY (AIO)

Newest of the minority self-help organizations. Established February 19, 1970 by LaDonna Harris, a Comanche Indian and wife of Sen. Fred R. Harris (D-Okla), with the backing of John Gardner, head of the National Urban Coalition, the late Walter Reuther, and Steelworkers president I. W. Abel. Stressing the need for a new approach to Indian problems, the AIO concentrates on education, job development, training and providing opportunity for the young. Its plans include an Indian legal defense fund and "bank of expertise" to advise on new Indian programs. (In 1968, Mrs. Harris was appointed to the National Council on Indian Opportunity, a new government agency concerned with Indian affairs headed by Vice President Agnew, but resigned in April, 1970, reportedly because she felt the Council was "either unable or unwilling" to find solutions to Indian problems.) Mrs. Harris is president and acting executive director of AIO as well as Honorary President of the Oklahomans for Indian Opportunity. Headquarters: 1829 Jefferson Place, N.W., Washington, D.C.

EARL ANTHONY

Writer and black militant. First became a civil rights activist in 1965 when he helped organize the first public rent strike in San Francisco. Also helped start Independent Action Movement in the same city to fight for more rights for the black community. In 1967, joined the Black Panther party and later was made its deputy minister of information for Southern California. Was expelled in March 1969 when other high ranking members were purged from Panther ranks. His *Picking Up the Gun: A Report on the Black Panthers* (published by Dial Press, 1970) was written after his expulsion and gives an inside look at the organization and its leaders. Born Roanoke, Virginia, 1941; raised in New York and Los Angeles. Holds a B.A. from University of Southern California, 1963.

LOUIS ARMSTRONG

Perhaps the greatest of all jazz musicians, he once insisted "the horn don't know nothing about these race troubles," but in 1957 (Little Rock) he called off a tour of the Soviet Union for the U.S. government because "the way they are treating my people they can go to hell." Contributes generously to civil rights causes. In 1913, was sent to reform school, the "Colored Waifs' Home for Boys," for shooting off a pistol on New Year's Eve. There learned to play the cornet. Joined Kid Ory's band (1919) and was befriended by King Oliver who helped him develop jazz skills. Considered 1929 the turning point in career. Starred in the revue "Hot Chocolates" and made Fats Waller's "Ain't Misbehavin'" a hit. Acquired nickname Satchmo (short for satchel mouth) at London Palladium. Has played all over the world including Russia and Africa with the Louis Armstrong All-Stars. Appeared in several movies including *High Society* and *The Five Pennies*. Won the jazz prize at the first World Festival of Negro Arts in Dakar, Senegal, in 1966. Asked the secret of his success, he says, "I set myself to be a happy man, and I made it." Born New Orleans, c. 1900. Married four times.

ASSOCIATION ON AMERICAN INDIAN AFFAIRS

Oldest private organization concerned with Indian affairs. Founded in 1922 by white writer Oliver La Farge, its first president. The association turned activist in 1960 and currently has a membership of 50,000. Has initiated programs dealing with health, education, economic development, housing, and legal aid. In 1969, association lawyers worked closely with the American Civil Liberties Union for commutation of the death sentence for a South Dakota Indian, Tom White Hawk, considered by many as a landmark case. Gives grants to such groups as the Organization of Native American Students. Instrumental in establishing the Na-

tional Indian Council on Alcohol (president: George Melissy, executive
director: Harriet Paul) in Minneapolis. Publishes a bi-monthly newsletter, *Indian Affairs.* President: Roger S. Ernst (a former under-secretary of the interior in the Eisenhower Administration). Executive
director: William Byler. Headquarters: 423 Park Avenue South, New
York, New York.

JOAN BAEZ

Folk-singing heroine of the non-conformists. Active in peace marches,
ban-the-bomb campaigns, civil rights, and anti-Vietnam war protest
movements. Founded the Institute for Study of Nonviolence in Carmel
Valley, California. Arrested in 1967 for participation in an anti-draft
protest and served 45 days in jail in Oakland, California. Was sued for
refusing to pay income tax because of opposition to war. Wrote
Daybreak (published by Dial Press 1968), an explanation of her pacifist
ideas. Studied at Boston University Fine Arts School of Drama in 1958
and became a big hit the following year at the Newport Folk Festival.
Since then she has made extensive concert tours of college campuses and
has appeared at Carnegie Hall. Avoids television, Hollywood, and
Broadway. On August 8, 1969, her appearance at New York's Madison
Square Garden was a 20,000 sellout. Born Staten Island, New York,
January 1941. Married to David Harris, 1968 (who in July 1969 began
a three-year jail sentence in Arizona for failure to register for the draft),
one child, Gabriel Earl, born December 2, 1969.

JAMES BALDWIN

Novelist, essayist, and playwright. Became one of the most articulate
spokesmen for the Negro revolution with publication of his "Letter
from a Region in My Mind," in the *New Yorker,* November 17, 1962,
described by critics as the most indelible and frightening description
ever written of what it means to be a Negro in a white society. The
essay was subsequently incorporated into the 1963 best-seller, *The Fire
Next Time,* and for a while Baldwin was hailed on radio, television, and
in lectures across the nation and abroad as the nation's foremost inter-
preter of the "Negro problem," which he insisted was not a Negro
problem, but a white problem. "The victims of segregation are the
white people, because the myth of white supremacy prevents them from
facing their own weaknesses." Addressing the World Council of
Churches in Uppsala, Sweden in July 1968, he charged that the Christian
churches had betrayed the black man—and their own principles—by
their identification with racist institutions. Today, Baldwin is considered
somewhat passé by the new breed of black militants, and his latest novel,
Tell Me How Long the Train's Been Gone, was described as "a disaster"
by critics. Currently lives in Istanbul, Turkey, where he is writing a
new non-fiction work and a new novel. Born August 2, 1924 in New
York City, he attended Frederick Douglass Junior High School and

DeWitt Clinton High School. At 14, he became a Holy Roller preacher in Harlem storefront churches, and after graduating from high school worked as handyman, office boy, factory worker, dishwasher, and waiter, while writing book reviews and essays. In 1948, he won a Rosenwald fellowship and went to live in Paris, where he spent most of the next decade. His first novel, the partly autobiographical *Go Tell It on the Mountain*, was published in 1952. It was followed by *Notes of a Native Son* in 1955, *Giovanni's Room* in 1956. His first play, *The Amen Corner*, was first performed in 1954. His collection of essays, *Nobody Knows My Name*, was named one of the outstanding books of 1961. His novel *Another Country* appeared the same year. And a play, *Blues for Mister Charlie*, a story of racial murder dedicated to victims of racial violence in the South, ran for five months at the ANTA theater on Broadway, April through August 1964, and won the Foreign Press Association's dramatic award for the 1963–64 season.

MARION BARRY, JR.
Executive director of operations for Pride, Inc. since 1968. One of the founders of SNCC, and its first chairman in 1960. In ensuing years, played a leading role in civil rights projects throughout the South, spending time in 15 Southern jails. In January 1968, helped SNCC organize grassroots opposition to the proposed five-cent bus-fare increase in Washington, D.C. Formed "People's Party" slate of candidates for a pilot police district election, February 1970; won 14 of 28 seats. Has been called the "*enfant terrible*" of the civil rights movement. When he joined Pride, he resigned as director of the Washington office of SNCC. Born 1937. Attended LeMoyne College in Memphis, Tennessee and was a graduate student in chemistry at Fisk University. *See also:* PRIDE, INC.

BEDFORD-STUYVESANT DEVELOPMENT AND SERVICE CORPORATION (D & S)
Private, non-profit corporation formed in 1967 (sponsored by late Sen. Robert Kennedy) to develop programs improving living conditions and creating employment in central Brooklyn (New York). President is John Doar. Staffed with experts in law, education, finance, construction, its purpose is to give technical assistance. Works through the Bedford-Stuyvesant Restoration Corp., run by residents of the area and headed by Frank Thomas. Headquarters: 268 Ashland Place, Brooklyn, N.Y. *See also:* JOHN DOAR.

HARRY BELAFONTE
Member of CORE and board of directors of SCLC. Has been leading participant in civil rights marches. Reportedly provided funds for education of the children of the late Martin Luther King. Grew up in West Indies and New York City where he attended high school. Served in the navy 1943 to 1946. Since the early 1950's has enjoyed considerable

international success as a singer and actor. Now president of his own company, Belafonte Enterprises, which produces his records. Always in demand as an entertainer, he nevertheless strictly limits his appearances to allow time for outside activities. Born New York City, March 1, 1927. Married, two children.

CLYDE BELLECOURT
Chippewa Indian, executive director of American Indians Movement and staff member of Minneapolis Urban Coalition. Spent many of his early years in jail, where, he says, he received his only education and learned that he was "not a dirty savage." *See also:* AMERICAN INDIANS MOVEMENT.

L. HOWARD BENNETT
Acting deputy assistant secretary of defense for civil rights, 1968–70. Headed panel looking into racial unrest in the military. According to a *New York Times* November 28, 1969 account, he recommended to the Pentagon "that all services follow the Marine Corps in permitting such open expressions of black pride as the clenched-fist black power salute and the Afro hair style." Joined the defense department in 1963; civil rights director from 1965. Previously a municipal judge in Minneapolis. Born Charleston, South Carolina, February 22, 1913. Attended University of Chicago, LL.D. 1950. Married, one child.

LERONE BENNETT, JR.
Writer and fellow of the Institute of the Black World, Atlanta, Ga. Author of *Black Power U.S.A., Before the Mayflower, A History of the Negro in America, 1919–1966.* Worked as a reporter for the Atlanta *Daily World* (1949–53). Now with the Johnson Publishing Company as senior editor of *Ebony* magazine. Born Clarksdale, Miss., October 17, 1928. Attended public schools in Jackson, Miss. and Morehouse College, A.B. (1949). Married, four children.

REV. JAMES BEVEL
Heads SCLC's direct-action program and had been one of Martin Luther King's chief lieutenants in Northern cities, principally Chicago. Also was director of the nonviolence workshop for the Poor People's Campaign in the summer of 1968. A Baptist minister, became civil rights activist in 1960 with the first sit-in protest in Nashville, Tennessee. Considered among the more radical of King's followers. With his wife, helped found Student Non-violent Coordinating Committee. A bitter critic of American involvement in Vietnam, in 1967 he headed Spring Mobilization to End the War in Vietnam, which organized protest marches in Washington and New York. Says of SCLC: "Christ got the movement started; we are just trying to keep it going." Born Laflore County, Mississippi, 1937. Married to the former Diane Nash. Currently based in Philadelphia.

BLACK ACADEMY OF ARTS AND LETTERS

Formed early in 1969 by a group of black scholars, artists and authors to provide "recognition and encouragement" to those contributing to the interpretation and projection of the black experience in America. In July, 1970, announced that the late W. E. B. DuBois, historian Carter G. Woodson, and the artist Henry O. Tanner had been named to its newly established Hall of Fame. Academy also protested denial of visa to the widow of DuBois, who wanted to visit U.S. from her home in Cairo. Academy president: Dr. C. Eric Lincoln, of Union Theological Seminary; Executive director: Mrs. Julia Prettyman. Address: 475 Riverside Drive, New York City.

BLACK DEVELOPMENT ADVISORY COUNCIL

Formed by 40 middle-class black organizations and civil rights leaders in 1968 to act as advisor to the Small Business Administration. Also advises SBA on Operation Business Mainstream (which promotes businesses owned by blacks and other minorities in the nation's ghettos, by encouraging extension of private bank credit through government guarantees and by supplying advisory services). Also serves as a national communication forum for black economic development groups. Council chairman: Dr. Walter Cooper. Headquarters: 1441 L Street, N.W., Washington, D.C. *See also:* WALTER COOPER.

BLACK ECONOMIC DEVELOPMENT CONFERENCE (BEDC)

Organization in whose name James Forman demanded $500 million "reparations" from white churches and synagogues in a series of dramatic appearances in May 1969, including disruption of communion service at New York City's Riverside Church, May 4. Forman later raised demand to $3 billion, but on August 17 lost his position as acting chairman. The organization under its new chairman, Dr. Calvin Marshall (a Methodist Zionist minister), made it known that its aims were now more "realistic." BEDC developed as a permanent agency from a conference sponsored by the Internal Foundation in Detroit in April 1969. The conference's aim was to dramatize the need for financial aid for its community projects. It adopted a "Black Manifesto," written largely by Forman, setting forth the demand for the $500 million which, it explained, represented $15 for every black in the United States. Marshall estimates that between $60–90 million have been promised by churches due to the pressure of the "manifesto." Today, the organization operates out of Dr. Calvin Marshall's New York office, with a staff of 30. Forman remains a committee member. Marshall's office: 806 Quincy St., Brooklyn, N.Y.

BLACK ECONOMIC UNION (BEU)

Formerly called Negro Industrial and Economic Union. Founded in 1967 by football star Jimmy Brown. Encourages blacks to go into business for themselves by making low interest loans available. Has offices in New York, Washington, Cleveland, Los Angeles, Kansas City, and Oakland. Brown and associates began the organization with their own capital before receiving grants from the Ford Foundation and the Economic Development Administration for around $750,000. After two years of operation had made over 200 loans to aspiring black business-men across the country. *See also:* JAMES NATHANIEL BROWN.

BLACK MUSLIMS
Veteran Chicago-based black nationalist group (also called Nation of Islam) with secret membership estimated between 50,000 and 250,000. Headed by Elijah Muhammad since 1930. Preaching racial separatism and black supremacy, movement did not gain popularity until 1950's. By early 1960's, had gained reputation as a fanatic and anti-Christian organization whose rigid discipline and doctrines threatened violent rebellion, despite proclaimed policy of nonviolence. Discipline includes rigid personal health habits, abstention from tobacco and alcohol, and extreme modesty for women. Muslims maintain their own police force, and refuse to vote or perform military service. Today, image is less fierce, with chief emphasis on "black capitalism." Aim is reportedly a Muslim-owned financial empire as cornerstone of self-sufficient "Black Islam Nation." In 1968, Muslims invested $6 million in business ventures. In March 1969, reported negotiating $20 million in loans. In November 1969, more than 2,000 whites protested Muslim plans to buy farmland near Birmingham, Alabama, reportedly part of Muslim program to buy thousands of acres in the South. Following the purchase, the Muslim-owned land was subjected to months of harassment, including poisoning of the water, which killed 30 head of cattle. Muslims announced in March 1970 that they were selling the land—to the Ku Klux Klan. How-ever, Muslims have pursued purchase of farmland elsewhere, including Michigan and Georgia, for produce and livestock to supply their stores and restaurants in Chicago, and eventually in other cities. Plans include a new headquarters to handle such diverse operations as meat-processing, garment-making, central accounting, and publishing. Muslims also run 47 schools and a University of Islam. Their newspaper, *Muhammad Speaks*, has a reported weekly circulation of 500,000. Among prominent Black Muslims were Malcolm X who left the movement in 1964, declar-ing himself against racism and segregation, and Cassius Clay, who was expelled in April 1969. *See also:* CASSIUS CLAY, ELIJAH MUHAM-MAD.

BLACK PANTHER PARTY FOR SELF-DEFENSE (BPP)
Organized in 1965 after the Watts riots, by early 1969 the Black Panther party had a membership estimated at three to five thousand with as many as 40 chapters in major cities such as New York, Chicago, and De-troit, and in Georgia, Tennessee, and other states, as well as Cali-

fornia. Its headquarters are in Oakland. Organized by Huey Newton and Bobby Seale while they were students at Merritt College in Oakland, purpose was to provide armed patrols to follow the police and intervene when they felt police were out of line. The Black Panther symbol was adopted, Newton explains, to signify that, like the panther, they would not attack unless attacked. The party's purpose is also said to be to break the "oppressive grip of the white power structure on black communities." Panthers stress pride, discipline, and clean living among followers, discouraging the use of drugs and alcohol.

On May 2, 1967, 30 armed Panthers invaded the chambers of the California state legislature in Sacramento, to protest pending legislation to ban the carrying of loaded weapons in public. On April 6, 1968, Panther member Bobby James Hutton, 17, was killed during a gun battle between Negroes and police in West Oakland. Panther education minister Eldridge Cleaver was injured, along with two policemen. On September 8, 1968, Panther founder Huey Newton was convicted of manslaughter in the October 28, 1967 shooting of Oakland patrolman John Frey. Newton was sentenced to 2 to 15 years imprisonment. The 7-week trial touched off extensive "free Huey" demonstrations.

In November 1968, police and Panthers fought gun battles in Berkeley and San Francisco, and there were incidents between Panthers and police in New York and New Jersey, including the machine-gunning of a Jersey City police station on November 29, and a fire-bomb attack on Newark Panther headquarters on December 1.

In an apparent move to improve the Panthers' image, Bobby Seale stated in January 1969, that efforts were being made to prevent the use of the organization by "provocateur agents, kooks, and avaricious fools" seeking a base for crime, and announced that a number of criminal suspects had been expelled.

On January 17, 1969, two Panther members were shot to death during a student meeting at UCLA, and a Panther spokesman described the deaths as "political assassinations" by a rival organization. On April 2, 1969, 21 members of the Panthers were indicted in New York on charges of conspiring to blow up several public buildings, including five department stores. Bail was set at $100,000 each. Lawyer William Kunstler described the case as a "turning point" in authorities' offensive against militant blacks. After stormy pre-trial hearings in Feb.-Mar. 1970, a trial date had not been set as of June 1970. July 14, 1969, FBI Director J. Edgar Hoover reported that "of black groups, the Black Panthers without question represent the greatest threat to internal security of the country." July 21, five policemen were shot in a gunfight at Panther offices in Chicago, in a growing series of police-Panther clashes across the country. These appeared to culminate in the killing of Panther leader Fred Hampton in a pre-dawn apartment raid in Chicago on December 4, 1969, and a raid on the Panthers' Los Angeles headquarters December

8, 1969, in which three Panthers and three policemen were wounded in a four-hour gun battle. The raids, particularly the Chicago incident, touched off a wave of protests, public sympathy and demands for investigation of police actions. A federal investigation led by Assistant Attorney General Jerris Leonard later sharply criticized police and other authorities' procedures in the case and in June, 1970, a special grand jury investigation was ordered.

On December 5, 1969, Panthers' lawyer Charles R. Garry claimed that a total of 28 Panther members had been killed by police. A study by the ACLU issued December 9 listed 12 Panthers killed and 12 wounded since October 28, 1967. During the same period, three policemen had been killed and 24 wounded in clashes with Panthers, ACLU reported.

Panther leader David Hilliard was arrested December 3 on charges that he had threatened the life of President Nixon in a speech at the November 15 Moratorium Day rally in San Francisco, in which he allegedly accused the President of being "the man responsible for all the attacks on the Black Panther party nationally" and added "we will kill Richard Nixon."

On December 28, the American Civil Liberties Union announced that after a survey in nine metropolitan centers it was their conclusion that law enforcement agencies across the country were "waging a drive against the Black Panther party resulting in serious civil liberties violations." Among other investigations of the Chicago shooting was that of the all black Ad Hoc Committee of U.S. Congressmen, headed by Rep. Charles C. Diggs, Jr. (D-Mich.), which according to Panther leader David Hilliard was the only group the Panthers themselves had faith in. Among critics of police methods was Seattle Mayor Wesley C. Uhlman, who declared in a speech that he had refused to permit a raid on the local Panther headquarters, saying the police raids reminded him of "midnight Gestapo-type" operations. One of the more unusual demonstrations of sympathy for the Panthers was a fund-raising party in January, 1970, at the fashionable New York apartment of conductor Leonard Bernstein, which highlighted a number of similar gatherings between Panther representatives and New York socialites.

A major Panther trial in 1970 involved national chairman Bobby Seale and 13 other Panthers, on charges concerning the murder of Panther member Alex Rackley, in New Haven, Connecticut. Among continuing investigations of the Panthers was one by the Internal Security Committee of the House of Representatives, whose chairman, Rep. Richard H. Ichord (D-Mo.), said in February 1970, that his panel wanted to "expose the party's finances, its objectives, its connections with what may be hostile foreign powers." The American Jewish Committee released a report February 14, 1970, linking the Black Panthers with the Arab guerilla organization, Al Fatah. By early 1970, Panther party membership was reported to be under 1,000. Its national headquarters is at 3106 Shattuck Avenue, Oakland, California. *See also:* STOKELY CARMICHAEL, ELDRIDGE CLEAVER, KATHLEEN CLEAVER, WILLIAM KUNTSLER, HUEY NEWTON, BOBBY SEALE.

BLACK P. STONE NATION

Biggest, best-organized youth gang in the United States and active force in Chicago's Coalition for United Community Action, formed 1968. Began in 1960 as a gang of 30 Blackstone Avenue youths on Chicago's South Side, who as Blackstone Rangers gained notoriety in battles with rival gang, the East Side Disciples. In 1967, Office of Economic Opportunity funded a "high-risk" job-training program involving Rangers and Disciples. This led to charges at Senate Permanent Investigations sub-committee hearings in June 1968 that the aim of the $927,341 program was merely to "buy peace" on Chicago's South Side. The committee charged that funds had been misused for extortion and drug and gun traffic. The federal funds were discontinued. Today, the Rangers claim a membership of more than 7,000, mostly in the predominantly black Woodlawn area. Under their new name, the Black P. (Peace) Stone Nation, they often appear as a bodyguard for SCLC's Rev. Jesse Jackson, a moderating influence on the gang. Headquarters: Chicago Black P. Stone Nation Youth Center, 6700 South Blackstone Avenue, Chicago, Illinois. *See also:* COALITION FOR UNITED COMMUNITY ACTION.

BLACK UNITED FRONT (BUF)

Founded during a January 1968 secret meeting called by Stokely Carmichael with some 100 Negro leaders representing about 20 organizations participating. BUF is a coalition of all-black organizations in Washington, D.C. that are concerned with the struggle for equal opportunity. Its structure is informal. In the winter of 1969, the organization's militant faction wanted to adopt a platform calling for the organization of a vigilante black force to protect the ghetto and oust local police from Negro areas altogether. This action was provoked after the killing of a patrolman in July 1968. Some members of the BUF issued a resolution stating that the slaying was justified. Mayor Walter E. Washington denounced the resolution and called it inflammatory and irresponsible. This issue split the organization. Rev. Channing Phillips was one of the active early leaders and considered the brains of the organization. In 1970, the organization was headed by Rev. Douglas Moore. Unrelated black united fronts have also been formed in other communities. *See also:* REV. CHANNING PHILLIPS.

JULIAN BOND

Georgia state representative. His name was put in nomination for vice-president at 1968 Democratic National Convention, but later withdrawn. Considered one of the most articulate and attractive moderate Negro voices, is a professed admirer of both Martin Luther King and Stokely

Carmichael. Believes emphasis should be on providing jobs and dividing power more equitably, rather than on integration or black nationalism. "As power begins to be divided more equitably, then you are going to see a lessening of what you call the racial problem. . . . I don't think it's going to happen quickly." Has been critical of student radicals, black and white: "All they do is talk, but they never do anything."

In 1965, at age 25, elected to Georgia state legislature for new seat created by Supreme Court decision on reapportionment. He and seven others were the first Negroes to be elected in 58 years. But by vote of 184–12, the house refused to permit him to take his seat, citing "disloyalty" in a statement by Bond in which he stated he admired draftcard burners. Bond, at the time an official of SNCC, also endorsed a SNCC statement opposing the Vietnam war. He resigned from SNCC in September 1966, "for personal reasons," and was reelected to the legislature in a special election in November 1966, but again denied his seat. On December 5, 1966, the Supreme Court ruled that the Georgia House of Representatives had violated Bond's constitutional rights by excluding him, and he was sworn in on January 9, 1967. (Bond later explained that his draft-card statement had been widely misquoted, that he had stated that he would not burn his draft card, but he understood why people did burn theirs, and admired their courage in view of the known penalties.)

Born in 1940 in Pennsylvania, the son of educator H. M. Bond (currently dean of the University of Atlanta), attended a white Quaker private school near Lincoln University (where his father was then president). Later studied philosophy under Martin Luther King at Morehouse College but left during his senior year to work full-time for SNCC as communications director. Also worked as reporter and later managing editor of the *Atlanta Inquirer*. Married to the former Alice Clopton, four children.

THOMAS BRADLEY

Los Angeles city councilman and former police lieutenant who in April 1969, appeared close to becoming the first black mayor of Los Angeles. In a nonpartisan primary on April 1 he defeated incumbent Sam Yorty by 293,753 to 183,334 votes in a city only 18 percent black. However, Bradley fell short of the majority needed to win. A runoff was held May 27, in which Yorty came back to win by 447,030 (53 percent) to 392,379 (47 percent), after accusing Bradley of running a "racist" campaign. Yorty himself was widely accused by the press of playing on racial fears. Bradley's performance and near victory was nevertheless considered highly impressive, and his campaign—with some 10,000 volunteers—attracted national attention. He was endorsed by leaders of the Democratic party including former Vice-President Humphrey, and Senators Edward Kennedy, Edmund Muskie, Fred Harris, and Alan Cranston, and received contributions from thousands of donors across the nation.

In May 1970, after an extensive tour of black communities across the country, he concluded that "black Americans today are more bitter and frustrated than ever before. . . ." He was born in 1918.

MARLON BRANDO
Leading white actor who withdrew from two motion pictures in 1968, to devote himself to aiding the SCLC and Martin Luther King Foundation. In April 1968, he demonstrated his sympathy with the Black Panther movement by attending the funeral of 17-year-old Bobby James Hutton, killed by a policeman in Oakland, California. Has said major problem in civil rights is communication: "We must inform the blind, bigoted and uninformed people. If not, there will be a revolution in this country unless we change our thinking. I don't believe it will come from the black community, or from the Indians or Mexican-Americans, but from white college students and other young people." He has traveled across country studying problems of poor and raising money for minority groups. Born Omaha, Nebraska, April 3, 1924. Attended Shattuck Military Academy, 1939–41. First Broadway success, *A Streetcar Named Desire*, 1948. Won Academy Award for best actor in *On the Waterfront*, 1954.

ANDREW FULTON BRIMMER
First Negro to be appointed a member of the Board of Governors of the Federal Reserve System (1966) and as such, the highest ranking black in government. He has been highly critical of the merits of black capitalism, which has put him at odds with the Nixon Administration. In a March 1970 speech at Tuskegee Institute in Alabama, he said that while Negroes had made significant economic progress during the 1960's, the gains were so unevenly distributed that there was a "deepening schism in the black community." Born in Kentucky in 1926 in a log cabin, son of a Mississippi farmer, and one of five children. Served in the army infantry during World War II and resumed his education afterwards. Graduated from the University of Washington in 1947 with a B.A. in economics and in 1951 received an M.A. Won a Fulbright Fellowship to India the same year. From 1953–54, served as a research assistant on India at M.I.T. From 1955–58, served as economist with New York Federal Reserve Bank. Received Ph.D. at Harvard in 1957 in monetary economics employment theory and international trade and economics. Taught at Wharton School of University of Pennsylvania in 1961 and joined the Department of Commerce in 1963, where he became assistant secretary in 1965. Married to the former Doris M. Scott, one daughter.

EDWARD BROOKE
Republican senator from Massachusetts, first Negro elected to the Senate since Reconstruction. Served on Boston Finance Commission and

was the first Negro in Massachusetts to become state attorney general (1962). Won his Senate seat in 1966. Supported Rockefeller for president in 1968 and seconded his nomination at the Republican National Convention in Miami in July 1968. Turned down a possible cabinet appointment for secretary of housing and urban development after a meeting with President-elect Nixon on November 27, 1968. Born in Washington, D.C. on October 26, 1919. Received a B.S. from Howard University in 1941. Inducted into an all-Negro infantry unit in World War II, rose to the rank of captain and won the Bronze Star for intelligence work. Received LL.B. from Boston University law school in 1948, admitted to the Massachusetts bar the same year. Married to the former Remigia Ferrari-Scacco, at Genoa, Italy, on June 7, 1947, two daughters.

BROWN BERETS
Established in December 1967 to protect the rights of Mexican-Americans, the Brown Berets now claim representation in many areas of the Southwest and West, with some 30 chapters and over 2,000 members. Activities include a free medical clinic. Founded by David Sanchez. First named the Young Citizens for Community Action. Name later changed to Brown Berets, Sanchez said, to "symbolize the culture of my people." Sanchez describes the organization as neither violent nor nonviolent, but an emergency operation to combat the racial crisis. Its motto is "Serve—Observe—Protect." *See also:* DAVID SANCHEZ.

CLAUDE BROWN
Author of 1965 best-seller *Manchild in the Promised Land*, a searing account of his Harlem upbringing. Star witness at Senate crime committee hearings on August 30, 1966, when he provided colorful testimony on drugs, drinking, and delinquency. Testified again, August 5, 1969, before House Select Committee on Crime (created May 1, 1969), at which he urged legalization of drugs. Argued that drugs are necessary for release from ghetto life, and the legalization would help curb crime. A street fighter at age six, at 11 he was a member of the Buccaneer "bopping gang" and its elite stealing group known as the Forty Thieves. After several stints in the Wiltwyck school for disturbed and deprived boys and the Warwick reform school, he finished high school and graduated from Howard University in 1965. Afterwards attended Rutgers law school. In summer 1969, taught creative writing course at University of California at Santa Barbara while working on his second book, dealing with the last 12 years of Malcolm X's life. Lectures widely. Once announced his intention to unseat Adam Clayton Powell. Born February 23, 1937, in New York.

H. RAP BROWN
Succeeded Stokely Carmichael as chairman of SNCC in May 1967. Did not seek reelection in 1968, but reelected chairman July 22, 1969.

Earned notoriety with his televised statement that "violence is as American as cherry pie" at a Washington, D.C. rally on July 27, 1967. Full statement was: "This country was born of violence. Violence is as American as cherry pie. Black people have always been violent, but our violence has always been directed toward each other. If non-violence is to be practiced, then it should be practiced in our community and end there." At same rally, declared: "If Washington, D.C., doesn't come around, Washington, D.C. should be burned down." At Senate Judiciary Committee hearings, August 2, 1967, police chief cited an inflammatory speech by Brown as "sole reason" for Cambridge, Maryland riot, July 28. Indicted by Maryland grand jury, August 14. Arrested New York, August 19, 1967, on federal charge of carrying gun across state lines while under indictment. In statement August 20, claimed he was being held as a political prisoner. After release on bail, August 22, told crowd of Negroes on courthouse steps: "We're at war . . . and you better get yourself some guns." During 1968 Columbia University disorders, Brown and Carmichael met with demonstrators at Hamilton Hall, April 26. On May 22, 1968, Brown was convicted by a federal court in New Orleans for violating the Federal Firearms Act. He was sentenced to five years in prison and fined $2,000, the maximum sentence. After serving time in Port Allen jail, near New Orleans, Brown was released in July 1969, into the custody of his lawyer, on two $15,000 bonds, his movements to be restricted to eastern Louisiana and southern New York (Bronx and Manhattan). He was released when the Court of Appeals vacated the conviction, pending a wiretapping appeal.

On May 4, 1970, after failing to appear for the long-delayed trial at Ellicott City, Maryland (for the Cambridge, Md. 1967 indictment) Brown automatically forfeited his $10,000 bail. On May 22, 1970, it was widely reported that Brown was in Algeria.

Born in Batan Rouge, Louisiana, October 4, 1943. Attended Southern University, but left in his senior year to work for SNCC. Author of *Die Nigger Die*, published April 1969 by Dial Press. Married (May 3, 1968) New York City school teacher Lynne Doswell.

JAMES BROWN
Nation's king of soul music. Proclaims his faith in America, but adds: "I can't rest until the black man in America is let out of jail, until his dollar's as good as the next man's." Advises kids to stay in school—the name of his fan club is "Don't be a Dropout." Reportedly gives 10 percent of his income to youth groups and charities. By appearances on radio and television in Boston and Washington, D.C., he helped cool riots which followed Martin Luther King's assassination. Unlike some other soul singers, he believes that the good life is in reach of the Negro, and according to a *Newsweek* article of July 1, 1968 he is the man who speaks for the black man on the street. Said *Newsweek*, "It's symptomatic of America's agonizing dilemma that most white people have

never heard of him. But to Negroes he is king, the man who made it."
Born in 1932 and raised in Augusta, Georgia, he dropped out of school
in the seventh grade. Was arrested at 16 (car theft, breaking and enter-
ing) and paroled three years later. Earned a precarious living as shoeshine boy, cotton picker, and prize-fighter before singing spirituals in a
Toccoa, Georgia church. Today employs around a hundred people in a
business empire that brings in $4 million a year and includes two radio
stations, music publishing companies and extensive real estate. Has sold
more than 50 million records, and in 1968 attracted 40,000 fans to hear
him one night at Yankee Stadium. Is separated from his wife, has one
son.

JAMES NATHANIEL BROWN
Played professional football with the Cleveland Browns. Has been called
the greatest offensive back in history. Retired from pro ball in 1966 to
devote himself to the improvement of Negro businesses and to a movie
career (first major film, *Dirty Dozen*). In 1967, he helped form the Black
Economic Union, which aims at encouraging blacks to go into business
for themselves by making low interest loans available. Has been brought
to court several times in recent years, on charges usually involving
illegal use of hands on both men and women. Says Brown: "I walk tall.
I do my thing. They try to break you. They won't break me." Born
February 7, 1936 on St. Simon Island in Georgia. Moved to Manhasset,
New York at the age of seven and after graduating from Manhasset High
School had a choice of 42 college scholarships as well as professional
offers to play football. Chose Syracuse University where he became
All-American in football and lacrosse. Graduated in 1957 with B.A.
degree. *See also:* BLACK ECONOMIC UNION.

ROBERT J. BROWN
Special assistant to President Nixon at the White House. A former
businessman, he was born Feburary 26, 1935 in Highpoint, North Carolina. He is a former president of B & C Associates in Highpoint, a public
relations and market research firm. In August '70, he stated that the
president was "becoming more sensitive to the problems of blacks."

WILLIAM H. BROWN III
Chairman of Equal Employment Opportunity Commission. A Republi-
can appointed by President Nixon, Brown replaced Clifford Alexander,
Jr., a Democrat, in April 1969 after Alexander resigned. Holds a B.S.
degree from Temple ('52) and LLD from Univ. of Penn. ('55). Born
Jan. 19, 1928 in Philadelphia.

LOUIS R. BRUCE
Commissioner of the Bureau of Indian Affairs in the Department of the
Interior, appointed by President Nixon in September 1969. Member of
the Oglala Sioux tribe of South Dakota. Before present appointment

was in public relations and executive director of Zeta Psi foundation and fraternity. In 1961, organized the first National Indian Council on Housing. Recipient of the American Indian Achievement Award. Received Medal of Freedom from President Eisenhower for "outstanding contributions in promoting the American way of life." Born in 1906. Office: 1951 Constitution Ave., N.W., Washington, D.C. *See also:* BUREAU OF INDIAN AFFAIRS.

RALPH BUNCHE

Under-secretary for political affairs at the United Nations since 1958. On April 12, 1967, took issue with what he called Dr. Martin Luther King's suggestion that the civil rights and peace movements merge. As a NAACP director, Bunche persuaded the NAACP board to adopt a resolution criticizing King's position. King denied the charges and Bunche accepted King's disavowal on April 13, 1967. Born in Detroit, Michigan on August 7, 1904. Received a B.A. from University of California at Los Angeles, an M.A. from Harvard University in 1928, and a Ph.D. from Harvard in 1934. Did post-doctoral work in anthropology and colonial policy at Northwestern University, attended the London School of Economics, and the University of Capetown, South Africa. Has taught at the University of California at Los Angeles, Howard University, and Swarthmore College. Was the recipient of the Nobel Peace Prize in 1950. Was with the Office of Strategic Services (1941–44) and various state department posts before his United Nations appointment. Married Ruth Ethel Harris in 1930, three children.

BUREAU OF INDIAN AFFAIRS (BIA)

Agency within Department of the Interior responsible for the administration and welfare of some 400,000 Indians, including 28,000 Aleuts and Eskimos. As trustee of lands owned by the Indians, it controls over 263 separate reservations, pueblos, and colonies, as well as scattered lands in 26 states from Florida to Alaska. With an annual budget of approximately 300 million dollars it attempts to provide improved housing, schools, job training, and health service programs. Despite its status as the nation's largest employer of Indians, the bureau has been described as "a major hurdle to Indian progress" (*Christian Science Monitor,* January 13, 1970), and is criticized for its power over Indians' private and public lives and its fumbling bureaucracy. However many Indian spokesmen claim that, for better or worse, the bureau is their only defense against extinction as a racial and cultural entity.

The BIA was created in 1834 as part of the Department of War to negotiate with hostile Indian tribes. In 1849 it was transferred to the Department of the Interior. In 1969, Secretary of the Interior Walter Hickel announced a major reorganization of the BIA, including, for the first time in the bureau's history, top administrative positions for established Indian leaders. Office: 1951 Constitution Ave., N.W., Washington, D.C. *See also:* LOUIS R. BRUCE.

EUGENE S. CALLENDER
President of the New York Urban Coalition. Elected August 21, 1969, he is currently on leave of absence as deputy administrator of the Housing and Development Administration of New York City. In 1967 he served as a member of the President's Task Force on Manpower and Urban Unemployment. A resident of New York City, he has been actively involved in programs for social change in local communities. Chaired committee that drafted the proposal for HARYOU-Act, the nation's first federal program for youth in the ghettos, and for three years was chairman of its board of directors. Former executive director of the New York Urban League. Founder of the street academies program and of Harlem Prep. Born Cambridge, Massachusetts, in 1926, he graduated from Boston University and Westminster Theological Seminary in Philadelphia. An ordained minister, he lectures frequently at colleges across the nation. Married to the former Lemoine DeLeaver, assistant to the dean of faculty at Barnard College. Three children.

GODFREY CAMBRIDGE
Comedian and actor, noted for his racial satire. In December 1968, became a charter member of a committee to help pay off the $50,000 promissory note for Eldridge Cleaver when he forfeited bail. He has said, "You're not going to find me on any picket lines. In the first place, I'm not non-violent." Born in Harlem, he was sent to Nova Scotia for elementary schooling "to miss the Harlem schools." Returned to New York for high school and attended Hofstra University for two and a half years. Made his Broadway debut in *Nature's Way,* and won an Obie award for his performance in *The Blacks* in 1961. Frequently appears on television. In 1969 made the film *Cotton Comes to Harlem,* in which he plays a Harlem detective. Divorced.

STOKELY CARMICHAEL
Former chairman of SNCC and one of the most charismatic of the new breed of militant black leaders. First popularized the phrase "black power" during a voting rights march in June 1966. Carmichael asserted the phrase meant nothing more than "a way to help Negroes develop racial pride and use the ballot for education and economic development." In his book *Black Power: The Politics of Liberation in America,* which he wrote with Professor Charles V. Hamilton, he states "the concept of Black Power rests on a fundamental premise: before a group can enter the open society, it must close ranks. By this we mean that group solidarity is necessary before a group can operate effectively from a bargaining position of strength in a pluralistic society." Carmichael broke with SNCC in May 1967. Officially expelled in August 1968 when the alliance between SNCC and the Black Panther party

ended at a meeting of the two groups in New York City, SNCC leaders voted to terminate their relationship with Carmichael, who was then prime minister of the Panthers.

From May to December 1967, he went on a world tour, visiting Britain, Czechoslovakia, Cuba (for which the United States revoked his passport), North Vietnam, Algeria, Egypt, Syria, and Guinea. While in Havana, he was quoted as saying: "We must internationalize our struggle, and if we are going to turn into reality the words of Che [Guevara] to create two, three and more Vietnams, we must recognize that Detroit and New York are also Vietnam."

Carmichael returned to the United States amid a storm of legislative protest. His passport was lifted and indictment proceedings were initiated against him by the justice department for preaching sedition. Carmichael settled in Washington, D.C. in 1968 and helped organize the Black United Front. He called a secret meeting of 100 black leaders representing some 20 organizations in Washington, D.C., on January 9, 1968 and formed the front to organize Negroes in the nation's capital. He married South African singer Miriam Makeba in April 1968 and in the spring of 1969 they went to live in Conakry, Guinea. Carmichael publicly broke with the Black Panthers in July, 1969, saying he could no longer support "the present tactics and methods which the party is using to coerce and force everyone to submit to its authority" and was denounced for his action by fellow Panther-in-exile Eldridge Cleaver. In an interview in Algiers Carmichael said he intended ultimately to return to the United States, but first wanted to work for the return to power of Ghana's Kwame Nkrumah.

However, Carmichael returned to the United States on March 18, 1970, and declared that he intended to wage "a relentless struggle against the poison of drugs in the black community." A few days later, on March 25, he was called before a closed session of the Senate Internal Security Subcommittee and questioned about his activities while abroad.

Carmichael was born in Trinidad, June 21, 1941. He moved to New York City at age 11, and grew up in a predominantly white neighborhood in the Bronx. Has degree in philosophy from Howard University (1964).

DIAHANN CARROL

Singer and actress, currently starring in her own television series, "Julia," the first network series focusing on a black family. In 1963 testified before a congressional hearing on racial discrimination in the entertainment world where she called herself "living proof of the horror of discrimination." Born July 1935 in the Bronx, New York. Won a Metropolitan Opera scholarship at the age of 10 but gave it up after a month. Graduated from the High School of Music and Art and went to New York University but left after a year to go into show business via modeling. Began her career as a night club singer. First musical was

House of Flowers. Has made several movies (*Carmen, Porgy and Bess*). In 1962 starred in Richard Rodgers' *No Strings.*

ROBERT (SONNY) CARSON
Heads the Brooklyn chapter of CORE and is widely regarded as an extremist. During the 1968 CORE national convention in Columbus, Ohio, he and 16 heads of other CORE chapters walked out of the convention. At issue was whether Negroes should lead a reform or a revolutionary movement, as Carson's group advocated, and this caused an ideological split in the organization. Teaches at the School of Common Sense, 7 Monroe Street, Brooklyn, New York. Office: 429 Clinton Ave., Brooklyn, New York.

LEONARD H. CARTER
West Coast regional director of the NAACP. A native of Minneapolis, Minnesota. Before joining NAACP staff, was secretary-treasurer of the Dining Car Employees Union Local 516, of the Great Northern Railway Company and later auditor to the National Joint Council of Dining Car Employees. Married, four children. Office: 948 Market St., San Francisco, California.

LISLE CARTER
Vice President for Social and Environmental studies at Cornell University, Ithaca, N.Y., since September 1968. First black assistant secretary in the Department of Health, Education, and Welfare. Appointed January 1966. Born in New York City on November 18, 1925, he graduated from Dartmouth in 1944 and St. John's University law school in 1950. Before working for the government, he practiced law in New York and was on legal staff of NAACP. Married to the former Emily E. Ellis in 1950, five children.

ARTHUR A. CHAPIN
Director of Office of Equal Opportunity in the Department of Labor. Has been with the labor department since 1961, and is an assistant to the secretary of labor. Earlier he served as assistant to the president of the New Jersey Congress of Industrial Organizations Council concerned with civil rights legislation, minimum wage, and unemployment compensation. Also served as a member of the New Jersey Committee on Housing and of a state wage panel for restaurant employees. Since joining the labor department has helped compile an annual directory of Negro college graduates for business and industry.

CESAR CHAVEZ
California grape-pickers' leader who since 1965 has won widespread national support for strike and boycott actions against table-grape growers. Executive director of the United Farm Workers Organizing Committee (AFL-CIO), which he founded in 1962. Began strike against San

Joaquin Valley growers in September 1965. In March and April 1966, led 300-mile protest march to Sacramento to gain support of Gov. Pat Brown. By end of 1966, several San Joaquin Valley growers, including the big Di Giorgio Corporation, agreed to sign contracts with the union. In 1967, when bitterness led to outbreaks of violence, Chavez fasted for 25 days "to recall farm workers to the nonviolent roots of their movement."

After being bedridden for a year with a back ailment, Chavez began touring the country early in 1969 to broaden support for "La Causa." In May 1969, he led 100-mile march to the Mexican border to urge Mexican farm workers who crossed border to join the union. Won support of Mexico's Confederation of Workers. March was joined by Rev. Ralph Abernathy, who said it symbolized "a black and brown coalition of the poor," and by Sen. Edward Kennedy, who on May 18 told the marchers that "the voice of Cesar Chavez is being heard in Congress." In September 1969, Chavez charged before the Senate Sub-committee on Migratory Labor that grape growers were "systematically poisoning" field workers with pesticides.

By the end of 1969, Chavez claimed that California grape sales were down 27 percent. The growers responded with a $75 million suit for damages against the union and a $4 million anti-boycott campaign. A major breakthrough came April 1, 1970, when three Coachella Valley table-grape growers (constituting 10 percent of table-grape producers) signed a contract with the union, to be followed soon by others. Recognition of the union, including the use of the union label, came after four and a half years of union picketing and was hailed by Chavez as, an essential victory. Married, 8 children.

SHIRLEY CHISHOLM

Democratic representative from New York, she is the first Negro woman ever elected to Congress. Elected November 5, 1968, from New York's Twelfth Congressional District (Bedford-Stuyvesant), she defeated former CORE chairman James Farmer. Elected to House Veteran Affairs Committee February 18, 1969, after rejecting original assignment to House Agriculture Committee. At a caucus of House Democrats, January 29, 1969, Mrs. Chisholm defied tradition for new members by requesting reassignment, preferably to a committee involved in urban affairs. Commenting upon her request for committee reassign-ment in January, she said: "It seems to me that it is time for the House of Representatives to pay attention to other considerations than its petrified, sanctified system of seniority which apparently is the only basis for making most of its decisions. There are only nine black members of the House, and the House has a moral duty to somewhat right the balance by putting the nine members it has into positions where they can work effectively to help the nation meet its critical problems of racism, de-privation and urban decay."

In maiden speech, March 26, 1969, declared she would vote against every defense money bill "until our values and priorities have been turned right-side-up again."

She is a member of the all-black Congressional Ad Hoc Committee formed in December 1969 to investigate Panther/police clashes. She has been a director of a child care center in the Bedford-Stuyvesant section of Brooklyn. Worked behind the scenes in politics until becoming a New York state assemblywoman in 1964. Considers herself part of the "new politics" of Julian Bond and Congressman John Conyers.

Born in 1925 in Brooklyn, New York, she moved to Barbados with her family but returned to Brooklyn at age 11 to finish grade school. Graduated from Brooklyn College, received a M.A. from Columbia University. Married Conrad Chisholm in 1950, no children.

CIVIL RIGHTS COMMISSION
Federal agency established by Civil Rights Act of 1957 to investigate allegations that citizens are being deprived of their civil rights. Also studies and collects information concerning civil rights legal developments and appraises the laws and policies of the federal government with respect to civil rights. Under the staff direction of Howard A. Glickstein serves as a national clearinghouse for civil rights information. It is solely a fact-finding agency with no enforcement or legislative powers. However, its recommendations carry great weight, and roughly 70 percent of them have been passed into law. Greatest achievements include recommendations leading to the 1965 Voting Rights Act and the 1965 Law Enforcement Assistance Act. Its report to President Nixon and Congress in April 1970 demanded stronger safeguards for the rights of Mexican-Americans. A board of six commissioners, appointed annually, listens to grievances throughout the year. It has field offices located in Chicago, Los Angeles, Memphis, and New York. Headquarters: U.S. Commission on Civil Rights, 1405 I Street N.W., Washington, D.C. Chairman: Rev. Theodore Hesburgh.

CIVIL RIGHTS DOCUMENTATION PROJECT
A Ford Foundation funded civil rights documentation center which began work in May 1967, with the aim of collecting documents, interviews, recordings, etc., both published and unpublished, for the benefit of future scholars. The project's policy committee is headed by Dr. Ralph Bunche and its director is Dr. Vincent J. Browne, dean of the College of Liberal Arts at Howard University. The current staff consists of a director, associate director (Norma Leonard), and a staff of eleven consisting of consultants who conduct field interviews, a librarian, staff assistants, and clerical help. To date, the project has taped interviews with about 750 persons. Some of the tapes are not available as they include rioters who have incriminated themselves on the tapes, and high-echelon officials and congressmen who have revealed details of closed-

door sessions on civil rights issues, and requested delayed release. The project is also collecting relevant transcripts of radio and television broadcasts. Given a $200,000 grant from the Ford Foundation in 1967, the project plans to increase its funding and hopes to extend its activities to 1975. Headquarters: 1527 New Hampshire Ave. N.W., Washington, D.C.

KENNETH B. CLARK
Distinguished educator and psychologist. Professor of psychology at City College of New York and first Negro to receive permanent appointment as a professor there (1960). Also the only black member of New York Board of Regents. In 1967 founded the Metropolitan Applied Research Center (MARC), a social research organization to "alleviate desperation in ghettos in northern cities not helped directly by Federal court decisions or civil rights legislation." Also director of the New York Foundation.

Testified before Supreme Court on school desegregation issue, 1954. Prominent role as arbiter in New York City school strike, 1968. With his wife Dr. Mamie Phipps Clark, also a psychologist, opened the Northside Center for Child Development, a guidance center for emotionally disturbed children, 1946. At Washington conference of black elected officials, September 1969, Dr. Clark stated: "Elected Negro officials are now the only civil rights leaders who are representatives of the aspirations, desires, and the quest for answers posed by their constituents and elected by their people to speak for them. The time has passed when self-appointed individual leaders . . . can speak for the masses of American Negroes." A foe of separatism in schools, which he contends is bad for blacks as well as whites, he testified before a Senate hearing on school desegregation April 20, 1970. Dr. Clark was born July 14, 1914 in the Panama Canal Zone, graduated from Howard University in 1933, and received Ph.D. at Columbia University in 1940. Author of four books, the latest of which is *Dark Ghetto*, "a summation of personal . . . experience as a prisoner within the ghetto," published in 1965. Office: City College, New York, New York.

JOHN HENRIK CLARKE
Associate editor of *Freedomways* magazine since 1962. Also teaches African and Afro-American history at both New York University and the New School for Social Research. In 1968, developed format for WCBS-TV series "Black Heritage" and acted as special consultant for the program. Born in Union Springs, Alabama in 1915, he moved to New York City in 1933. Attended high school in Columbus, Georgia and New York City and graduated from New York University in 1952. Founding member of the Black Academy of Arts and Letters and the author of five books. His most recent book, published in the fall of 1969, is *Malcolm X: The Man and His Time*.

CASSIUS CLAY (Muhammad Ali)

Undefeated former heavyweight boxing champion of the world, whose title was lifted by the World Boxing Association in 1967 because he refused to be drafted. Adopted Black Muslim faith and name Muhammad Ali in 1964, but was expelled by Muslims (for one year) in April 1969, following his announcement that he would return to boxing to pay off $300,000 worth of debts. His expulsion from the Black Muslims meant that he could no longer claim draft exemption status as a Black Muslim minister. Clay first refused to be drafted in 1965. He was convicted for draft evasion and sentenced to five years in jail in 1967. He appealed and in 1968 the conviction was upheld by the Fifth Circuit Court of Appeals which rejected his plea for exemption as a Black Muslim conscientious objector. In May 1969, a U.S. District Court judge in Houston set a hearing to determine if the 1967 conviction was based on evidence obtained by illegal government wiretapping. But in July 1969, the judge ruled that the government had not used wiretapping information in his conviction and Clay was resentenced to the same five years and a $10,000 fine.

Born in Louisville, Kentucky in 1942, he was educated in public schools there. First fought at the age of 12, and at 18 (1960) had fought 108 amateur bouts, losing only eight. Won an Olympic Gold Medal (1960) in Rome and turned professional. Defeated Sonny Liston (1964) in Miami to become heavyweight champion of the world, and again beat Liston in Lewiston, Maine (1965). Also successfully defended his title against Floyd Patterson (1965), George Chuvalo (1966), Henry Cooper (1966), Brian London (1966), Karl Mildenberger (1966), Cleveland Williams (1966), Ernie Terrell (1967), Zora Folley (1967). Married twice (presently to Belinda Boyd, August 18, 1967), one child.

WILLIAM CLAY

Democratic representative from Missouri's First Congressional District, he was elected in 1968 as his state's first Negro congressman. Has been in politics since 1959, when he was elected alderman in St. Louis. Won reelection in 1963. In that year, as an alderman, served 112 days of a 270-day jail sentence for demonstrating to give Negroes white-collar jobs at a St. Louis bank. Shortly thereafter became his ward's committeeman and occupied this powerful political seat until election to the House of Representatives. Had been race relations coordinator for Steamfitters' Union Local 526 but resigned this position when he became a congressman. A member of the all-black Congressional Ad Hoc Committee formed in December 1969 to investigate Panther/police clashes. Born in 1931, he served in the army during the Korean War. In 1955 joined the NAACP and became head of its Youth Council, then joined CORE. Holds a B.S. degree in political science from the University of St. Louis. Married, three children.

REV. ALBERT J. CLEAGE

Leading spokesman of Detroit militants. Heads the Federation for Self-Determination, formed late in 1967 as a unifying force and clearing-house for Negro programs and proposals. In January 1968, the Ford Foundation awarded Cleage's federation two grants totaling some $100,000 which Cleage said his federation refused to accept because "whites have tried to absorb blacks paternalistically and on terms set by whites." Nominated at National Council of Churches eighth general assembly (1969) in Detroit for its presidency. Defeated by Mrs. Theodore O. Wedel, first woman to hold the office, receiving 93 votes to Mrs. Wedel's 387. Supported Eugene McCarthy for president in 1968. Pastor of the Shrine of the Black Madonna, formerly the Central United Church of Christ, which is located in the heart of the 1967 riot area of Detroit.

ELDRIDGE CLEAVER

Minister of information of the Black Panthers, living in exile abroad since end of 1968. Disappeared from public view in late November 1968, after refusing to surrender himself for a parole violation. Had been paroled since 1966, after serving nine years of a 14-year sentence on a 1958 conviction for assault with intent to kill. Parole was rescinded after he was involved in a gun battle between Black Panthers and police in Oakland, April 6, 1968. He was released on bail June 12, but this decision was overturned and further appeals were exhausted November 26.

Cleaver joined the Panthers in February 1967, and in a period of less than two years emerged as a dynamic black leader, journalist (*Ramparts* magazine) and author (*Soul on Ice, Post-Prison Writings and Speeches*). In speeches and articles, he expounded the Panthers' demands for the liberation of black America. In August 1968, he became the presidential nominee of the Peace and Freedom Party, said his campaign was aimed at "laying the base for a revolutionary movement that will unite black . . . and white radicals," and in the November 5 election received 36,385 votes, mostly from California.

In October 1968, Cleaver lectured at the University of California at Berkeley on "the roots of racism," and received a standing ovation from students. The lecture took place after weeks of public debate in which Gov. Ronald Reagan led opposition to Cleaver's appearance, denouncing him as "an advocate of racism and violence." Cleaver's lecture, intended as the first of a series, was described as "moderate" and "scholarly."

Cleaver's whereabouts were unknown from November 1968 until May 1969, when he was discovered by reporters living in a small apartment in Havana. In July 1969, Cleaver and his wife Kathleen arrived in Algiers as guests of the Algerian government, to attend the Pan-African Cultural Festival. The festival was marked by a public clash between Cleaver and Stokely Carmichael when the latter announced his break with the Panthers. Reportedly the issue was cooperation with whites, which Cleaver supported and Carmichael denounced. Cleaver told reporters he was homesick and intended eventually to return to the United States either legally or illegally. However, after the festival, Cleaver remained in Algiers with his wife who gave birth to a son there, July 29, 1969. In October 1969, Cleaver was reported to have begun discussions with North Vietnam for the return of U.S. military prisoners in exchange for Black Panther leaders in custody in the United States. In Aug. 1970, he led Panther delegation to Hanoi for "Solidarity Day" between North Vietnam and American blacks.

KATHLEEN CLEAVER
Wife of Eldridge Cleaver and active spokesman for his causes. Daughter of foreign service officer Ernest Eugene Neal, with whom she had traveled widely in Asia and Africa. Born 1945. Educated at Oberlin and Barnard College. Worked in the Peace Corps and for SNCC. Met Eldrige Cleaver at black student conference at Fisk University in March 1967 and married him December 27 the same year. On July 29, 1969, in Algiers, she gave birth to a son, named Antonio Maceo after a nineteenth-century black Cuban revolutionary. She appeared in a cameo role in the Michelangelo Antonioni film *Zabriskie Point*.

COALITION FOR UNITED COMMUNITY ACTION
Chicago group of militant organizations, South Side neighborhood groups, and street gangs formed in early summer of 1969 to force an end to discrimination in the city's construction industry. After it began harassing tactics in late July, more than 20 construction sites representing contracts exceeding $80 million were shut down. Coalition aimed at 10,000 on-the-job training positions for black youths, and more business for black contractors. An agreement, called the Chicago Plan, was reached between Coalition and union and construction officials on January 13, 1970. This agreement scaled down the coalition's demands to fewer black trainees, rather than continue the impasse. Three major gangs are involved, the Conservative Vice Lords (gold berets), the Black P. Stone Nation (red berets), and the East Side Disciples (black berets). SCLC leader Jesse Jackson and his Operation Breadbasket also form part of the coalition, which represents a total of about 100 organizations with combined membership of 50,000. Coalition Chairman is C. T. Vivian, and chief organizer is David Reed, a former aid to Illinois governor Richard Ogilvie. Office: 1369 East 53rd Street, Chicago, Illinois. *See also:* BLACK P. STONE NATION, JESSE JACKSON, OPERATION BREADBASKET.

ROBERT COARD
Heads Action for Boston Community Development. Born 1928, graduated from Dillard University in New Orleans in 1950. Received a master's degree in sociology from Boston University, and a doctorate in city planning from Massachusetts Institute of Technology. The Coards live

in Roxbury and have two sons and two daughters. *See also:* ACTION
FOR BOSTON COMMUNITY DEVELOPMENT.

ELLA MAE COLLINS

Chairman of the Organization of Afro-American Unity since death of
her brother, Malcolm X. Born in Butler, Georgia, 50 years ago. A
former member of the Black Muslims, she left the movement in 1959
because, she says, she believed it was "fishing for suckers." Still considers herself a Muslim, but is not affiliated with any mosque. Has run a
non-sectarian school in Boston called the Sarah A. Little School for
Preparatory Arts. Says she hopes to bring about brotherhood and
understanding between races through the OAAU. In an interview in
May 1969, she urged a greater unity among militants and moderates. *See
also:* ORGANIZATION OF AFRO-AMERICAN UNITY.

CONGRESS OF MEXICAN-AMERICAN UNITY

Loose confederation of some 300 small Mexican-American groups in
Los Angeles county, which arose out of a successful campaign to put a
Mexican-American on the Los Angeles Board of Education in 1967.
Hopes to increase influence of *chicano* votes in future elections and
eventually develop community action programs. Financed by contributions from member groups, it has no government or foundation support.
Founded by Rev. Antonio Hernandez. President since February 1970
is Esteban Torres, an official of the United Auto Workers. Headquarters: 274 South Atlantic Boulevard, Los Angeles, California.

CONGRESS OF RACIAL EQUALITY (CORE)

Founded in 1942 by James Farmer and a group of students at the University of Chicago. CORE pioneered such techniques as the sit-in,
which it first used in June 1943 at Jack Spratt's restaurant in Chicago's
Loop, and the freedom ride, challenging southern bus segregation.
Made headlines in May 1961 when freedom-riders tested integration
of bus terminal facilities following a 1960 Supreme Court decision.
Freedom-riders were attacked by mobs in Birmingham and Montgomery, Alabama, and were arrested in Jackson, Mississippi. In 1965,
CORE began an intensive drive for voter registration and desegregation
in Bogalusa, Louisiana, which frequently erupted into violence. In
March 1966, Farmer resigned from leadership of CORE and was succeeded by Floyd McKissick. Later that year, as McKissick embraced
the new slogan of "black power," Farmer denounced it. CORE continued in a black separatist direction under its next leader, Roy Innis,
who succeeded McKissick in 1968.

In July 1968, CORE proposed a Community Self-Determination
Act, designed to promote black capitalism, which was introduced before
the Ninetieth Congress. It was not acted upon but was reintroduced to
Congress in 1969.

At one time, CORE was a broad-based organization with a reputed membership of 180,000, including many whites. But in late 1969 the NAACP's Roy Wilkins said CORE was virtually non-existent as a national civil rights group. (Innis had called on Wilkins to "withdraw from the state" and leave the struggle to younger men.) In October 1969 *Ebony* magazine reported that CORE was $300,000 in debt and that its ideological switch to black nationalism had been costly in terms of membership. Its Harlem headquarters reportedly maintains a permament staff of seven. Office: 200 West 135th Street New York, New York. *See also:* JAMES FARMER, ROY INNIS, FLOYD McKISSICK.

JOHN CONYERS, JR.
Democratic representative from the First Congressional District in Detroit, Michigan. Elected in 1965 and reelected in 1968. He serves on the House Judiciary Committee, the first black to do so. As a member of the Congressional Ad Hoc Committee investigating Panther/police confrontations, declared on March 11, 1970, that the committee's investigation showed "absolutely, positively, definitely yes" that police and federal agencies had conspired to wipe out the Black Panther party. A native of Detroit, Conyers was born on May 16, 1927 and holds a B.A. and LL.B. from Wayne State University. He worked for three years as legislative assistant to Congressman John Dingell before going into politics for himself. Always active in union affairs, was a referee for Michigan's Workmen's Compensation Department. In 1963, President Kennedy appointed him to the National Lawyers Committee for Civil Rights under Law. In 1965 had difficulty in winning the primary from his district but did win it by a mere 45 votes. Went on to trounce his opponent in the election, winning by 138,000 votes. He was a co-sponsor of the Medicare program under President Johnson and a supporter of 1965 Voting Rights Act.

WALTER COOPER
Chairman of the Black Development Advisory Council. Has been active in civil rights since age 14 when he organized a strike of the football team at his high school in Clairton, Pennsylvania because they would not allow black cheer leaders. Born July, 1928 in Pennsylvania. Graduated from Washington and Jefferson College in 1950 with a B.A. in chemistry. Received a Ph.D. in 1956 from the University of Rochester in physical chemistry. Before going to Washington was a research associate with Eastman Kodak Company, in Rochester, New York, and returned there in 1969 after a year in Washington, D.C. Married, two children.

BILL COSBY
First Negro actor to star in a network television series ("I Spy"), he won Emmies in 1967 and 1968. Cosby is also one of the most prominent entertainers committed to the Negro cause and is noted for assistance to

young black performers. Has announced his intention to leave the entertainment world at age 35 (1973) to devote himself to teaching. In 1968, narrated program in CBS series "Of Black America." Born in 1938 in Philadelphia, Cosby dropped out of high school to become a Navy medic and eventually earned his diploma in the service. Attended Temple University, and started in show business in 1962. In much demand on the night club circuit. In fall of 1969 began a new Sunday night series, the "Bill Cosby Show." Married, three children.

GEORGE CROCKETT

Controversial judge of Detroit Recorder's Court, who has frequently clashed with police over the handling of Negro defendants. A storm of public protest followed his action in freeing suspects following a shoot out between police and militants at the New Bethel Baptist Church on March 29, 1969, in which a policeman was killed. When the county prosecutor, William L. Cahalan, ordered one of the men held for further questioning, Crockett charged the prosecutor with contempt of court. On March 31, the police commissioner charged that Crockett had hindered police investigation and there were further protests by Detroit Police Officers Association, City Councilman Nicholas Hood, Jr., and Mayor Jerome P. Cavanagh. On April 3, in a public demonstration in sympathy with police, some 2,000 whites marched in the funeral procession for the dead policeman. At the same time, several hundred Negroes marched in support of Judge Crockett. At a news conference, Crockett insisted his actions were correct. "Can any of you imagine the Detroit police invading an all-white church and rounding up everyone in sight to be bused to a wholesale lockup in a garage? Can any of you imagine a (white) church group . . . being held incommunicado for seven hours . . . without their constitutional rights to counsel? . . . Can anyone explain in any other than racial terms the shooting by police inside a closed and surrounded church?" In an earlier case, when suspending sentence of a repeat offender, whom he felt had been mistreated by police, Crockett said: "I think the only thing we can do to bring a stop to that is to prevent the police at least from getting whatever vicarious pleasure there is out of beating up a person and then seeing the person being sentenced. So it's my position that I can take into consideration, in imposing sentence, what the police did to the man after he was arrested." Judge Crockett graduated from the University of Michigan Law School (1934). Was appointed judge in 1966 and comes up for reelection in 1972. Born 1910.

CRUSADE FOR JUSTICE
(LA CRUSADA PARA LA JUSTICIA)

Self-help organization for Mexican-Americans in Denver. Conducts "liberation classes" (to teach leadership, identity, etc.) and publishes a newspaper, *El Gallo* (The Fighting Cock). It also runs a nursery, a gymnasium and a job-skill "bank." Provides legal aid and a bail-bond service and sponsors a program to develop young artists through its "revolutionary theater" and art gallery. In April 1969, organized Youth Liberation Conference attended by 100 youth and student groups from across the country. Crusade claims about half of Colorado's 185,000 *chicanos* as followers. Headed by Rudolfo Gonzales. Headquarters: 1362 Downing Street, Denver, Colorado. *See also:* RUDOLFO GONZALES.

HAROLD CRUSE

Author of *The Crisis of the Negro Intellectual* (1967), which was described at the time as "the theoretical base, the intellectual argument for national and ethnic separation of the Negro in America." (*New York Times*, November 21, 1967). An angry tract, it heaped blame for the Negro condition on white intellectuals, liberals, left-wingers, labor, and heavily on the Jewish community. He was equally scathing of much of the black community. Rejecting integration, he called for Negro power base—economic, cultural and political—and, if necessary, an all-black political party. Currently author-in-residence at University of Michigan. Cruse contributes to the *New Leader, Liberator,* and other publications. Born in Petersburg, Virginia, his formal education did not go beyond high school. After military service, 1941–45, he worked in civil service jobs, as a film editor, and in 1960 visited Cuba to study the Castro revolution.

OSSIE DAVIS AND RUBY DEE

Successful husband-wife acting team for more than 20 years (they have been called "Mr. and Mrs. Broadway"). In recent years they have been closely associated with the civil rights movement and its leaders. Davis delivered an eloquent eulogy at the funeral of Malcolm X, was prominent in raising money for the legal defense of LeRoi Jones, attended the King funeral in Atlanta, and took part in the Martin Luther King memorial march in Memphis in May 1968. Lectures widely on campuses where, he says, "there is a tremendous hunger among blacks and whites for the truth about black experience in this country. This is why I can increasingly be part of the cultural arm of the revolution." Davis wrote screenplay and directed 1969 United Artists production, *Cotton Comes to Harlem.* Film is described as the first major motion picture to be made about black America which is entertaining without either preaching or demeaning the black community. Davis was born December 18, 1917, in Cogdell, Georgia, and was a student at Howard University, 1935–38. After war service, he made his stage debut (1946) in *Jeb.* Another member of the cast was Ruby Dee, and they were married in 1948. In 1959 they were in *Raisin in the Sun.* In 1961–62, Davis authored and costarred with Ruby Dee in the Broadway hit *Purlie Victorious,* a racial satire which was basis for Broadway smash musical *Purlie* in

1970. They later starred in the film version *Gone are the Days*. Davis won an Emmy nomination for his role in *Teacher, Teacher,* and has appeared widely in television series and specials. Recipients of the Frederick Douglass Award (May 1970) for "distinguished leadership toward equal opportunity" and the first living black couple ever to receive it. Ruby Dee was born in Cleveland, Ohio, but raised in Harlem. She graduated from Hunter College in 1942. They have three children and live in Mount Vernon, New York.

SAMMY DAVIS, JR.

One of the most involved of the nation's top entertainers, Sammy Davis has made numerous personal appeals and appearances on behalf of civil rights causes. He took part in the March on Washington in 1963. In 1965 he was named man of the year by B'nai B'rith "for untiring labors on behalf of human rights and the Jewish people." When Martin Luther King was assassinated, Davis called NBC and asked to speak for a few minutes on the "Tonight Show." He announced that he would attend the funeral in Atlanta and called on "black brothers to cool it— white brothers to come forward now, we need each other desperately." In 1968, he campaigned for Robert Kennedy for the presidency. Born December 8, 1925 in New York City. Made his stage debut at four as part of the Will Mastin Trio and stayed with them until he joined the army in 1943. Since the war he has been one of the world's top nightclub entertainers, and has starred in numerous Broadway shows and motion pictures. Converted to Judaism in 1956. His autobiography, *Yes, I Can,* appeared in 1965. Divorced from his second wife, Mai Britt, in 1968. Three children.

WILLIAM DAWSON

Democratic representative from the First Congressional District of Illinois from 1943 through 1970, when he announced he would not seek reelection. Longest serving Negro member of Congress and at 84 the oldest member of the House of Representatives. Long considered close to Chicago's Mayor Daley and the Democratic establishment of that city, is regarded by militants as an "Uncle Tom." Joined the American Expeditionary Force in 1917 as an officer and after the war went to law school at Northwestern University and set up a law practice in Chicago. Ran for Congress in 1929 as a Republican and lost. In 1935 was elected to the City Council and became a Democrat when Roosevelt was president. In 1940 was elected Democratic Committeeman from Chicago's Second Ward before taking his seat in the House of Representatives. In 1944 was assistant chairman of the Democratic National Committee, and campaigned for Harry Truman in 1948. Born on April 26, 1886 in Albany, Georgia. Graduated magna cum laude from Fisk University in Nashville, Tennessee. Married, two children.

DEACONS FOR DEFENSE AND JUSTICE

Based in Bogalusa, Louisiana, the deacons are an armed, semi-secret organization pledged to acts of retaliation against systematic Ku Klux Klan harassment and terrorization of Negro communities. It is chartered by the state of Louisiana to "instruct, train, and teach citizens, especially minority groups, the principles of democracy." Founded by Charles Sims of Bogalusa, Louisiana, in July 1964. Other known leaders are Ernest Thomas, a vice-president and organizer, and Henry Austan. Claims to have 62 chapters in the South and one in Chicago. In 1965 CORE passed a motion at its national convention not to endorse the group because of its proclaimed military convictions. In July 1969, *Bogalusa News* reported Deacon's organization no longer active.

VINE DELORIA, JR.

Author of *Custer Died For Your Sins: An Indian Manifesto*, published by Macmillan in September 1969, and executive director of the National Congress of American Indians, 1946–67. A Standing Rock Sioux from a distinguished family of American Indians with scholar, churchman and warrior-chief ancestors, he has served on the executive council of the Episcopal Church and is a board member of the Southwest Intergroup Relations Council in Austin, Texas. Received degrees from Iowa State University and Lutheran School of Theology and later studied at University of Colorado Law School. Served in the Marines in the 1950's. Born on the Pine Ridge Indian Reservation in North Dakota, 1935.

SISTER MARTIN DE PORRES (GREY)

The only black nun in the 500-member order of the Sisters of Mercy and chief organizer of the first National Black Sisters Conference held in Pittsburgh in the fall of 1968. The conference, held at Mount Mercy College, was attended by 150 black nuns. They met to discuss how they could make themselves more relevant to the needs of the black community by trying to determine their responsibility to their people, their church, and religious community. Sister Martin said the reason for the conference was that "the Church is predominantly a white institution and it caters to white communities. Since white racism is behind the race problem, then we, as black religious women, have to help white clergy and our white sisters teach their people the truth." Sister Martin is from Sewickley, Pennsylvania and has been a nun since 1960. Born in 1943, she is the daughter of Edgar W. Grey, a steelworker.

ADOLPHUS SUMNER DICKERSON

Has been active in civil rights movement for over 20 years and is chairman of a grievance committee on civil rights in Atlanta. Is considered a pivotal person on civil rights issues in Georgia because of his ability to communicate with both sides. Currently pastor of Central Methodist Church in Atlanta. He was born in 1914 in western Georgia and educated at the University of Atlanta and Boston University. Was ordained in 1937.

CHARLES C. DIGGS

Democratic representative from Michigan's Thirteenth Congressional District and senior black representative from Michigan, was first elected in 1954. Heads the all-black Congressional Ad Hoc Committee, formed in December 1969 to investigate Panther/police clashes. Born December 2, 1922 in Detroit. He was educated there and enrolled first at the University of Michigan, then transferred to Fisk University in 1942. Drafted into the air force, he spent two years in service, 1943–45. After the war, enrolled at Wayne State University in mortuary science. (His family owns House of Diggs, the largest funeral home in Michigan.) Began his political career in 1951 with election to the state senate.

IVAN DIXON

Organized the Negro Actors for Action, which is now disbanded. Has said, "There should be an integrated curriculum that teaches about Frederick Douglass as well as George Washington . . . To identify only with whites makes Negro kids negate themselves. The time has come when my kids won't have to even think of their heritage." Born April 6, 1931 in Harlem. Attended Lincoln Academy in King's Mountain, North Carolina, and graduated from North Carolina College with degree in political science and history. Returned to New York and joined Department of Welfare as a social case investigator. Studied with American Theater Wing in New York and at Western Reserve University as a graduate student in drama. Broadway debut was *Raisin in the Sun*. In 1966 won best actor award given by the first World Festival of Negro Arts, in Dakar, Africa. In 1967, starred in CBS's "The Final War of Olly Winter." Movie parts include the much acclaimed *Nothing But a Man*. Now featured in the CBS series, "Hogan's Heroes." Married, four children.

JOHN DOAR

Assistant attorney general in charge of Department of Justice Civil Rights Division, 1964–67. President of New York City Board of Education, 1968–69. Head of the Bedford-Stuyvesant Development and Service Corporation since 1968 and a board member of investment banking firm of Bear, Stearns and Company. A white man, Doar was born December 3, 1921 in Minneapolis. Received a B.A. from Princeton in 1944 and law degree from University of California at Berkeley in 1949. After practicing law in Wisconsin (1950–1960), he joined the Civil Rights Division of the justice department in July 1960 as deputy to Burke Marshall, who was assistant attorney general in charge of the division under Robert Kennedy. Rode with the freedom riders in 1960's, shepherded James Meredith through the first weeks at the University of Mississippi, prosecuted more than 30 Southern voting-rights cases in federal courts, and in 1965 was the government's chief representative during civil rights march from Selma to Montgomery. Left the justice department in 1967. Married to the former Anne Leffingwell, four children.

RICHARD L. DOCKERY

Southwest regional director of the NAACP (area includes Arkansas, Louisiana, Oklahoma, New Mexico, and Texas). Prior to his appointment in 1966 was president of the San Antonio branch of the NAACP and also employed as a procurement data specialist at Kelly Air Force Base. A native of Camden, Alabama, in 1951 he was appointed director of the city recreation department in Pensacola, Florida, becoming the first Negro city director in the South. Married, one son. Office: 2600 Flora Street, Dallas, Texas.

ADRIAN DOVE

Sociologist working as a program analyst for the Bureau of the Budget. Was chairman of Watts Construction Employment Committee (1965–67). In 1968, he was a member of White House task force on programs for hard-core unemployed. Author of "Soul Folks Chittlings Test," which he devised as a parody of employment and IQ tests that reflect the culture of white, middle-class America. (Sample question: If I were playing the dozens, I'd be talking most about a) waterbread, b) your mamma, c) the digit man, d) wrinkles, e) a together set). Born in Dallas, Texas of Jamaican parents in 1934, he was raised in Los Angeles. Graduated from California State College in Los Angeles and did graduate work at University of Southern California, Loyola at Los Angeles, and University of Hawaii.

HARRY EDWARDS

Tried to organize a boycott by black field and track athletes on the U.S. Olympic team at 1968 games in Mexico because of an International Olympics Committee decision to admit South Africa to the games. (The committee later reversed its decision and barred South Africa from the competition after U.S.S.R. and 40 other countries threatened to withdraw.) Edwards called off his boycott when he failed to get support of all 26 black athletes on the team. However, Tommie Smith, a gold medal winner, and John Carlos, a bronze medal winner, used the victory ceremony for a black power demonstration. Both men appeared without shoes and in black socks and raised their black-gloved fists in a "black power" salute during the U.S. national anthem. "The revolt of the black athlete is the newest phase of the black liberation movement in America," Edwards has said. In commenting on the boycott he remarked, "It seems as though the only way we can reach a lot of people is by showing them all is not well in the locker room." Received a B.A. from San Jose State College and an M.A. from Cornell University. Taught at San Jose State (1967), and currently is a lecturer and graduate fellow at Cornell. Author of *The Revolt of the Black Athlete*, published by Free Press in September 1969. Born 1942, unmarried.

RALPH W. ELLISON

Best known for his novel *Invisible Man* published in 1952, which won for him the National Book award the following year. Attended Tuskegee Institute (1935–36). In 1955, American Academy of Arts and Letters awarded Ellison the Prix de Rome which enabled him to write in Italy for the next two years. Has lectured on writing at N.Y.U., Columbia, Rutgers, Princeton, and Bennington College. Last published work was *Shadow and Act*, a collection of essays, in 1964. Born March 1, 1914 in Oklahoma City, Oklahoma. Married to the former Fanny McConnell.

PROJECT ENTERPRISE

Nixon Administration's major program to encourage and expand minority business enterprises. Launched in the fall of 1969, the program expanded the availability of venture capital and management advice and training, chiefly through a series of local investment companies set up for this purpose. The investment companies, sponsored by major U.S. corporations and private-sector organizations in partnership with the federal government, are known as Minority Enterprise Small Business Investment Companies (MESBIC). By August 21, 1970, 16 such companies were in operation and commitments had been received for over 100. One of the first and most successful of the companies, the Arcata Investment Company of Palo Alto, California, had financed some 50 minority businesses, including stores, soul-food restaurants, a bus service, beauty shops, nightclubs and a delivery service. The companies, licensed by the Small Business Administration work in conjunction with the Commerce Department's Office of Minority Business Enterprise (OMBE). *See also:* ARTHUR McZIER, ABRAHAM S. VENABLE.

FRED (AHMED) EVANS

Cleveland militant sentenced to death by all-white jury May 12, 1969, for first degree murder of three policemen and a civilian in what was described as nation's first armed attack by group of black nationalists. Was scheduled to die in electric chair, September 22, 1969, but won stay of execution and lawyers continued efforts to obtain new trial. Evans allegedly instigated attack by group of his supporters (the Black Nationalists of New Libya) on a squad car in Glenville ghetto area of Cleveland on July 23, 1968. Attack led to gunfights and rioting in which 11 persons died, and an estimated $1.5 million worth of property was damaged. Violence commission report released after Evans' trial stated Evans had been unaware of the attack on police until after it started. Before arrest, Evans directed a summer program to train Negro youngsters in African crafts and operated store for African products. An attempt to free Evans by fellow black nationalist prisoners at Cuyahoga County jail was reported by UPI, May 9, 1969. Since his sentence, Evans has been in Ohio State Penitentiary in Columbus. Born April 23, 1928 in Greenville, North Carolina, Evans served two enlistments in the regular army, attaining rank of sergeant before dishonorable discharge (1955), for striking an officer.

(JAMES) CHARLES EVERS

Elected mayor of Fayette, Mississippi, May 14, 1969. Ran on an all-black slate opposing five white men in a bid for Fayette's five alderman seats. Defeated 77-year-old incumbent, who had held the office for the last 20 years, by 131 votes, thus becoming first Negro mayor in a southern town with white residents since Reconstruction. Also Mississippi field director of the NAACP. Joined the national staff in June 1963 following the rifle slaying of his brother, Medgar W. Evers. Born in 1921 in Mississippi, had been a businessman and disk jockey in Chicago before joining NAACP staff. In 1964 helped avert a riot by Jackson State College students after police had ringed the college campus with shotgun-carrying patrolmen, armored tanks, and dogs. The incident occurred after an automobile struck a coed on a campus street. The subsequent shotgun wounding of three demonstrators resulted in student anger. Made unsuccessful bid for Congress in March 1968, when he led the field against six white candidates in preliminary election for Mississippi's Third Congressional District, but lost the run-off. At the 1968 Democratic convention, along with Dr. Aaron E. Henry, state chairman of the NAACP, and Hodding Carter III, white publisher of the *Delta Democrat-Times* in Greenville, Mississippi, Evers led the bi-racial coalition known as the Loyal Democrats in their successful challenge which barred the seating of the all-white regular Mississippi delegation. Office: 1070 Lunch Street, Jackson, Mississippi. *See also:* MISSISSIPPI FREEDOM DEMOCRATIC PARTY.

JAMES FARMER

Appointed assistant secretary of health, education, and welfare in 1969 by President Nixon. One of the nation's leading civil rights activists for more than two decades, he was born in Marshall, Texas in 1920, the son of a college professor (who was the nation's first Negro Ph.D.). Received a B.S. in chemistry from Wiley College at 18, and a divinity degree from Howard University, but was not ordained. In 1942, he founded CORE in Chicago, pioneered the sit-in to desegregate public facilities and later was one of the original Freedom Riders, for which he was jailed in 1961. Led 2,000-strong Pilgrimage of Prayer, 1959, to protest closing of Virginia's public schools. Also led major civil rights actions in Louisiana. After leading CORE to some of its greatest successes in the 1960's, Farmer left the organization in 1966 in disagreement with increasing emphasis on separatism. Ran as Liberal party candidate for Congress in November 1968, losing to Shirley Chisholm.

Since his appointment to HEW, Farmer has incurred criticism from some former civil rights colleagues for not being more outspoken against Nixon Administration policies. Married to the former Lula Peterson, two daughters. *See also:* CONGRESS OF RACIAL EQUALITY (CORE).

WALTER FAUNTROY

Washington head of the SCLC. Also heads the Model Inner City Community project and is a founder of the Black United Front. He resigned as vice chairman of the Washington, D.C. city council in January 1969. Born in 1936, he is a graduate of the Yale Divinity School.

C. CLYDE FERGUSON, JR.

United States ambassador to Uganda since May, 1970. During Nigerian civil war, he served as State Department's special coordinator for relief to civilian victims. He was Dean of Howard University Law School, 1963–69. During Kennedy Administration, he was general counsel to the U.S. Commission on Civil Rights. He also served as an alternate delegate and expert to the United Nations sub-commission on prevention of discrimination against minorities, 1963–65. Represented U.S. at UNESCO conference on human rights, 1965, and helped draft UNESCO statement on race, 1966. Born November 4, 1924 in Wilmington, North Carolina. Graduated from Ohio State University and Harvard Law School. Served with U.S. army in Europe and Asia, 1942–46. Widower. Three daughters.

ARTHUR A. FLETCHER

Assistant secretary of labor in Nixon Administration. Recognized as originator of the controversial "Philadelphia Plan" to integrate construction unions. Previously was special assistant to Governor Daniel Evans of Washington, coordinating relations between local communities and state government. Born Dec. 22, 1924, in Phoenix, Arizona.

JAMES FORMAN

Field director for the Black Economic Development Conference. Had been acting chairman of organization, April through August 1969, when he wrote and presented the "Black Manifesto" calling for reparations from white churches. Made headlines (May 4, 1969) when he disrupted communion services to read manifesto at New York's Riverside Church. A former Chicago schoolteacher and veteran civil rights activist, he was one of the early leaders of SNCC and its executive secretary from 1964–66. During that period he took a prominent role in voter registration drives and demonstrations in Mississippi and Alabama. In 1966, he lost his SNCC leadership position in the shake-up which saw Stokely Carmichael replace John Lewis as chairman, but he remained a member. At the July 1969 meeting of SNCC he was named director of international affairs. Born in Chicago on October 5, 1929. Graduated Roosevelt University, 1951. After serving in the army, joined Juvenile

Research Center in Chicago. Separated, one child. *See also:* BLACK ECONOMIC DEVELOPMENT CONFERENCE, STUDENT NATIONAL COORDINATING COMMITTEE.

ARETHA FRANKLIN
Top pop singer of soul music, described in a *Time* magazine cover story, June 1968 as "Lady Soul: Singing it like it is." Born March 25, 1942 in Memphis, Tennessee, one of five children of nationally known revivalist minister Rev. Clarance L. Franklin, pastor of Detroit's New Bethel Baptist Church. (Scene of a shoot-out between police and militants in March 1969, *see* George Crockett entry.) Brought up on gospel music at home, at 14 she was a featured performer in her father's evangelist show that traveled across the country. In 1967, her first recording hit "I Never Loved A Man," sold a million copies. This was quickly followed by four other gold single records. Today, she reportedly commands $15,000 to $20,000 a performance. As a star, she has helped define the new Negro sense of identity, and in 1968 was invited to give a "soul" rendition of the national anthem at the Republican National Convention in Miami Beach. Her Grammy and Golden Mike award winning record "Respect" (a song written by the late Otis Redding) has been called "the new Negro national anthem." In 1967, SCLC awarded her a special citation. Married to Ted White, who manages her career, three sons.

FREEDOM INDUSTRIES, INC.
A Boston-based black conglomerate involved with food, electronics, engineering, and advertising. Organization owns two supermarkets operating in black communities and is negotiating for more stores in other Boston areas. It is privately financed and based firmly on the profit motive. Its president and founder, Archie Williams, was born in 1934 in North Carolina. He graduated from Brown University and holds a law degree from Boston University. Served in the navy and had a successful law practice before forming Freedom Industries in 1968. Considered one of the best examples of Negroes helping themselves in taking substantial roles in the business community.

ERNEST J. GAINES
Author, has written *Of Love and Dust* (1967) and *Bloodline*, a collection of short stories (1968) both published by Dial Press. Born on a Louisiana plantation in 1933, he worked as a field hand at the age of nine. Served in the army from 1953–55 and graduated from San Francisco State College in 1957. In 1958 won the Wallace Stegner Creative Writing Fellowship at Stanford University and the Joseph Henry Jackson Literary prize in 1959.

MILTON GALAMISON
Militant civil rights activist, and vocal critic of New York City school policies for the last decade. Has been arrested nine times in an effort to

end segregation in that city's school system. First became involved in the school integration issue in 1956 when he made an unsuccessful attempt to integrate an all-Negro high school in Brooklyn. In 1964, organized the first city-wide school protest to demand integration. In 1965, organized another boycott to support demands for community control of schools. In May 1968, organized still another boycott during the Ocean Hill–Brownsville school decentralization controversy. Appointed a member of the Board of Education by Mayor Lindsay on July 14, 1968, was elected vice president of the board, October 16, 1968. His term was to expire July 30, 1971 but on May 1, 1969, the New York state legislature in Albany voted to replace the board with an interim one of five members, one from each borough, to deal with the decentralization issue. Galamison has said of decentralization: "The forces that oppose decentralization are concerned about keeping power away from the black community, not obtaining integration. I for one have not abandoned the long-range goal of integration." Is pastor of the Siloam Presbyterian Church in Brooklyn (since 1949) and holds divinity degrees from Lincoln and Princeton Universities. Currently working with the Opportunity Industrial Center, the Bedford-Stuyvesant Development Association, and the Parents' Workshop for Equality in New York City Schools, which he organized in 1959 and serves as chairman. Taught a course on education and urban studies at Harvard University in 1969 for one year. Born 1923. Married, one son, a student at Wesleyan University.

CARLOS "CHINO" GARCIA
Director of downtown branch of New York's Real Great Society. Born on the Lower East Side of Manhattan, in 1942. At 12 joined his first gang and at 17 became the leader of the Assassin Lords, a gang whose membership numbered some 500. In 1967, New York police gave him the option of exile in Puerto Rico, or staying in New York to face charges. He chose Puerto Rico and spent a year there. Returned to New York in 1968 to take his present position. He has no formal education and taught himself to read and write. *See also:* THE REAL GREAT SOCIETY.

JOHN W. GARDNER
Distinguished white educator and social critic who, as President Johnson's secretary of health, education, and welfare, 1965–68, substantially reorganized and strengthened that department. Resigned March 1, 1968, to head the newly formed National Urban Coalition. A Republican, he was known as one of the most energetic backers of Johnson's "Great Society," and urged the nation to tackle the problems of the cities with "barn-raising enthusiasm." A president of the Carnegie Corporation in New York (1955–65), sponsored study that led to the new math, and the famous Conant study of education in the United States. Known as a perfectionist, he coined the phrase "pursuit of excellence." In December

1967 warned: "We are in deep trouble as a people. And history is not going to deal kindly with a rich nation that will not tax itself to cure its miseries." In February 1969, presented follow-up to Kerner report entitled *One Year Later*, which declared that the nation was "a year closer to two societies . . . increasingly separate and scarcely less unequal." In July 1970, he announced plans to form a national lobby of 400,000 citizens to exert pressure for governmental reforms and action on domestic issues. Born in Los Angeles, October 8, 1912, he graduated from Stanford University and University of California at Berkeley and became a professor of psychology. In World War II he served with the marines in Italy and Austria. He joined the Carnegie staff in 1946. Married, two daughters. Author of *Excellence, Self-Renewal, No Easy Victories*, and *Recovery of Confidence*.

CHARLES R. GARRY

California lawyer who has defended Black Panther leaders since 1967 and whose absence through illness from the trial of the Chicago Eight was nominally the cause of defendant Bobby Seale's numerous outbursts. Seale claimed that he would accept only Garry as his counsel, but Judge Hoffman refused to postpone the trial until Garry was well enough to take part. In addition to Seale, Garry had defended Huey Newton, Eldridge Cleaver, David Hilliard and others. Born March 17, 1909 in Bridgewater, Mass. to Armenian immigrant parents named Garabedian. Garry's family later moved to Selma, California, where he grew up on a farm. He has said: "I guess one of the things that makes me so incensed about what's happening to black people is I relate it to my early life and the discrimination I received by just being an ethnic Armenian. I was called a Goddamned Armenian and up until the time I finished grammar school I think I had a fight every single night." Worked his way through school and went to law school at nights. Admitted to the bar in 1939. Married to the former Louise Evelyn Edgar. No children.

GILBERTO GERENA-VALENTIN

Militant who has been described as the most influential Puerto Rican in New York City. In July 1969, was dismissed from his $16,000 a year job as an official on the city's Commission on Human Rights because he adopted a "destructive role, inflaming and dividing the community" according to the commission's chief, Simeon Golar. Jailed twice, July 12 and 15, 1969, for refusing to vacate his office after his dismissal. Released July 18 when his case was postponed. Born January 15, 1925 in Puerto Rico. Separated from his second wife, two daughters.

KENNETH ALLEN GIBSON

Mayor of Newark, New Jersey since July 1, 1970—the first black mayor of a major northeastern city and only the third black man in recent times to be elected mayor of any large American city (after Carl Stokes in Cleveland, Ohio and Andrew Hatcher in Gary, Indiana). Gibson defeated Hugh J. Addonizio, the white two-term incumbent, in a mayoral runoff June 16, 1970 by an unexpectedly large margin of more than 11,000 votes (54,892 to 43,339) in a record 73 percent voter turnout.

Gibson describes himself as only a nominal Democrat, a moderate, and a liberal. However, he was criticized by opponents in the campaign for accepting support of the city's militant black and Puerto Rican factions, particularly the New Ark (sic) Fund headed by LeRoi Jones.

Born in Enterprise, Alabama, May 15, 1932, Gibson is the son of a seamstress and a butcher who moved to Newark when he was eight. He worked his way through Newark College of Engineering after U.S. army service, receiving a civil engineering degree in 1963. He was active in community work, the YMCA and NAACP. By 1966, when he first ran unsuccessfully for mayor, he was chief engineer of the Newark Housing Authority, where he had specialized in urban renewal projects. Married, two daughters.

SIMEON GOLAR

Chairman of the New York City Housing Authority, appointed by Mayor Lindsay in January 1970. Had previously served as vice-chairman of the agency 1967–69. In May 1970, he charged that the federal housing program was being "dismantled" and "destroyed" because of Administration policies which were beginning "to spell out a pattern that threatens to reverse the historic, social, and humanitarian goals . . ." Has also been chairman of the New York City Human Rights Commission. A member of the Liberal party, he ran as candidate for attorney general of New York state in 1966. Born 1929. Married, two daughters.

RODOLFO "CORKY" GONZALES

Leader of the *chicano* movement in Denver. In 1965, founded the Crusade for Justice (*La Crusada para la Justicia*), a self-help organization for Mexican-Americans. Born in 1928 in a Denver *barrio*. The son of a Mexican emigrant laborer, at 10 he was working in the sugar beet fields beside his father. After graduating from high school at 16, became a boxer. He retired in the mid-1950's as the third ranking contender for the world's featherweight title in the National Boxing Association. For the last 15 years has been working in the civil rights movement and in 1968 led the Southwest *chicano* delegation with Reies Tijerina, in the Poor People's March on Washington. A published poet and playwright, best known works: *A Cross for Maclovic* (a play), and *Joachim* (an epic poem which has sold more than 50,000 copies and is being made into an educational film). Married, eight children. Office: 1362 Downing Street, Denver, Colorado. *See also:* CRUSADE FOR JUSTICE.

CHARLES GORDONE

He has been called "the most astonishing new American playwright to come along since Edward Albee." First black playwright to win the

Pulitzer Prize, Gordone received the award in 1970 for his play *No Place To Be Somebody*, described by one reviewer as a "searing look into racial hangups, black and white, in terms of misfits who frequent a Greenwich Village bar." A former actor, Gordone entered the theater in New York after graduating from California State College at Los Angeles in 1952. In 1961, he joined the off-Broadway company producing Jean Genet's "The Blacks." Married to a white woman, the former Jeanner Warner, who reportedly coached him in his writing. Gordone describes himself as "part Indian, part French, part Irish, and part nigger." On black militants he says, "I have respect for their politics. I think it's viable. I mean it's happening ain't it and we have to look at what's happening. But these cats (the black militants) today are discovering they need to join with other elements." Born 1925 in Cleveland, he grew up in Elkhart, Indiana. Enlisted in the Air Corps in 1944. Married several times, one child.

JESSE GRAY

Controversial Harlem leader who organized hundreds of Harlem tenants in a 1963 rent strike, he founded the Harlem Tenants Council and ACT Associates (1964). In June 1969 won the Democratic nomination for New York city councilman from Harlem's Fifth District, to succeed retiring J. Raymond Jones, but was defeated in the November 4 election by Liberal party candidate Charles Taylor (18,059 to 11,604). In January 1970, announced he would run against Adam Clayton Powell. Has been called everything from a "grass-roots kind of guy with a finger in every pie in Harlem" by a Harlem welfare worker, to a "venomous little demagogue with a long record of Communist associations, who made a name of sorts for himself (in 1963) when he instigated a rent strike in Harlem" by *Time* magazine (July 31, 1964). In an interview with *New York Post*, June 27, 1969, declared "I'm pro-black, not anti-white." Born May 14, 1923 in Tunica, Louisiana, he attended Xaxier College in New Orleans and Southern University in Baton Rouge but never graduated. Married Rosa Lee Brown in 1947 and has been separated since 1965, two children.

JACK GREENBERG

Director-counsel of the NAACP Legal Defense and Educational Fund, Inc. (LDF), and directs the activities of 25 staff and 250 cooperating attorneys for the LDF and the National Office for the Rights of the Indigent (newly organized by Greenberg).

Greenberg, a white, succeeded Supreme Court Associate Justice Thurgood Marshall as director-counsel in October of 1961. He has since become nationally known for winning an impressive string of civil rights legal victories. Has argued successfully before the Supreme Court in matters of school segregation, protest demonstrations, recreation, voting, criminal, and other cases. Also served as executive director of the New

York State Bar Association's Special Committee to Study the New York Anti-Trust Laws, for which he wrote *New York Anti-Trust Law in the Federal System* (1957) and *The New York Law of Unfair Competition* (1950). Author of *Race Relations and American Law*, and has written for *The New York Times Magazine*. Born 1924. A lieutenant in the navy during World War II. Married the former Sema Ann Tanzer of Wilmington, Delaware, four children. Home: Great Neck, New York. *See also:* NAACP LEGAL DEFENSE AND EDUCATIONAL FUND.

DICK GREGORY

Successful $350,000-a-year nightclub comedian turned independent crusader for civil rights and peace in Vietnam. In 1968, ran as presidential candidate of Freedom and Peace party (splinter group of Peace and Freedom party), receiving 148,622 votes. Took "oath of office" as "president-in-exile" in Washington, March 6, 1969. Much in demand as campus lecturer, in 1968 spoke at 150 colleges in 36 states, reportedly earning $5,000 a week in fees. Author of *From the Back of the Bus* (1964) and three other books. Twice went on prolonged fasts to protest Vietnam war, the first in November 1967 for 40 days, and the second in June 1968 for 47 days.

First ventured into politics in 1967 when polled 22,000 votes as write-in candidate against Chicago's Mayor Richard Daley. Since beginning civil rights career in 1962 has been jailed some 20 times, the latest during 1968 Democratic convention in Chicago, for leading marchers through police barricades. During 1965 Watts riots, was shot in leg while attempting to quiet a rioter. In June 1969, attended World Assembly of Peace in East Berlin, "to emphasize racism as the prime cause of war."

Married, eight children. Born in St. Louis, Missouri in 1932. Attended Southern Illinois University where he was an outstanding athlete. Served in the army and worked in the United States Post Office in Chicago, from which he was fired, reportedly for impersonating his colleagues and for flipping letters addressed to Mississippi into the overseas mail slot. Became a nightclub comedian in 1958. In 1961 he auditioned at the Playboy Club in Chicago and was an instant hit. From then on he commanded large salaries. Gregory has said: "This is the only country in the world where a man can grow up in a filthy ghetto, go to the worst schools, be forced to ride in the back of the bus, then get $5,000 a week to tell about it."

JAMES E. GROPPI

An Italian-American priest, assistant pastor of St. Boniface Church in Milwaukee's ghetto area. He has shocked many of Milwaukee's whites and irritated city and state authorities by his militant leadership of local civil rights causes. He first received national attention in 1967, when he led 100 days of marches and demonstrations for open housing, despite repeated warnings and pleas from Milwaukee officials and statements of non-support by his church superiors. For resisting arrest during the marches, in February 1968 he was sentenced to six months in jail, but the sentence was stayed and after paying a $500 fine he was placed on probation for two years.

On September 29, 1969, Father Groppi led a take-over of the assembly chambers in Madison, Wisconsin to protest cuts in state's welfare budget. He was sentenced to six-month jail term on October 17, on grounds that his actions had violated the terms of his probation. However, he was released October 27 by the order of Supreme Court Associate Justice Thurgood Marshall, who declared that Groppi was entitled to freedom on bail until the Supreme Court had ruled on the earlier case.

Father Groppi has been jailed at least a dozen times since beginning his civil rights activities and has said he considers going to jail for the cause "a holy act." Born 1931 in Milwaukee, he was appointed assistant pastor at St. Boniface in 1963, and became an advisor to the NAACP's local youth council. He marched in Mississippi in 1964, and in Selma, Alabama in 1965. In answer to some white critics of his militancy, he once declared: "I am white only in complexion. I will picket with the Negro. I will go South with him. I will go to jail with him. And I will hang with him if it need be."

Father Groppi left St. Boniface June 1, 1970 and was reassigned to St. Michael's, a racially mixed parish in Milwaukee.

KENNETH GUSSCOTT
President of the Boston branch of NAACP since 1963, and since March 1969 president of the New England Conference of NAACP. Under Gusscott leadership the NAACP Boston office launched a Positive Program for Boston in 1968. Designed to improve Negro opportunities, it is supported by private businesses, which in 1968 invested some $174,000. A native of Boston, he is regarded as the originator of that city's civil rights movement. Parents were both part of the Garvey movement in the 1920's and they formed the first all-black credit union in the city. Attended Boston Technical High School, Northwestern University and graduated from the Merchant Marine Academy. Served in the air force during World War II and later joined the defense department as a marine engineer. Later he was chief nuclear test engineer for Bethlehem Steel. Currently is project engineering supervisor for General Dynamics.

JOSÉ ANGEL GUTIERREZ
Leader of the Mexican–American Youth Organization (MAYO) in Texas, and organizer of the successful Crystal City, Texas, school boycott which made national headlines in January 1970. The boycott set a precedent with direct negotiations between students and the predominantly white Crystal City school board to effect demanded curriculum

changes. Gutierrez, 25, is the son of a doctor, formed MAYO with four others in 1967 while a student at St. Mary's College in San Antonio. Home: 124 West Edwards, Crystal City, Texas. *See also:* MEXICAN-AMERICAN YOUTH ORGANIZATION (MAYO).

WILLIAM F. HADDAD

Award-winning reporter for *New York Post* 1957–61, associate director of Peace Corps, 1961–63, and a leading official in Office of Economic Opportunity until 1965. Since 1966 has headed own group, the New York-based U.S. Research and Development Corporation, which conducts training programs for hard-core unemployed. Is co-publisher, with CORE director Roy Innis, of *Manhattan Tribune*, an experimental West Side community paper aimed at greater black-white dialogue. Paper also serves as a training ground for black newsmen. Aide to Senator Estes Kefauver, 1954–57. Special assistant to Robert Kennedy in 1960 presidential campaign. In 1964, ran unsuccessfully as reform candidate in New York's Nineteenth Congressional District. Born in Charlotte, North Carolina, July 25, 1928. Received B.A. from Columbia University in 1954. Studied Russian and Chinese at Georgetown University, 1954–56. Married Kate Roosevelt, 1959, three children.

FANNIE LOU HAMER

Charismatic leader of the Mississippi Freedom Democrats at the 1964 Democratic National Convention, "the mammy-style grandmother . . . became the symbol of the downtrodden Southern Negro" (*Washington Post* 7/14/68). Given an ovation at the 1968 Convention, when her group successfully unseated the regular Mississippi delegation. First became involved in the civil rights movement August 31, 1962 when she was barred in her attempt to register to vote in Rulesville (Sunflower County), Mississippi. She then joined SNCC (1962) and became an activist in the voter registration drive. In 1963, joined James Meredith in his march on the University of Mississippi. And, at the 1964 Democratic National Convention, she was the vice-chairman of the predominantly black Mississippi Freedom Democratic party that sought to unseat the all-white regular delegation. In 1968, worked toward the coalition of her Freedom party with other black and liberal white groups, to be known as the Loyal Democrats of Mississippi. This group successfully challenged the state's all-white delegation at the 1968 Democratic convention. Born in 1918, the youngest of 20 children, and the daughter of a sharecropper. She is married to Perry (Pap) Hamer.

CHARLES V. HAMILTON

Professor of Government at Columbia University since September 1969 and formerly chairman of the Department of Political Science at Roosevelt University, Chicago. One of the nation's most articulate authorities on black power. Co-author with Stokely Carmichael of *Black Power: The Politics of Liberation in America.* Was board member of SNCC and is currently adviser to several civil rights groups. Lectures widely on the black revolution. Graduate of Roosevelt University, Loyola University (Chicago) and the University of Chicago. Has taught at Tuskegee Institute, Albany State College (Georgia), Rutgers and Lincoln Universities. Married, two daughters.

HARLEM UNEMPLOYMENT CENTER (HUC)
Privately funded organization founded in 1964 to bring together black and white workers by supporting them in their struggle for employment, training, and democratic trade unionism. With rank-and-file representation from longshoremen, freight, utility, transit, restaurant, hotel, and garment industries, HUC gives counsel to individual workers with specific union and work related grievances and represents them before federal, state, and city agencies. Primarily concerned with job placement in construction work. Currently active membership is 450. Supported by membership dues ($3.00 per month) with an annual budget of $15,000. Director and founder is James Haughton.

LaDONNA CRAWFORD HARRIS
Half-Comanche, half-Irish wife of Sen. Fred Harris, Democrat of Oklahoma. In 1969–70, Mrs. Harris emerged as a leading and attractive spokesman for Indian interests. In February 1970 she founded the Americans for Indian Opportunity. Earlier she had resigned from the President's National Council on Indian Opportunity, on the grounds that too little progress was being made. She is a member of the Urban Coalition national steering committee. Born February 15, 1931 and raised by Comanche grandparents in Walters, Oklahoma. Three children. *See also:* AMERICANS FOR INDIAN OPPORTUNITY, NATIONAL COUNCIL ON INDIAN OPPORTUNITY.

PATRICIA ROBERTS HARRIS
Ambassador to Luxembourg, 1965–67, and first Negro woman to head an American embassy. In 1966, appointed alternate delegate to the United Nations. In 1968 President Johnson appointed Mrs. Harris to the seven-member Commission on Causes and Prevention of Violence. In February 1969, was central figure in dispute at Howard University. Appointed dean of the law school February 1st, she was confronted by a student boycott and resigned February 27, charging that Howard President James Nabrit had placed her in "untenable position" by negotiating with student protesters behind her back. Was member of Howard's law faculty for several years. Long active in civil rights and Democratic politics, she has held office in Washington chapters of the NAACP, Urban League, ACLU, and other groups. Was chairman of the National Women's Committee on Civil Rights, 1963–64, and is a director of the NAACP Legal Defense Fund. Born in Mattoon, Illinois, May

31, 1924, the daughter of a railroad waiter, she graduated from Howard
University in 1945 and later studied at University of Chicago and
American University. Married to lawyer William Beasley Harris.

JERU-AHMED HASSAN
Born in 1924 in Washington, D.C. as Albert Roy Osborne, changed his
name to Hassan when he organized the Washington-based Blackman's
Volunteer Army of Liberation in the mid-1960's. A back-to-Africa
movement, the organization's purpose was said to be to create a mer-
cenary army of American Negroes (called the "Black Star Regiment")
to fight for independence in Central and South Africa, and thereby to
win a nation for themselves. Hassan's para-military organization later
established the Blackman's Development Center in Washington, D.C.,
which in July 1970 received financial backing from the city government
for its successful anti-drug program which treats 2,800 addicts a week.
Hassan testified before a special Senate subcommittee on alcoholism and
narcotics in April 1970. Declared that heroin reaches Washington through
a conspiracy of the Mafia, Cosa Nostra, and "the black syndicate."

WILLIAM H. HASTIE
First Negro to be made a federal judge. Born in Knoxville, Tennessee
on November 17, 1904, he received an A.B. degree from Amherst College in 1925 and an honorary M.A. in 1940 also from Amherst. Earned
an LL.B. from Harvard University in 1930, admitted to the bar the same
year. Made a federal judge on the Third Circuit Court of Appeals in
Philadelphia in 1949. Married the former Beryl Lockhart, two children.

RICHARD GORDON HATCHER
Mayor of Gary, Indiana, since November 1967. Along with Carl Stokes
of Cleveland, one of the first blacks elected mayor of a major American
city. Democrat Hatcher's victory was a triumph over the active and bitter opposition of the regular Democratic machine. Election was fraught
with notorious examples of harassment and attempted vote-rigging. At
Hatcher's request, Attorney General Ramsay Clark ordered 22 FBI men
to Gary to get purged names restored to the registration lists. On November 6, just prior to the election, a special three-judge federal court
ordered 1,000 false names from the lists and the reinstatement of 5,000
Negro voters. The court acted after consolidating separate suits brought
by Hatcher and the justice department. Hatcher finally defeated Joseph
B. Radigan by 39,330 votes to 37,941. Since taking office, Hatcher has
been faced with a series of civic problems and racial unrest: garbage
collectors' strike, a school boycott, complaints from whites that he padded
black payrolls, an outbreak of violence (sniping and looting) after Martin
Luther King's death and a 65 percent crime increase over 1968.

In April 1969, he was confronted with losing some 40,000 white residents, almost a quarter of Gary's 180,000 population. A drive was launched by city councilman Eugene Kirtland, a Republican, to disannex the white (ethnic) neighborhood of Glen Park. The reason, some say, sprang from racism but Glen Park residents who supported the move claimed that it would lower their taxes. Born 1933, the son of a factory worker, Hatcher worked his way through Indiana University and Valparaiso University law school. After graduation he moved to Gary to practice law. He became a deputy prosecutor and, in 1963, a member of the city council.

JAMES HAUGHTON
Director and founder of Harlem Unemployment Center. Born in 1930 in Brooklyn, New York. Holds bachelor's degree from City College of New York and Master's in public administration from New York University. Served in the Korean War. Married to Dr. Eleanor Leacock, an anthropologist. *See also:* HARLEM UNEMPLOYMENT CENTER.

AUGUSTUS F. HAWKINS
Democratic representative from California's Twenty-first Congressional District, elected in 1963. In 1934, elected to state assembly and worked particularly on juvenile delinquency until election to Congress. He has been a vigorous supporter of legislation in civil rights, labor relations, health, welfare, and housing and more than 300 laws on the statute books in California bear his name or acknowledge his co-authorship. He is a member of the all-black Congressional Ad Hoc Committee formed in 1969 to investigate Panther/police clashes. In private life, has an insurance and real estate business and automobile appliance business. Born in Shreveport, Louisiana on August 31, 1917, he moved to California at age 11, went to high school there and graduated in economics from the University of California.

NATHAN C. HEARD
Author whose first novel, *Howard Street,* published November 1968 (Dial Press), is based on his adolescence in the Newark ghetto. Taught himself to write during three spells in prison between 1958 and 1968 (the last time for armed robbery). He was finally released December 1968, a month after his book was published. Born 1936 in Newark, New Jersey, is currently working on a second book. From September 1969, he lectured in creative writing at Fresno State College in California.

BRENT L. HENRY
Princeton University graduate, class of 1969, and the first black and youngest man ever elected to serve on the Board of Trustees at Princeton. His four-year term expires July 1973. A participant in the student take-over of a campus building there early in 1969, his election was part of a new arrangement designed to have four persons of approximately

college age on the Board of Trustees at all times after 1972. (Previously, the median age had been about 60.) He was born in 1947.

HERBERT HILL

National labor director of NAACP since 1948 and a veteran of hundreds of legal battles against discriminatory unions. A white man, he was an organizer for the United States Steel Workers of America in his teens. Joined the NAACP in 1938, first working with its Harlem branch and in 1945 joined the national staff as a field worker. Born January 24, 1924 in Brooklyn, New York, he attended public schools there, and attended New York University and the New School for Social Research but did not receive a degree. Is co-author of *Citizen's Guide to Desegregation: A Study of Social and Legal Change in American Society* and *Anger and Beyond*. A frequent lecturer and magazine writer. Married.

JULIUS W. HOBSON

Economist with Department of Housing, Education, and Welfare for 20 years until his resignation April 1, 1970. He is known as an uncompromising civil rights activist. As local chairman of ACT, filed suit against Washington, D.C. school board that resulted in landmark decision by U.S. District Judge J. Skelly Wright, June 19, 1967 that "de facto" segregation in D.C. schools was unconstitutional. Served as school board member until 1969 when he failed to get re-elected. Currently heads Washington Institute for Quality Education, a research organization concerned with minority problems. Also teaches Sociology at the American University in Washington. Has been on FBI monthly surveillance list. Born 1922 in Birmingham, Alabama and a graduate of Tuskegee Institute. Married twice, currently to the former Tina Lower, a white woman, two children.

JEROME H. HOLLAND

Ambassador to Sweden, appointed January 13, 1970 by President Nixon. The post, which had been vacant for the previous year, has been made difficult because of a growing rift in U.S./Swedish relations over the Vietnamese War. Prior to his appointment, Dr. Holland had been president of Hampton Institute in Virginia since 1960. He holds a B.S. from Cornell University (1939), a Ph.D. from University of Pennsylvania (1950), an LL.D. from University of Cincinnati (1960). Married the former Laura Mitchell in 1948, two children. Born January 9, 1916.

BEN HOLMAN

Director of Community Relations Service, Department of Justice. Formerly a reporter with the *Chicago Daily News* and with CBS News in New York. On WNBC-TV program on integration, November 15, 1969, said: "I've personally found that I've drifted away from the integration goal, and I think I'm mirroring the attitude of a lot of blacks. How can you really have integration when 85 percent of the country doesn't want it?" Born December 18, 1930. Unmarried.

HAMILTON HOLMES

Desegregated the University of Georgia in Athens on January 10, 1961 along with Charlayne Hunter. Graduated valedictorian and class president from high school, and while waiting for admission to University of Georgia, attended Morehouse College. Was under police protection during his first days at the university but afterwards shunned public attention and stuck close to his books. Graduated in 1963 and entered Emory University Medical School in Atlanta graduating in 1967. Completed his first year of residency at Detroit General Hospital in 1969, after which he fulfilled his military service in Germany.

JAMES A. HOOD

Desegregated the University of Alabama in 1963 along with Vivian Malone. But withdrew two months later, on doctor's orders, "to avoid complete mental and physical breakdown," following state-backed demands for his expulsion for alleged remarks at a Negro rally. Went to live in Detroit, where he worked at Ford Motor Company while studying for B.A. in sociology at Wayne State University. Graduated 1969. Became director of central city programs of Interfaith Action group in Detroit, providing ghetto with educational opportunities and other aid. Planned graduate study at Michigan State University in police administration. Born Gadsden, Alabama, November 10, 1942. Married, one son.

LENA HORNE

Singer and actress, and the first Negro woman ever to be signed to a long-term Hollywood contract. Considers herself part of the revolution. Has spoken in Mississippi, marched on Washington, sung for SNCC. In 1963 with James Baldwin met Robert Kennedy to discuss segregation in North, but identifies more particularly with Southern Negro. "My identity is finally very clear to me. I'm a black woman and I'm not alone." "Am I hopeful?" she repeated when a reporter asked her if the color problem might one day conceivably die out. "Honey, I'm so hopeful that sometimes it hurts." Born June 30, 1917 in Brooklyn, New York and joined the chorus line in the Cotton Club in 1933. Sang with the Charlie Barnett Orchestra 1939 and made her first records with him. Also has done films, records and TV. Wrote her autobiography LENA, in 1965. Starred in *Cabin in the Sky; Stormy Weather;* and played *Jamaica* on Broadway. Married to white musician Lennie Hayton.

CHARLAYNE HUNTER

Desegregated the University of Georgia, January 10, 1961, along with Hamilton Holmes. Graduated in 1963 with a degree in journalism. Married white student Walter Stovall in the spring of 1963, and their daughter Susan was born in November of the same year. After graduation, worked for the *New Yorker* magazine as an editorial assistant while her husband was a reporter for the *Bergen* (New Jersey) *Record*. Later worked for WRC, the NBC affiliate in Washington, D.C., and in July 1969, joined the staff of *The New York Times*. One of her first stories, "Panthers Indoctrinate the Young," appeared August 18, 1969. Born 1942.

RUBY HURLEY
Southeast regional director for the NAACP which includes states of Alabama, Florida, Georgia, Mississippi, Tennessee, North Carolina, and South Carolina. A native of Washington, D.C., she attended public schools there, Miner Teachers College and Robert H. Terrell Law School. Before joining the NAACP, worked in the Industrial Bank of Washington and later for the federal government. In 1951, sent to Birmingham, Alabama on a temporary assignment to coordinate NAACP membership campaigns for the branches of Alabama, Florida, Georgia, Mississippi, and Tennessee. Subsequently the southeast region was established and expanded to include North and South Carolina. This seven-state area leads all other NAACP regional groups in membership and consists of more than 90,000 adult members and 13,000 youths. There are also 448 adult branches and 144 youth councils and college chapters in her region. Office: 859½ Hunter N.W., Atlanta, Georgia.

PHILIP HUTCHINGS
Succeeded H. Rap Brown as SNCC chairman in June 1968. Previously a SNCC organizer in Newark, New Jersey, and then program director. Redefined SNCC's aims to include the formation of a black political party that, with its emphasis on black power, would end "racism and imperialism." On July 22, 1969 was replaced by H. Rap Brown as SNCC chairman.

INDIANS OF ALL TRIBES
A corporation formed in February 1970 by the Indians living on Alcatraz Island in San Francisco Bay. Its seven-member governing board is headed by Richard Oakes, a Mohawk Indian who was leader of the group of 89 that seized the island November 20, 1969, claiming ownership under the terms of an 1868 Sioux treaty (Alcatraz had stood abandoned since 1963, when the federal prison was closed down). The group claims that it wants to establish a cultural center on the 12-acre island, but more immediately wants title to the land and to provide adequate educational, health and food facilities for a resident population of 150. In March 1970, the Indians of All Tribes sent a proposal to Washington asking for a grant of $300,000 to finance their plans. The chief federal negotiator, Robert Robertson, met with them on April 18, 1970 and proposed the island be turned into a park with "maximum Indian qualities." Turning down the proposal, the Indians threatened to draw up their own ownership deed and seek private financing if agreement could not be reached. On June 8, 1970 electric power to the island was cut off. However, be-

sides coping with the problems of daily existence there, the Indians produced a weekly newsletter and radio program called Radio Free Alcatraz. Headquarters: 4339 California Avenue, San Francisco, Calif.

INNER CITY BUSINESS IMPROVEMENT FORUM

An all-black, non-profit corporation formed in Detroit after the 1967 riots, under the auspices of Rep. Charles Diggs, for the funding of black business enterprises. By mid-1970, had invested or loaned nearly $1 million and cooperated with Detroit banks and the Small Business Administration in another $3.7 million in loans, sponsoring nearly 100 black business and industrial projects, including a supermarket, a plastic toy manufacturer, and the city's first black-controlled bank, the First Independence National Bank (President, David B. Harper), which opened in June, 1970. The ICBIF has received funds from the Ford Foundation, the Office of Economic Opportunity and the Detroit Economic Development Corporation—which was set up in 1968 for the specific purpose of aiding black business. (The Economic Development Corporation is an offspring of New Detroit, a coalition of Detroit business and labor leaders formed by then Governor George Romney and Mayor Jerome Cavanagh after the 1967 riots.) Chairman of the ICBIF is the Rev. Charles E. Morton; president is Larry Doss, formerly with the Internal Revenue Service; executive director is Charles Brown, Jr. ICBIF address: 1672 14th Street, Detroit, Michigan. *See also:* CHARLES DIGGS.

ROY INNIS

National director of CORE since 1968, when he succeeded Floyd McKissick. Has continued to turn CORE from a broad-based civil rights organization into a black nationalist group with little influence outside Harlem. Defining his ideas of separatism in *Ebony* magazine, Innis said: "Under segregation, black people live together but their institutions are controlled by whites. Under integration, black people are dispersed and the institutions, goods and services are still controlled by whites. In effect, the two are the same. But under separatism, black people will control their own turf." In the New York mayoralty election in November 1969, Innis refused to endorse any of the candidates and urged Harlem voters to boycott the election. As part of his separatist program, he initiated the Community Self-Determination Bill, introduced in Congress July 1968. Has called for the drafting of a new Constitution, because the original ignored black people. Despite his separatist philosophy, Innis joined with former newsman William Haddad to launch the *Manhattan Tribune* in November 1968, with the stated aim of bridging the gap between "the frustrated, angry black community and the frightened white community" of New York City's Upper West Side. Innis also works with Haddad's organization, the Research and

Development Corporation. In March 1970, Innis proposed a unitary system plan for school integration which would create one white and one black school district, each autonomous and equal. Mobile, Alabama has been chosen as first test city for his plan. Born in St. Croix, Virgin Islands on June 6, 1934. Came to New York with his mother at age two and lived in Harlem. Quit high school at 16 to enlist in the army, fought in the Korean War (he lied about his age) and stayed in the army for two years. While in the service, he passed the high school equivalency exam. Went to City College of New York where he studied chemistry. He has been married twice, presently to the former Doris Funnye of Georgetown, South Carolina, four children.

INSTITUTE OF BLACK ELECTED OFFICIALS
Formed in 1967 to bring together black office holders, its second national conference was held in Washington, D.C., September 11–14, 1969. Conference attended by nearly 400 officials, the largest gathering ever held of elected black officials, and estimated to be about one-third of all elected black officials in the country. They discussed new approaches to common problems and were addressed by government and academic leaders. The institute's conferences are supported by foundation funds and its business is handled from the offices of Metropolitan Applied Research Center. Co-chairmen are: Woodrow Wilson, state assembly (Nevada); Louise Reynolds, alderman (Louisville, Kentucky); Percy Sutton, Manhattan borough president (New York); and Mervyn Dymally, state senator (California). Washington representative: Eleanor Farrar. Office: MARC, 1819 H. Street, N.W., Washington, D.C.

INTERRELIGIOUS FOUNDATION FOR COMMUNITY ORGANIZATION (IFCO)
A multiracial foundation dedicated to the pursuit of "self-determination" in the urban ghettos. Sponsored National Black Economic Development Conference in April 1969. Founded in December 1966 by 10 major Catholic, Protestant, and Jewish social action agencies—including the Executive Council of the Episcopal Church, the American Jewish Committee, and the Catholic Committee for Community Organization. Announced its intention to "help mobilize poor communities throughout the country to play a greater role in solving their problems" by coordinating the programs of the member agencies. Agencies now numbering 23, seek grants from other foundations, train community organizers, and sponsor research programs. From September 1967 to September 1969, received a total of one and a half million dollars in grants. Now funds local communities in more than 40 cities and such national organizations as the National Welfare Rights Organization and the National Association of Afro-American Educators. Sponsored the Black Economic Development Conference (BEDC) to dramatize the need for still more financial assistance to community organizations. Be-

cause of the publicity connected with the BEDC and James Forman's "Black Manifesto," the United Presbyterian Church pledged IFCO $100,000. Acts as a channel for funds donated to the BEDC, now a separate organization. Controlled by a racially balanced board of directors with 43 members and is based in New York. Rev. Lucius Walker is executive director. Office: 211 East 43rd Street, New York, New York.

JESSE JACKSON

Head of SCLC in Chicago and, after a series of successful actions there, is widely considered the city's leading Negro spokesman and probable next national leader of SCLC. Architect of Operation Breadbasket which has led successful boycott campaigns against Chicago's leading chain stores and other businesses. Now travels widely, guiding similar operations in other cities. Ordained a Baptist minister in 1968, he does not have a church but conducts Saturday morning meetings at South Side's Capitol Theater (79th & Halstead St. in Chicago), which have developed a phenomenal regular following of up to 5,000 people. In April 1968, it was Jackson who cradled Martin Luther King's head in his arms on the balcony of the Lorraine Motel in Memphis. In June 1968, he gained national prominence as manager of Poor People's Campaign Resurrection City in Washington, D.C. In October 1969, he launched Operation Breadbasket in New York's Bedford-Stuyvesant section.

Born in Greenville, South Carolina, in 1941, he received an athletic scholarship to the University of Illinois and later studied at North Carolina Agricultural and Technical College. Jackson led his first protest march in Greensboro in 1963. He later became president of the newly formed North Carolina Intercollegiate Council on Human Rights. It was after this that he joined King ("my father figure, my brother figure and my teacher"). "America is pluralistic," he has said. "There is talk about being a melting pot. But really it's more like vegetable soup. There are separate pieces of corn, meat, and so on, each with its own identity. The blacks have been pushed down to the bottom of the pot. We are going to come up and be recognized or turn the pot over." *See also:* OPERATION BREADBASKET.

MAYNARD HOLBROOK JACKSON

Vice-mayor of Atlanta since October 1969. The first Negro ever elected to one of the top two offices of the Georgia capital, he gained nearly 60 percent of the votes against white candidate, Alderman Milton G. Farris. A lawyer and vice-president of the Atlanta NAACP, Jackson is considered to be a progressive liberal.

In 1968, against the advice of local Negro leaders, he ran against former Governor Herman Talmadge in the Democratic primary for the U.S. senate and lost heavily.

Born March 23, 1938, in Dallas, Texas, he is a graduate of Morehouse College and North Carolina Central University. Married, two daughters.

JAPANESE AMERICAN CITIZENS LEAGUE

A national non-profit organization which campaigns for equal rights for Japanese-American citizens. Has an intensive information and education program and serves as a "watchdog" alert for movements and proposals both in Congress and state legislatures that would affect their welfare. Has approximately 20,000 members in 85 local chapters in 32 states. Publishes a weekly news magazine called the *Pacific Citizen*. National director is Masaow Satow. Office: 1634 Post Street, San Francisco, California.

JOHN H. JOHNSON

Millionaire publisher and founder of the $12 million Chicago-based Johnson Publishing Company, and chairman of Supreme Life Insurance Co., reputedly the nation's largest Negro business. Named by President Nixon to Advisory Commission on Minority Enterprise, "to eliminate roadblocks on the path of economic opportunity to every citizen." In 1942, Johnson started the monthly *Negro Digest* with a borrowed $500. In 1945, he launched *Ebony* "to emphasize the brighter side of Negro life and success." With more than one-million circulation, it is the nation's biggest Negro publication and chief moneymaker of the Johnson empire. It was followed by *Tan* (1950) and *Jet* (1951). In 1951, Johnson was named one of the 10 most outstanding men of the year by the Junior Chamber of Commerce. In 1957, accompanied the then Vice-President Nixon on a goodwill trip to nine African countries and in 1959 went with Nixon again to Russia and Poland. Was a special ambassadorial representative for United States at independence ceremonies of the Ivory Coast in 1961 and at Kenya's independence ceremonies in 1963. Received the Russworm, Spingarn, and Horatio Alger awards. In 1966 was a member of the National Advisory Council of President's Committee on Economic Opportunity. Is a vice-president of the National Urban League. Born in Arkansas City, Arkansas on January 19, 1918. Attended University of Chicago and Northwestern University. Married to the former Eunice Waller, two children.

LYNDON BAINES JOHNSON

According to the NAACP magazine, *Crisis*, January 1969, President Johnson was the first U.S. president so fully committed to the betterment of racial inequities. His achievements were cited as a major breakthrough. "During his administration, Congress passed three major civil rights laws (1964, 1965, and 1968), [which] enacted a halt to discrimination in employment, education, housing, public accommodations, voting and to assure equal protection of the law. As Senate Majority Leader he played a major role in the passage of the Civil Rights Acts of 1957 and 1960. He also set a new record in enlarging employment opportunities for Negroes in Federal Service."

J. RAYMOND JONES

Veteran New York City Democratic party official, who in 1964 was elected chairman of the New York County Democratic Committee

(Tammany Hall), reputedly the first black in the country to head a county political organization. Resigned as Tammany Hall leader in March 1967, after Senator Robert Kennedy denied him his support. In 1969 mayoralty campaign, broke his 48-year record of strict party loyalty by endorsing Mayor Lindsay, declaring Democratic candidate Mario Procaccino's campaign to be "anti-black." Active in Democratic politics since 1921, Jones became district leader in 1959, city councilman in 1962, and was sometimes known by fellow Democrats as "the Fox." Born in St. Thomas, V.I., November 19, 1899, he settled in New York City in 1918. Married, one daughter.

LEROI JONES (Imamu Ameer Baraka)

Poet and playwright who since 1967 Newark riots has led efforts to organize that city's black and Puerto Rican communities as a political force, through the United Black Brothers, Black Community Development, and the Committee for United Newark. In a city whose population is more than 50 percent Negro, he has declared: "We are out to bring self-government to this town by 1970 . . . it can be taken without a shot being fired." To this end, Jones has worked to prevent a repetition of rioting by promoting better communications with the authorities and white groups, and by providing a 24-hour "advice and help" service to members of the community. His organizations have also spurred voter education and registration (up 20 percent in a year) and "brought thousands of dollars worth of resources into the black community of Newark," according to *Ebony*, August 1969. Jones once summed up his philosophy: "I'm in favor of black people taking power by the quickest, easiest, most successful means they can employ. Malcolm X said 'the ballot or the bullet.' Newark is a particular situation where the ballot seems most advantageous. I believe we have to survive. I didn't invent slavery. I didn't invent white men. What we're trying to do is deal with him the best way we can." Jones has become a minister of the "Kawaida" faith, adopting the Swahili title Imamu (spiritual leader) and the Arabic name Ameer Baraka. Arrested in the July 1967 riots for possession of firearms and sentenced to three years, Jones and his two co-defendants were finally acquitted July 2, 1969, after a retrial. Born October 7, 1934, in Newark, he won a scholarship to Rutgers and later obtained an M.A. at Columbia. His poetry and fiction won him a John Hay Whitney Fellowship in 1961, and he received an Obie Award in 1964 for *The Dutchman*, as the best off-Broadway play of the season. Married to second wife, Amina Jones, has six children.

PERCY L. JULIAN

One of the nation's most noted Negro scientists and a pioneer in the chemistry of hormones and steroids. Director of the Julian Research Institute in Chicago, a non-profit organization engaged in pure and applied research on drugs, particularly in the areas of sex hormones, oral contraceptives, and pro-vitamin D3. In 1967 was one of 47 leading Negro business and professional men who formed a fund-raising organization to finance the activities of the NAACP Legal Defense and Educational Fund. Also a generous contributor to civil rights causes. Born in Montgomery, Alabama, 1898. Atttended DePauw University (Indiana) by working his way through as a waiter, graduating Phi Beta Kappa (1920) and taught at Fisk and Howard Universities. Did postgraduate work at Harvard (1923) and the University of Vienna (1931). Married, two children.

JUSTICE DEPARTMENT, CIVIL RIGHTS DIVISION
Responsibilities include enforcement of civil rights laws and executive orders prohibiting discrimination; authorizing intervention in cases brought by private litigants involving the denial of equal protection of the laws on account of race; supervision and direction of criminal prosecutions of any person acting under cover of the law and private persons acting in conspiracy to interfere with or to deny the exercise of federal rights. Division is headed by an assistant attorney general. Noted previous holders were Burke Marshall (1960–64), and John Doar (1964–67). Present head is Jerris Leonard. Division has field offices in Montgomery, Alabama, Los Angeles, California, New Orleans, Louisiana, Jackson, Mississippi, and Dallas, Texas. In August 1969, a group of 40 of the division's lawyers publicly protested the Nixon Administration's desegregation policies. On October 1, the leader of the dissident lawyers, Gary J. Greenberg, was forced to resign after criticizing Attorney General John Mitchell in open court. On October 14, the justice department filed suit to end alleged racial segregation in the elementary schools of Waterbury, Connecticut, the first such action by the federal government in a Northeastern state. In July, 1970, the Department launched widespread legal action against remaining southern school districts which had not desegregated. *See also:* JOHN DOAR, JERRIS LEONARD, BURKE MARSHALL.

RON KARENGA
Founder of the Los Angeles-based black nationalist organization "US" (as opposed to THEM) and considered one of the most articulate and influential of the new breed of black militant leaders. Karenga urges blacks to foster their own distinct Afro-American culture instead of trying to adapt to white values. His adopted Swahili name, Karenga, means "keeper of tradition." Among those he has influenced is LeRoi Jones, whose Black Community Development program in Newark is patterned on U.S. Though he uses violent language ("When it's 'burn,' let's see how much you can burn. When it's 'kill,' let's see how much you can kill."), and though he adopts a somewhat fearsome pose (shaven head, Genghis Khan mustache, dark glasses, and armed guards), Karenga is credited with a major role in keeping Los Angeles calm

after the King assassination, and his aim has been described by a Negro lawyer as "to exploit the fear of violence without actually using it." Played key role in formation of the Black Congress in 1967, an umbrella organization of Negro groups in Los Angeles, including moderates and militants, which sponsors supplemental schooling for ghetto children, cooperative food stores, etc. Karenga has also had private meetings with Governor Reagan and Los Angeles police chiefs. Former chief Reddin has praised Karenga's peacekeeping efforts. Motto of Karenga's organization is: "Anywhere we are, US is." But actual membership is small, estimated at less than 100. There has been conflict between US and Black Panthers, and when two members of the Panthers were shot dead at UCLA meeting on black studies January 23, 1969, the Panther group accused US of the assassinations. Three members of US were later convicted of the killings and sentenced to life imprisonment, September 17, 1969. Karenga was born Ronald Everett in 1943, the youngest of 14 children of a Baptist minister. Received an M.A. in political science at University of California at Los Angeles and was first Negro elected president of the student body at California Junior College. Says he switched from moderate to militant after Watts riots in 1965, when he took the Swahili name of Karenga and formed US. Married, three children.

NICHOLAS deB KATZENBACH

With the Department of Justice from 1961–66, first as assistant attorney general, then attorney general (1965–66). During his time in the department, he faced Governor George Wallace on the steps of the University of Mississippi with James Meredith in 1962 and helped draft and steer through the Civil Rights Act of 1964, and the Voting Rights Act of 1965. In 1966 he was switched by President Johnson from the justice department to the state department as undersecretary of state, a position he held until November 1968. Currently a vice-president and general counsel of IBM. A white man, he was born in 1922 in Philadelphia. Graduated from Phillips Exeter Academy (1939), Princeton University (1945), and Yale University (1947) LL.B. A Rhodes Scholar (1947–49) at Balliol College, Oxford. Admitted to the New Jersey bar 1950. Worked for the firm of Katzenbach, Gildea and Rudner in Trenton until joining the justice department. Married the former Lydia King Philips Stokes in 1946, four children.

CHARLES 37X KENYATTA

Leader of the small, armed Harlem Mau Mau organization, who became an important link between the ghetto and New York's city hall. Kenyatta was shot and seriously wounded June 8, 1969, by unknown assailants believed to be linked to an extortionist ring posing as civil rights activists. Kenyatta himself accused the Black Muslims. Kenyatta had been one of Malcolm X's bodyguards at the time the latter was slain in 1965 (two of the men convicted for the murder were Black Muslims). Later, Kenyatta's Mau Maus often appeared in Harlem armed with machetes and bayonets, and were shunned as too extremist by other civil rights groups. But since 1967, Kenyatta has worked with city officials on Harlem improvement projects, and in 1968 was credited with a major role in keeping violence to a minimum when he led a peace-keeping group which toured the ghetto, urging restraint. Walked arm-in-arm with Governor Rockefeller at Central Park rites for Martin Luther King, Jr., April 7, 1968, and accompanied Mayor Lindsay to King's funeral in Atlanta, April 9. Kenyatta campaigned vigorously against Harlem narcotics pushers and "blacks who use other blacks." Born Charles Roberts in 1920.

CORETTA SCOTT KING

Widow of Dr. Martin Luther King, Jr. Since his death has emerged as an eloquent speaker and internationally recognized public figure in her own right. In January 1969, announced plans for Martin Luther King Memorial in Atlanta, to include a park, library, museum and Afro-American study center. In same month, traveled to India to receive Nehru Award for international understanding, in behalf of her husband. Received further awards in Italy, where she met with Pope Paul VI. In London, in March 1969, became first woman ever to preach in St. Paul's Cathedral, where she called for "a new ministry of conciliation." In April 1969, led 2000-strong march through streets of Charleston, South Carolina, in support of striking hospital workers. In February 1969, conferred with Henry Kissinger at White House as representative of anti-war group. Gallup Poll (February 1, 1969) placed her fourth on list of nation's most admired women (after Mrs. Ethel Kennedy, Mrs. Rose Kennedy, and Mrs. Mamie Eisenhower), and she was named Woman of the Year, 1968 by the National Association of Television and Radio Announcers. As principal speaker at Poor People's Solidarity Day in Washington, June 19, 1968, appealed to women of America to unite "and form a solid block of woman power to fight the three great evils of racism, poverty and war." Since her husband's death, Mrs. King has made several concert appearances with the Washington National Symphony as narrator of Aaron Copland's *A Lincoln Portrait*.

Born in Heiberger, Alabama, April 27, 1927. In 1945, she became one of the first Negro students accepted at Antioch College in Ohio, where she majored in education and music. Graduating in 1951, she went on to the New England Conservatory of Music in Boston, where she studied voice. While there, she met King, who was doing graduate work in philosophy at Boston University. They were married June 18, 1953, after which she gave up her plans for a singing career to help her husband. In 1954 they moved to Montgomery, Alabama, where King had been appointed a Baptist pastor—and the following year became nationally known for leading the Montgomery bus boycott. In the ensuing years, she participated in marches, meetings, etc. with her husband, and gave more than 30 "freedom concerts" to raise funds for SCLC. She has written a biography of her husband, *My Life with Martin Luther King, Jr.*, published by Holt, Rinehart & Winston in September, 1969. She lives in Atlanta with her four children: Yolanda Denise ("Yoki"), born 1955; Martin Luther, III, born 1957; Dexter Scott, 1961; Bernice Albertine, 1963.

EARTHA KITT
Renowned "down-to-Eartha" singer, she has been an outspoken critic of war in Vietnam. Made her feelings known to Mrs. Lyndon Johnson (then the First Lady) at a White House luncheon in January 1968, saying that the war was having a demoralizing effect on the nation's youth. "I got 5000 letters about that," she said, "only seven were critical." Born in North, South Carolina, January 26, 1928. Was a seamstress, dancer, and Parisian torcher, before capsizing Broadway (in *New Faces of 1952* with her show stopping rendition of "Monotonous") and Hollywood in *Anna Lucasta*, 1958. Author of *Thursday's Child* (1956) and *A Tart Is Not a Sweet*. Divorced, one daughter.

ELIZABETH DUNCAN KOONTZ
Director of Women's Bureau in the Department of Labor. Former teacher and first black president (elected 1968) of the National Education Association. Born 1919 in North Carolina, she holds a B.A. in English from Livingstone College (1938) and an M.A. from Atlanta University. Married.

WILLIAM M. KUNSTLER
Flamboyant defense counsel in the 1969 Chicago Seven conspiracy trial, whose conduct in court and frequent clashes with Judge Julius Hoffman made him a hero among students and radicals, a controversial figure within the legal profession, and the recipient of a four-year, 13-day jail sentence for contempt of court, believed to be the longest sentence for contempt ever imposed on an American lawyer. Kunstler, a white man who has been active in defending civil rights cases since 1961, said that the Chicago trial marked the first time in his life that he had openly disobeyed the court. Speaking to a crowd of 2000 in Los Angeles, March 1, 1970, Kunstler called for demonstrations to "let government, courts, the men who run this country, feel and see the power of the people." At the same time Kunstler cautioned against violence, declaring, "I don't think we should give the opportunity to the establishment to destroy our youth." Kunstler carried the same message to several campuses, including the Santa Barbara campus of the University of California, where the same night, February 25, rioting students set fire to a branch of the Bank of America. Governor Reagan

held Kunstler in part responsible for the rioting, but student leaders denied there was any connection.

Kunstler's active involvement in civil rights dates from 1961, when he witnessed the arrest of five "freedom riders" at a lunch counter in Jackson, Mississippi. Describing the incident in his autobiography, published in 1966, he wrote: "The sight of five frightened young people taught me what I had never known before—that only by personal involvement can one justify his existence." In the years following, Kunstler increasingly ignored his private practice in New York to devote himself to civil rights cases, usually without a fee. His clients included Martin Luther King, Jr., Stokely Carmichael, Adam Clayton Powell, Malcolm X, and H. Rap Brown. He appeared for the defense of numerous Black Panthers and also represented pacifists, draft protesters, school desegregation litigants, students and teachers involved in campus disorders and free speech issues. In 1966, Kunstler helped found a New York group, the Law Center for Constitutional Rights, to provide legal and financial help in cases involving personal rights, and now maintains his office at the center. He reportedly helped to raise $200,000 for the defense of the Chicago conspiracy defendants, in which his own services were given free. A black militant reportedly described him as "the blackest white man I ever saw," and in 1969, *Life* magazine termed him "the most sought-after civil rights lawyer in the country." However, U.S. Attorney Thomas Foran, chief prosecutor in the Chicago conspiracy trial, called Kunstler "incredibly unprofessional." Judge Julius Hoffman sentenced Kunstler to four years and 13 days on 24 counts of contempt of court, February 15, 1970.

Kunstler has written 10 books, mostly legal, but one is an account of the Hall-Mills murder case of the 1920's, for which film rights have been sold. Born July 7, 1919, in New York City, the son of a physician, Kunstler graduated from Yale in 1941, and served in the Pacific in World War II, being awarded the Bronze Star. He graduated from Columbia University Law School in 1949, and began a law firm with his younger brother, Michael. In the early 1950's, he began taking cases from the American Civil Liberties Union. He is a member of the bars of New York, District of Columbia, U.S. Supreme Court, U.S. Court of Military Appeals, and the U.S. District Courts for the Southern and Eastern Districts of New York. He was married in 1942 to the former Lotte Rosenberger, two daughters. Home is in Mamaroneck, New York. Office: 511 Fifth Avenue, New York, New York.

LEADERSHIP CONFERENCE ON CIVIL RIGHTS
Founded in 1949, a coalition of 118 national groups pushing for federal civil rights legislation and enforcement. In March 1970 launched a successful lobbying campaign against Senate confirmation of Judge G. Harrold Carswell for Supreme Court justice. To affiliate with the conference, a group must be a non-partisan, national organization with a

constituency. Issues a regular newsletter. Officers are: chairman: Roy Wilkins; legislative chairman: Clarence Mitchell; secretary: Arnold Aronson; counsel: Joseph L. Rauh; director of Washington office: Marvin Caplan; executive assistant: Yvonne Price. Office: 2027 Massachusetts Avenue, N.W., Washington, D.C. *See also:* CLARENCE MITCHELL, JOSEPH L. RAUH, JR., ROY WILKINS.

LEGAL DEFENSE AND EDUCATIONAL FUND, INC. (LDF)

Established in 1939 as an independent agency of the NAACP. Serves as legal arm of entire civil rights movement. Completely separate and distinct from the parent organization although NAACP is retained in the official name of the fund. Funded by Ford Foundation grants and public contributions. Director-counsel is Jack Greenberg. Office: 10 Columbus Circle, New York City. *See also:* JACK GREENBERG.

JERRIS LEONARD

Nixon-appointed assistant attorney general in charge of Civil Rights Division, Department of Justice. Though considered more conservative than predecessors in this office, he surprised critics by strong personal leadership of investigation of Panther deaths in Chicago and of student deaths at Kent State and Jackson State. In May, 1970, he flew to Jackson in middle of night to head off pre-dawn confrontation between students and officials. Urged dissident lawyers in his division to aim at integration through "persuasion and leadership." In July, 1970, he launched large-scale legal action to force school desegregation in Mississippi and other southern states.

A leader of the Republican party in Wisconsin, Leonard was candidate for U.S. Senate in 1968. Born January 17, 1931 in Chicago, he worked his way through Marquette Law School and at 25 was elected to the State Assembly. Chairman, Wisconsin Legislative Council, 1967. Married, four sons, two daughters.

JULIUS LESTER

Author, teacher, and broadcaster. Joined SNCC in 1966 as director of photo department and later became a field secretary (he has since resigned from the organization). Since July 1968, has hosted a weekly radio program on WBAI-FM in New York called "The Great Proletarian Cultural Revolution." Also teaches a course in black history at the New School for Social Research. His first book, *Look Out, Whitey! Black Power's Gon' Get Your Mama!*, published in 1968 (Dial Press), is described as a personal interpretation of black power. Also wrote *To Be a Slave* (1968), and *Search for the New Land: History as Subjective Experience*, published October 1969. Born in St. Louis, Missouri in 1939. Graduated from Fisk University in 1960. Married, two children.

JOHN LEWIS

National chairman of SNCC, 1963–66. A devout Baptist, he was one of the founders of SNCC in 1960, and one of the first to sit-in and make freedom rides. Jailed a total of 40 times. In 1966, when SNCC became more militant and the radical elements began to take over, he was replaced as chairman by Stokely Carmichael, who made "black power" the rallying cry. Resigned from the organization reportedly because he felt it was departing from its principles of nonviolence. At time of leaving SNCC, he stated that the organization had 50 members and offices in New York, Atlanta, Washington and San Francisco. Lewis has since dropped out of the public eye as an activist, but has continued to work in the civil rights field. After serving with the Field Foundation in New York, in 1969 he returned to the South as director of community organization projects for the Southern Regional Council in Atlanta, Georgia. Became director of Council's Voter Education Project (V.E.P.), March 1970. Married. *See also:* SOUTHERN REGIONAL COUNCIL.

C. ERIC LINCOLN

Professor of sociology and religion at the Union Theological Seminary in New York City. Is also adjunct professor of sociology at Vassar College. Born in Athens, Alabama, June 23, 1924. Holds an A.B. from LeMoyne (1947), M.A. from Fisk University (1954), a Ph.D. from Boston University (1960). Lectures frequently across the country as well as abroad. The author of several books including *A Profile of Martin Luther King,* and *The New Blacks and The Black Estate,* both published in 1969, and *Black Muslims in America,* 1961. He is also a published poet. He is the recipient of some 19 awards and honors from universities and foundations, and is on the board of directors of Manhattan Community Center, Boston University, the American Forum of African Study, Martin Luther King Memorial and the Black Academy of Arts and Letters. Married to the former Lucy Cook, four children.

ROBERT LUCAS

National chairman of the Black Liberation Alliance, a Chicago-based militant group claiming a national membership of 10,000, with 800 members in the Chicago area, forming part of the Chicago Coalition for United Community Action. Lucas achieved national prominence in September 1966, when as chairman of the Chicago chapter of the Congress of Racial Equality (CORE) he led 250 civil rights marchers through the tense all-white suburb of Cicero. The previous year, 1965, he led several marches protesting de facto school segregation and was one of several CORE members arrested for chaining themselves to the Alabama State exhibit at the Chicago boat show. Described as a loner who prefers action to talk, Lucas emerged as one of the new breed of militant black leaders who shunned structured organizations in favor of popular, action-oriented movements.

Born 1924 in Roncevert, West Virginia, Lucas served with the U.S. army in Europe in World War II and then settled in Chicago, where he completed his high school education and joined the Post Office in

1948. In March, 1966, he led a demonstration protesting discrimination in promotions at the Post Office. He is married, one son. Alliance headquarters: 75 East 35th Street, Chicago.

AUTHERINE LUCY

The first Negro to try to desegregate the University of Alabama in 1956, seven years before Vivian Malone and James A. Hood accomplished it. Enrolled in Mills College in Tuscaloosa, part of the University of Alabama, in 1953. After a three and a half year court fight—masterminded and argued before the Supreme Court by present Supreme Court Justice Thurgood Marshall, then a lawyer for the NAACP—won her legal right to register. At 26 and already a college graduate, her registration caused a series of violent outbursts in the white community and marked the first time federal and state law agencies clashed over the issue of school segregation. Staying only a few weeks, she withdrew and sued the university for conspiracy for barring her from the school dormitories. Born in 1930, she married Rev. Hugh C. Foster in 1956. Currently lives in Shreveport, Louisiana, where she teaches sixth grade. Three children. Has not been active in civil rights since 1956 and says she has no plans in that direction.

VIVIAN MALONE

Desegregated the University of Alabama in 1963. On June 11 of that year, Governor George Wallace of Alabama carried out a 1962 campaign promise to prevent integration of Alabama schools, and confronted Deputy Attorney General Nicholas Katzenbach at the university's Foster Hall to bar her and James Hood from registering. In spite of rioting and personal harassment, she became the first Negro to graduate from Alabama (1965). Worked for the Civil Rights Division of the justice department after graduation, then joined the Veterans Administration, working in both Atlanta and Washington. Born 1942. Married MacArthur Jones, a teacher, September 3, 1966, one son.

BURKE MARSHALL

Assistant attorney general for Civil Rights Division of the Department of Justice, from 1961 to 1964. Presently is general counsel for the IBM Corporation. Was Robert Kennedy's leading white authority on matters involving civil rights. Kennedy said of him: "he has the world's best judgment on anything." Born on October 1, 1922, in Plainfield, New Jersey, and graduated from Phillips Exeter Academy in 1940, from Yale University in 1943, and received LL.B. from the same university in 1951. Was admitted to the Washington, D.C. bar in 1951 and practiced law as a member of the firm of Covington and Burling until 1961. Married to the former Violet Person in 1946, three children.

THURGOOD MARSHALL

First Negro Supreme Court justice in United States history. Was appointed by President Johnson in 1968. A friend says of him, "Thurgood feels that the Constitution is a living document that has to be viewed in terms of today but I don't believe he wants to rewrite it. He's more of a legal conservative than one might assume from his civil rights and civil liberties advocacy." Admitted to the Maryland bar in 1933, he joined the NAACP the same year as special counsel and began a career of fighting for civil rights in the courts. Won 29 of the 32 cases he argued before the Supreme Court, including the landmark 1954 decision on school desegration. In 1956, helped integrate the University of Alabama. In 1957, was at Central High School in Little Rock, Arkansas. *Newsweek* magazine said of him "in three decades he has probably done more to transform the life of his people than any Negro today." Born in Baltimore July 2, 1908, he received an A.B. degree from Lincoln University (1930), and LL.B. from Howard University (1933). Did postgraduate work in Syracuse at the School of Social Research and at the University of Liberia. Married, two children.

THOMAS W. MATTHEW

Described as "perhaps the nation's number one practitioner of black economic power," Matthew is the founder and president of the Negro self-help group called NEGRO (National Economic Growth and Reconstruction Organization), which runs a string of self-supporting businesses in New York, Pittsburgh, Watts, and other cities. A successful neuro-surgeon who gave up a reputed $100,000-a-year private practice to launch NEGRO, Matthew is a foe of handouts and welfare programs, which he believes perpetuate the dependency of Negroes. Equally a foe of federal and state taxes on his projects which, he says, in fact save taxpayers' money by getting people off the relief rolls. Convicted October 2, 1969, for failure to pay 1968 income taxes, claiming he wanted to donate his personal resources to NEGRO. After serving 59 days in jail had his sentence commuted by President Nixon in his first act of executive clemency (January 1970). In February 1970, Matthew announced his support of Judge G. Harrold Carswell for the Supreme Court, and his organization placed a full-page advertisement in *The New York Times* endorsing the nomination. Born one of nine children of a New York City janitor in 1926, Matthew was the first black graduate of Manhattan College and the first black neuro-surgeon to graduate from Harvard Medical Center. He is director of the Negro-run Interfaith Hospital in Jamaica, Queens. *See also:* NEGRO.

RHODY ARNOLD McCOY, JR.

Past controversial administrator of New York City's experimental and troubled Ocean Hill–Brownsville school district, which was established in 1967 as an effort to provide effective education for an underprivileged area and to encourage community involvement. The community governing board's attempt to remove several white teachers led to teacher walkouts, pupil boycotts, physical clashes, and eventually a city-wide teachers' strike which closed all New York City public schools for three months in the fall of 1968. In 1969, the district opposed a decentralization bill passed by New York state to phase out the experimental school districts. In September 1969, he urged that the district's programs, which had been criticized as "questionable" by the United Federation of Teachers, be evaluated by a team of independent educators from outside the city school system. A group of parents in November 1969 called for McCoy's dismissal because of his "dictatorial" methods. In July 1970, the school district became part of newly formed District 23 and McCoy was forced to resign.

Born in Washington, D.C., January 16, 1923. Graduated from Howard University in 1947 and received his M.A. from New York University in 1949, after which he became a teacher in the city's public school system. Became a principal in 1965 and administrator of the Ocean Hill–Brownsville district in 1968. Married, seven children.

FLOYD B. McKISSICK

Joined CORE in the early 1960's and succeeded James Farmer as national director in 1966. Embraced the concept of "black power" the same year. Has said, "as long as the white man has all the power and money, nothing will happen because we have nothing. The only way to achieve meaningful change is to take power." In 1967, took a leave of absence from CORE to work on his cities projects—a program to prepare for the rise of Negroes to positions of civic, political, and economic responsibilities in cities where they will soon be the majority. He resigned from CORE in 1968 to devote himself full-time to black economic power. One of his projects is to build a new city in North Carolina called "Soul City." Author of *Three-Fifths of a Man* (published by Macmillan in August 1969), which focuses on Negro economic equality through a combination of Constitutional rights and black nationalism. McKissick has denounced the war in Vietnam, decrying "black men going over to Vietnam and dying for something they don't have a right for here." Born in Asheville, North Carolina, March 9, 1922, he was reared with three sisters. Did undergraduate work at Morehouse and North Carolina Colleges. Graduated from University of North Carolina Law School. Married to the former Evelyn Williams, four children. Office: McKissick Inc., 360 West 125th Street, New York, New York.

ARTHUR McZIER

Head of Small Business Administration's Minority Enterprise Program since 1968. Responsible for establishing Operation Business Mainstream, May 1969, to coordinate agency's various programs and services for minority enterprises, particularly in ghetto areas. During 1969, Operation Mainstream made more than 5,000 loans totaling some $128 million. Before joining the government in 1968, McZier was a marketing analyst for the Ford Motor Co. Born Atlanta, 1935, he attended Loyola University on an athletic scholarship and graduated in business management, 1959. In the same year he was all-star basketball player, captain of Loyola team, and named "most valuable player" and "athlete of the year."

JAMES H. MEREDITH

Desegregated the University of Mississippi in 1962. In June of that year, the United States Court of Appeals ruled that Meredith's application for enrollment to "Ole Miss" had been rejected solely on racial grounds and ordered that he be admitted. When he entered the university, he underwent a grueling ten-day ordeal, during which there were riots, and federal troops accompanied him everywhere. Made the decision to desegregate "Ole Miss" while attending Jackson State College in Mississippi. He then asked help from NAACP and Medgar Evers assisted him. "Nobody handpicked me. I made the decision myself. I paid my own tuition." (He later broke with NAACP in 1963.) Considered a loner, an idealist who goes his own way as he sees it. Currently a Harlem landlord and businessman, who according to *The New York Times*, May 10, 1969, experienced difficulties with his tenants and his enterprises because of a series of bad breaks and mismanagements. Was convicted on August 9, 1969 (and spent two days in jail) for harassing tenants in the 34-family apartment house in the Bronx which he bought in December 1967. Tenants charged that he cut off hot water, did not clean halls, or fix the plumbing and the elevator, or make other repairs. In July 1969, staged a cross-country walk from Chicago to New York, to "build and promote Negro pride and positive goals in the black community." On June 5, 1966 went on his now historic 220-mile march from Memphis to Jackson to encourage voter registration. Was shot in the back June 6, and hospitalized. Returned to march June 24 and attended the windup rally in Jackson, June 26. Meredith was born in Kosciusko, Mississippi, June 25, 1933, one of ten children. Attended high school in Florida and spent six years in the army. Graduated from Columbia Law School. On March 7, 1967, announced his intention to run against Adam Clayton Powell for his congressional seat, but withdrew on March 13, after severe criticism from other Negro leaders. Author of *Three Years in Mississippi*, published in 1966. Married to the former Mary June Wiggins, one son.

MEXICAN–AMERICAN LEGAL DEFENSE AND EDUCATIONAL FUND

Formed in San Antonio, Texas, in 1968, by a group of Mexican-American lawyers to provide legal representation for poor *chicanos*. Modeled after the NAACP legal fund and financed by a $2.2 million Ford Foundation grant for eight years of operation. By April 1970, the fund claimed to be involved in 155 cases affecting 100,000 *chicanos* from Texas to California. However, disagreement was reported between executive director Pete Tijerina (no relation to Reies Tijerina), a San Antonio lawyer, and the Ford Foundation, which wanted to move the fund's headquarters to New York or Washington to give it a national image. Tijerina argued that most of the nation's five million *chicanos* were in the Southwest, and said he would return to private practice if the fund's headquarters were moved. Officers: president, Associate Justice Carlos C. Cadena, executive director, Pete Tijerina. Headquarters: 302 International Building, San Antonio, Texas.

MEXICAN-AMERICAN YOUTH ORGANIZATION (MAYO)
Formed in 1967 by five students at St. Mary's College in San Antonio, Texas. Has since become a nationalistic organization. Has chapters in nine communities in the Rio Grande Valley and San Antonio areas; membership numbers about 1,000. In 1960, MAYO set up a college headed by José Angel Gutierrez that is working for accreditation with Antioch College in Ohio. *See also:* JOSÉ ANGEL GUTIERREZ.

MISSISSIPPI FREEDOM DEMOCRATIC PARTY
A predominantly black group that made headlines by challenging the regular Mississippi delegation at the 1964 Democratic National Convention, charging that the all-white slate did not adequately represent blacks. Under a compromise settlement by the Credentials Committee, the freedom delegates received two seats as special delegates. At the 1968 Democratic convention, the Freedom Democrats formed part of a coalition of black and liberal white groups, known as the Loyal Democrats of Mississippi, which this time successfully barred the state's all-white regular delegation from being seated. The bi-racial coalition based their argument before the Credentials Committee on the ground that discrimination by whites on the precinct level prevented blacks from being selected as delegates to the county convention. Since the county convention chose the delegates to the state convention, which in turn named the delegates to the national convention, Mississippi's regular delegation, it was argued, failed to meet national standards that would assure full participation of blacks in the political process. The Loyal Democrats were a coalition of the state branch of the NAACP, the Freedom Democratic party, the state's Young Democrats, the Prince Hall Masons, the Mississippi Teachers Association and the state AFL-CIO. The chairman was Dr. Aaron E. Henry, state chairman of the NAACP; vice-chairman was Hodding Carter III, white publisher of the *Delta Democrat-Times* in Greenville, Mississippi, and chairman of the state's Young Democrats; Charles Evers was the campaign coordinator.

CLARENCE M. MITCHELL, JR.
Director of the Washington bureau of the NAACP since 1950 and as chief NAACP lobbyist closely involved with all civil rights legislation of recent years. "All Americans are in debt to him," commented *Washington Post* after passage of 1968 open housing bill. Was close to President Johnson. Outspokenly out of sympathy with black nationalists and rioters, whom he has denounced as "hoodlums." Critical of media for

publicity given to minority dissidents. Former newspaperman in Baltimore, where he was born March 9, 1911. Received LL.D. from Morgan State College, Baltimore. Married to the former Juanita Jackson, four children. Office: 100 Massachusetts Avenue, Washington, D.C.

JOSEPH M. MONTOYA

Senator (D-New Mexico) since 1965 and only *chicano* currently serving in the U.S. Senate. Born September 24, 1915 in Pena Blanca, New Mexico. Worked his way through school, graduating from Regis College (1934), and Georgetown University Law School (1938). Entered politics in 1936, being elected to New Mexico's House of Representatives while still a law student. Married to the former Della Romero (1940), three children.

ANNE MOODY

A new writer. Her first book, *Coming of Age in Mississippi*, an autobiography of her childhood, was published December 1968 by Dial Press. Worked for CORE in 1964 and most recently was coordinator of the School of Industrial and Labor Relations at Cornell University. The daughter of a sharecropper, she was born in 1940 and worked her way through school, graduating from Tougaloo College (Jackson) in 1964. Married.

CECIL B. MOORE

Controversial Philadelphia civil rights leader and president of the Philadelphia chapter of the NAACP, 1962–68, during which period the chapter tripled its registration to upwards of 30,000. A lawyer, he has twice run for Congress and lost both times. Born in 1951 in West Virginia and graduated from Bluefield College there. Holds a law degree from Temple University (1953). He joined the marine corps during World War II and stayed in the service for nine years. Came under investigation by the Bar Association of Pennsylvania for making anti-semitic remarks in 1967 and was subsequently suspended from his job with the NAACP the next year. Currently practicing law privately. Office: 1831 Chestnut Street, Philadelphia, Pennsylvania.

CHARLES MORGAN, JR.

White lawyer who heads American Civil Liberties Union activities in the South, with headquarters in Atlanta. As a young lawyer in Birmingham, Alabama, he received national attention in 1963 by publicly denouncing the white community for harboring extremists, following the bombing of a church in which four Negro children were killed. Joined ACLU in 1964 and responsible for expanding its activities throughout the South. Has defended Julian Bond, Stokely Carmichael, H. Rap Brown, and Muhammad Ali (Cassius Clay), among others. Author, *A Time to Speak*, 1964. Born 1930. Graduated from University of Alabama, 1955. Married, one son. Office: 5 Forsyth Street, N.W. Atlanta, Georgia.

E. FREDERIC MORROW

First Negro to serve as executive assistant to the President (1955–61) and author of *Black Man in the White House*. Presently a vice-president of the Bank of America in New York. Born in Hackensack, New Jersey in 1910, and educated at public schools there. Graduated from Bowdoin College and Rutgers University Law School. Worked as field secretary for NAACP for five years and then joined the Public Affairs Department of CBS. In 1952, he joined the late General Eisenhower's presidential campaign as adviser and administrative assistant. He became administrative assistant to the secretary of commerce after Eisenhower's election and in 1955 went to the White House. In 1961 he became vice-president of the African-American Institute in New York and in 1964 joined the Bank of America. In 1967, he was made a full vice-president. Mr. Morrow is married to the former Catherine Gordon of Chicago. Office: 41 Broad Street, New York, New York.

CONSTANCE BAKER MOTLEY

First black woman to become federal judge (January 25, 1966), when she was named U.S. District Judge for Southern District of New York. An active Democrat, in 1965 was first woman (black or white) to hold office as borough president of Manhattan. State senator, 1964–65. Assistant counsel, NAACP, 1947–65. Born in New Haven, Connecticut on September 14, 1921, she attended grammar and high schools there. Received a B.A. degree from New York University in 1943 and LL.B. from Columbia University Law School in 1946. Married to Joel Motley, real estate and insurance broker. One son.

ELIJAH MUHAMMAD

Leader of the Black Muslim movement since 1930. Born Elijah Poole in Sanderville, Georgia, on October 10, 1897. One of 13 children, he is believed to have finished only the fourth or fifth grade in school. Left home at age 16, married Clara Evans and produced six sons and two daughters. Worked as a field hand and railroad laborer before moving to Detroit in 1923, where he worked for Chevrolet until 1929. When the Depression came, went on relief and met the founder of the Nation of Islam, W. D. Fard. In 1930 Muhammad took over leadership of the Black Muslims (Fard mysteriously disappeared in 1934), and changed his name from Poole to Muhammad. Embracing a doctrine which later became known as "black supremacy," he founded his Temple Number 1 in Detroit in 1931. Two years later, Muhammad was arrested by Detroit police for refusing to transfer his child from a Muslim school to a public school, and moved to Chicago. Jailed from 1942–1946 in Chicago by the FBI for draft-dodging during World War II. Once released, again began recruiting followers, and by 1959 he had 50 temples in 22 states. Over the years he has steered clear of publicity but in 1963, nation-wide publicity was unavoidable when Malcolm X, his right-hand man for many years, resigned from the Black Muslims. (Malcolm X was shot to death in 1965 in what many observers believe was a vendetta murder and Muhammad was forced to publicly disavow any involvement, although at least one of the men arrested was said to have been a Black Muslim enforcer.) Muhammad has homes in both Chicago and Phoenix, Arizona. *See also:* BLACK MUSLIMS.

NATIONAL ALLIANCE OF BUSINESSMEN

Organization representing nation's business leaders which conducts program to provide special training and jobs for hard-core unemployed, with support of federal government. Formed in 1968, it provided more than 100,000 jobs in first year, aimed at 600,000 by June 1971. Program is known as JOBS. Address: 726 Jackson Place, N.W., Washington, D.C.

NATIONAL ASSOCIATION FOR THE ADVANCEMENT OF COLORED PEOPLE (NAACP)

Established in 1909 on the 100th anniversary of the birth of Abraham Lincoln. The organization was the outgrowth of and based on the principles of the Niagara Movement, the first Negro protest organization, which was founded in 1905 by W. E. B. DuBois. Largely the brainchild of William English Walling, a white Southerner who feared racists would carry "the race war to the North," Mary Ovington, a white newspaper reporter, and Dr. Henry Moskowitz, a New York social worker. Its purpose was to achieve by peaceful and lawful means, equal citizenship rights for all Americans by eliminating segregation and discrimination in housing, employment, voting, schools, the courts, transportation and recreation. Since it was founded, the organization's scope has widened and gone into every phase of civil rights activity, its principal task now being the implementation of civil rights acts. Has disassociated itself publicly, at its July 1966 national convention, from the "black power" concept of reaching its objectives. In 1969, launched nationwide campaigns for school desegration, more jobs and training for blacks in the building industry, and abolition of housing discrimination, especially in suburbs.

In an unusual departure at its 1970 convention, NAACP chairman Bishop G. Spottswood denounced the Nixon Administration as "anti-Negro."

Today, the NAACP is the oldest and largest civil rights organization, with an overall membership of nearly 500,000, with 1,800 chapters, seven regional offices and an annual budget (for 1969) of $3,635,500. Publishes monthly magazine, *Crisis.* Roy Wilkins is executive director. Headquarters: 1790 Broadway, New York, New York. *See also:* ROY WILKINS, LEONARD H. CARTER, RICHARD L. DOCKERY, (JAMES) CHARLES EVERS, HERBERT HILL, RUBY HURLEY, CLARENCE M. MITCHELL, JR., JULIUS E. WILLIAMS.

NATIONAL COMMITTEE OF BLACK CHURCHMEN

Founded in Dallas, Texas in November 1967, to direct the strategy of black churchmen within their various denominations, helping them make more effective contributions to their communities. With total membership about 400, the Committee has been actively involved in social activities in the Mississippi delta and took part in the Charleston, South Carolina hospital workers strike, June 1969. Holds convocations annually; the last one was held in Oakland, California, November 11–14, 1969. Some of its members attended the All-Africa Conference of Churches in the Ivory Coast in September 1969. In June 1970, the Committee urged the black community not to participate in July 4th activities but to celebrate instead Black Liberation Day, June 28. Chairman of the 65 man board of directors is Rev. M. L. Wilson. Office: 354 Convent Avenue, New York, New York.

NATIONAL CONFERENCE OF BLACK LAWYERS

Created at a conference of lawyers and students in Chicago, June 1, 1969 to establish "a permanent and on-going body of all black lawyers determined to join the black revolution and committed to taking all steps necessary to assist black people to attain the goals to which they are rightfully entitled by the most fundamental principles of law, mortality, and justice." Temporary co-chairman of the conference was Floyd B. McKissick. Most of the lawyers (some 4,000) who attended belong to the National Bar Association; the students are members of the Black American Law Students Association whose transportation and lodging for the conference were paid by a $27,500 grant from MARC—the Metropolitan Applied Research Center of New York.

NATIONAL CONGRESS OF AMERICAN INDIANS (NCAI)

Founded in 1944 by Indians, it claims to be the largest and only national Indian-controlled group. With a membership of 400,000 (including a large Eskimo constituency) it represents 108 tribes and lobbies for Indian interests in Washington. It also publishes a quarterly magazine, *The Sentinel*. President, Earl Old Person, a Blackfoot, born 1929 in Browning, Montana; executive director, Bruce Wilkie. Headquarters: 1346 Connecticut Avenue, N.W., Washington, D.C.

NATIONAL COUNCIL ON INDIAN OPPORTUNITY

Established by President Johnson on March 6, 1968, to encourage and coordinate federal programs and to appraise and suggest new ways to "help Indians help themselves." Council is headed by the vice-president and a 13-member board consisting of seven cabinet members and six Indians appointed by the president for a two-year term. Annual budget (1969) is $300,000. At the council's first meeting under the Nixon Administration, January 26, 1970, Mrs. LaDonna Harris, a spokeswoman for the council's Indian members, presented a petition of 50 requests for alleviation of the most serious problems facing the Indian community. Mrs. Harris, a Comanche, the wife of Senator Fred Harris (D-Okla), resigned in April 1970. In addition to the heads of government departments concerned with Indian affairs (interior, labor, commerce, HEW, HUD, agriculture, and the OEO), the council includes the following Indian representatives: Cato Valandra, member of Rosebud Sioux tribe, South Dakota; William L. Hensley, Eskimo, member of Alaska state legislature; Wendell Chino, past president of National Congress of American Indians and chairman of the Mescalero/Apache tribe, New Mexico; Roger Jourdain, chairman of Redlake/Chippewa tribe, Minnesota; Raymond Nakai, chairman of Navajo tribe, Arizona. Executive director: Robert Robertson. Office: 726 Jackson Place, N.W., Washington, D.C. *See also:* AMERICANS FOR INDIAN OPPORTUNITY.

NATIONAL COUNCIL OF NEGRO WOMEN, INC.

A charitable and educational organization with objectives of achieving equality of opportunity and eliminating prejudice and discrimination based on race, creed, color, sex, or national origin; reducing neighborhood tensions and fostering understanding and cooperation among people of different races, creeds, colors and backgrounds; strengthening family life; relieving human suffering among the aged and poverty stricken; combating juvenile delinquency; and educating the public generally to a sense of better citizenship. Has claimed membership of 3,850,000 in 25 national affiliates. Has 106 local offices in 40 states. Issues newsletters, press releases, has a quarterly publication and gives special reports on civil rights problems. National president: Miss Dorothy I. Height.

NATIONAL WELFARE RIGHTS ORGANIZATION

One of the newest, fastest-growing, and currently most militant of the nation's civil rights movements. Specializes in representing welfare recipients and deliberately shuns ideological issues such as black separatism. Membership has been depicted in early 1969 as "an army of 30,000 angry welfare mothers." Mostly black, though open to all races. Founded in 1966, the organization now claims a membership of 75,000 with 300 chapters across the nation. Headed by former CORE official George A. Wiley, it has staged demonstrations at city halls and welfare department offices. On May 25, 1969, broke into the convention of the National Conference on Social Welfare in New York, to demand $35,000 from convention registration fees "to help organize welfare recipients." In February 1969, the group's leaders met with HEW Secretary Robert Finch, who described them as "an important constituency of HEW." He promised to investigate their charges that the department's policies were being "flagrantly violated" in many areas. The organization adopted a more militant program at its 1969 convention, to fight for $5,500 guaranteed annual income for family of four and to pressure welfare agencies across the country for supplementary payments for children's clothing. In June 1970, some 500 members stormed city welfare offices in Washington, D.C., demanding money to buy furniture. Damage to the offices was estimated at $5,000. A welfare official commented that the rights group apparently felt the need to do "something dramatic" because it was losing membership. The organization's national headquarters is in Washington, D.C. *See also:* BEULAH SAUNDERS, GEORGE A. WILEY.

NEGRO (NATIONAL ECONOMIC GROWTH AND RECONSTRUCTION ORGANIZATION)

An economic self-help organization for Negroes on welfare rolls, started in 1964 and incorporated in 1966. By 1969 employed more than 800 persons in more than 15 business enterprises in New York, Pittsburgh, and Watts. Financed through the sale of bonds, in denominations as small as 25 cents, NEGRO assets exceeded $3 million. Its businesses include an advertising agency, newspaper, chemical plant, clothing factory, bakery, laundry, bus lines, and a hospital. The hospital is the 160-bed Interfaith Hospital in Jamaica, Queens (New York), operated entirely by Negroes and directed by neuro-surgeon Dr. Thomas W. Matthew, founder and president of the self-help organization. Dr. Matthew declares that NEGRO "accepts no federal or philanthropic funds, no handouts from anyone." He opposes increased welfare programs and guaranteed incomes as "guaranteed dependency" and instead urges the government and big business to make loans available to help Negroes help themselves. Several thousand persons support NEGRO by the purchase of bonds and the organization's future plans include expansion into the construction industry. It has already carried out repairs and renovation of several buildings in Queens and Harlem. In 1970, Matthew proposed a plan for New York's Ellis Island to President Nixon. Since the island is no longer actively used by the government, Matthew had wanted to set up experimental self-help communities there where 1,000 families would build homes and be taught skills. After "occupying" the island for 32 days in July, the group was given official permission in August 1970, by the National Park Service, to develop it over the next five years. *See also:* THOMAS W. MATTHEW.

HUEY P. NEWTON

Co-founder and minister of defense of the Black Panther party, and hero of American radicals since his 1968 trial and 2-to-15 years sentence for "voluntary manslaughter" in the death of an Oakland policeman the previous year. The trial was marked by numerous "free Huey" demonstrations, and the phrase subsequently became a favorite slogan of both black and white radicals. A blow-up of Newton in an African chair, with zebra skin and black beret, rifle in one hand and spear in the other, became a popular poster. In May 1970, the California Court of Appeals reversed Newton's conviction on the grounds that the trial judge had failed to instruct the jury on the defense position that Newton was unconscious during the shooting. In interviews with reporters following the decision, Newton said he felt embarrassed by the famous poster and it did not represent his view of himself. He said he was opposed to violence, but remained a dedicated revolutionary. Once free, he would aim to broaden the base of the Panther movement among the black population, and it would advocate a "democratic socialistic society, free of racism." Newton said he would also seek the return of exiled Panther leader Eldridge Cleaver, possibly through the United Nations. But Newton added that he would never choose exile for himself, even if he were convicted again on a retrial.

While in prison, Newton was reportedly denied privileges for refusing to work for the prison pay of three to ten cents an hour, which he denounced as exploitation. He demanded that prisoners receive the legal minimum wage for work performed.

Newton was born 1942 in Louisiana, the son of a minister. He was raised in Oakland, California, where he graduated in social sciences from Merritt College. With fellow student Bobby Seale, he founded the Black Panthers in 1965. *See also:* BLACK PANTHER PARTY FOR SELF-DEFENSE.

OPERATION BOOTSTRAP

Successful self-help operation begun in Watts after 1965 riots, and by 1969 employed more than 100 persons in businesses grossing more than half a million dollars a year. Main elements are a job-training center, printing shop, and doll factory (specializing in black dolls). Operation started by Lou Smith and Robert Hall, who refused on principle to accept government or private financing. Instead, adopted policy of asking business and education centers for know-how, training, and money as and when needed. Organizers emphasize aim of helping Watts residents discover their own potential and among other activities organize group therapy sessions. "The thrust is inward rather than outward," Bootstrap president Lou Smith has said.

Smith was born in Philadelphia in 1929 and worked with CORE for five years (1964–68). He says he began Bootstrap "without a red cent." Office: 4161 South Central Avenue, Los Angeles, California.

OPERATION BREADBASKET

Operation Breadbasket is the name given to the SCLC program to gain jobs and other rights by effective use of the boycott. Patterned on the successful "selective buying" campaign conducted in Philadelphia in the early 1960's by Baptist minister Dr. Leon Sullivan. The first SCLC Breadbasket campaign was in Atlanta, Georgia, but the biggest and most successful operation has been in Chicago, where it was launched in 1966 by Martin Luther King, Jr., and some 60 ministers. Jesse Jackson was named its director, and he has been the principal architect of its success in Chicago and elsewhere. In 1968, the Chicago operation conducted 40 boycotts which resulted in the hiring of 8,000 blacks. The assistant director is Rev. Calvin Morris. Office: 366 East 47th Street, Chicago, Illinois. *See also:* JESSE JACKSON, LEON SULLIVAN.

OPPORTUNITIES INDUSTRIALIZATION CENTER (OIC)
Launched by Rev. Leon Sullivan as a job-training program in the Negro ghetto of North Philadelphia in 1964. Has expanded into one of the nation's biggest and most successful self-help operations, with seven branches in Philadelphia and others in 90 cities across the nation. In the Philadelphia area alone, the centers had trained more than 6,000 people and placed 5,000 in jobs by 1969. Three federal sources have contributed $15 million and private businesses $4 million. The first center was established in an abandoned North Philadelphia police station after a boycott program had revealed that there were not enough skilled blacks to fill all the jobs offered. The centers offer courses in electronics, drafting, cabinet making, and restaurant skills, welding, department store sales, dry cleaning and laundry work. They also give training in job interviews, attitude, grooming, wise shopping, etc. Eskimos and Japanese-Americans are trained at centers in such cities as Seattle; Mexican-Americans in San Jose, California. *See also:* LEON SULLIVAN, ZION INVESTMENT ASSOCIATES, INC.

ORGANIZATION OF AFRO-AMERICAN UNITY (OAAU)
Group founded by Malcolm X in 1963 after his break with Black Muslims. Since Malcolm X's death in 1965, it has been headed by his sister, Mrs. Ella Mae Collins, but today is considered largely inactive. In May 1969, however, conducted series of observances of Malclom X's birthday, including "open house" at the organization's Harlem offices. *See also:* ELLA MAE COLLINS.

ORGANIZATION OF NATIVE AMERICAN STUDENTS
A student group formed in 1968 by three high school students—Michael Benson, a Navajo, Howard Bad Hand, a Rosebud Sioux, and Steven Fast Wolf, an urban Indian from Chicago, who initiated regular meetings of Indian students being educated in New England schools. The group's purpose is threefold: to set up college programs aimed at helping Indian students; to provide a social outlet to ease the period of adjustment to college life; and to encourage students to return to their reservations after graduation to help their people. Group is run by an eight-member board, holds two conferences for total membership annually, and publishes a periodic newsletter, *ONAS Newsletter*. It is supported by grants from government and private sources, including the Association on Indian Affairs, the Bureau of Indian Affairs, and leading

Indian folksinger Buffy Ste. Marie. Membership of 50 is approximately half of the 100 Indian students currently enrolled in Eastern colleges. President: Michael Benson, Wesleyan University, born April 1950. Board member: Howard Bad Hand, Dartmouth College, born August 1948.

ROSA PARKS

On December 1, 1955, seamstress Rosa Parks refused to "move to the rear" of the Cleveland Avenue bus in downtown Montgomery, Alabama, was arrested and fined $10. Her action triggered a 381-day bus boycott led by Martin Luther King, Jr., bringing him to national prominence, and marking a turning point in the history of black protest. Mrs. Parks later joined the staff of Congressman John Conyers in Detroit.

BASIL A. PATERSON

As Ambassador Arthur Goldberg's running-mate in the New York Democratic primary, June 1970, he became the first Negro to win a major party's candidacy for Lieutenant Governor of New York. Until his nomination, he was little known outside Harlem's 27th district, which he had represented as a state senator since 1966. Born April 27, 1926, in Harlem, where he graduated from DeWitt Clinton High School in 1942. After two years of army service, he was graduated from St. John's (Catholic) University, Brooklyn, in 1948, and its Law School in 1951. Paterson is a member of the Manhattan law firm of Paterson, Michael and Murray and former president of the New York chapter, NAACP. Married to the former Portia Hairston, two children.

REV. CHANNING E. PHILLIPS

First Negro to be nominated for the presidency of the United States at a major party convention. At the 1968 Democratic National Convention in Chicago (he received 67½ votes), Phillips said he ran "to show the Negro vote must not be taken for granted." Was favorite-son candidate of the Washington, D.C. delegation, which he headed. The delegation's 23 votes had been originally pledged to Robert Kennedy. As member of Platform Committee, Phillips opposed administration's position on Vietnam. Pastor of Lincoln Memorial Temple in Washington since 1956. Is also president of the Housing Development Corporation, a nonprofit housing rehabilitation agency funded in part by Office of Economic Opportunity. Was one of the early leaders of the Washington based militant Black United Front. Participated in Selma marches, 1965. At 1964 Democratic National Convention was active supporter of Mississippi Freedom Democratic party. Born 1928, holds B.A. in sociology from Virginia Union University, divinity degree from Colgate Divinity School, and Ph.D. in theology from Drew University. Married, five children.

SAMUEL R. PIERCE

General counsel to the treasury department, appointed April 1970 by President Nixon, and one of the top black appointees in the Nixon Administration. A partner in the prominent New York law firm of Battle, Fowler, Stokes, and Kheel since 1961. Has been a faculty member, since 1958, of New York University Law School. Also a member of the Advisory Committee of New York CORE, a life member of the NAACP, and director of the Lawyers' Committee for Civil Rights Under Law (a committee initiated by the late President John F. Kennedy). Served as a judge to the New York Court of General Sessions (1959–60) and is a strenuous worker for Republican party causes (once ran for Congressman Adam Clayton Powell's seat on the Republican ticket). Received an A.B. from Cornell University (1947) and LL.B. (1949). Served with Office of Strategic Services during World War II. Born September 8, 1922 and married to physician Barbara Wright (1948), one child.

SIDNEY POITIER
In 1965 became the first Negro to win an Academy Award for a starring role (*Lilies of the Field*). Says he tries to work in films that make a positive contribution to the image of black people in America. Wrote *For Love of Ivy* for this reason. "I try to do and say nothing that might be a step backward." Born February 20, 1927 in Miami, Florida, but moved to the Bahamas. At 15 returned to the United States, first to Miami, then to New York where he worked as a dishwasher. In 1941 enlisted in the army for four years (served with a medical detachment). Studied with the American Negro Theater, which once rejected him because of his unintelligible West Indian accent. In 1950 made first movie *No Way Out*. Starred on Broadway in *Raisin in the Sun* (1959). Most recent movies: *To Sir with Love, In the Heat of the Night, For Love of Ivy, Guess Who's Coming to Dinner*, and *The Lost Man*. Divorced, four daughters.

POTOMAC INSTITUTE
Non-profit, private research agency that conducts studies of urban, educational, and racial problems. Financed by the Taconic Foundation of New York, the institute has been in operation since 1961. Currently conducting a two-year demonstration project in Baltimore called Equal Business Opportunity, to assist Negroes in starting or expanding their own businesses. President Harold C. Fleming (born 1922) was executive director of the Southern Regional Council before joining the institute in 1961. Headquarters: 1501 Eighteenth Street, N.W., Washington, D.C.

LEW POTTER
Editor responsible for the program composition of National Educational Television's series "Black Journal," the first nationwide series by and for black Americans. Graduated from Howard University in 1959, did post-graduate studies at Wharton School of Finance at the University

of Pennsylvania. Office: NET, 10 Columbus Circle, New York, New York.

ALVIN F. POUSSAINT

One of the country's leading black psychiatrists and an expert on the psychosis of oppression. Best known for his article, *Black Power, A Failure for Integration Within the Civil Rights Movement.* Currently associate professor of psychiatry and associate dean of student affairs at Harvard Medical School. Taught at Tufts University School of Medicine, 1967–69. Graduated from Columbia University (1956), M.D. from Cornell University Medical School (1960), and M.S. from University of California at Los Angeles (1964). Born May 15, 1934. Unmarried.

ADAM CLAYTON POWELL, JR.

Democratic representative from New York's Eighteenth Congressional District from 1945. Served as chairman on the Labor and Education Committee until 1967. Also pastor of Harlem's Abyssinian Baptist Church, which claims to have the world's largest congregation (over 70,000) where he succeeded his father in 1937. Commended by former President Johnson in 1966 for a "brilliant record of accomplishment" that had included passage of some 56 key bills under both Presidents Kennedy and Johnson. For the last decade has been involved in a series of legal congressional tangles. In 1966 he lost a $155,785 libel suit leveled at him by Mrs. Esther James, a Harlem widow (she had initiated the suit in 1960). For several years he stayed away from New York under threat of arrest for nonpayment. He then retreated to the island of Bimini. In 1967 the New York Court of Appeals reduced the damage award against him by $100,000 and Powell was to give Mrs. James the $33,000 profits from his record album *Keep the Faith Baby.* In 1967 his troubles with official Washington began. On January 9, he was stripped of his chairmanship and the next day barred from taking his House seat pending an investigation of his "qualifications." A select House committee, headed by Emanuel Celler, found he had misused congressional funds, acted contemptuously toward the New York courts in his libel suit, and kept his wife on the congressional payroll although she did not work in either his district or the District of Columbia as required by law. On March 1, 1967, following the committee's report, the House voted 301 to 116 to exclude Powell from the Ninetieth Congress. He was re-elected from his district in November 1968, but did not present himself for swearing in. Powell countered by taking his case to the Supreme Court, which on June 16, 1969 ruled that his constitutional rights had been violated by the House of Representatives in excluding him from the Ninetieth Congress, but referred to a lower court the issue of Powell's right to $55,000 back pay. He was reseated on January 3, 1969 after a five-hour debate and a 251–160 vote approving a proposal to seat him, but depriving him of his congressional seniority and imposing a $25,000 fine to be withheld from his congressional salary at $1,150 a month, until paid. On September 29, 1969, Powell said he would ask the Supreme Court to order restoration of his seniority and the $55,000 back pay, but on February 2, 1970, the Court refused Powell's request for a hearing. In December 1969, an anti-Powell group was formed in Harlem, led by Dr. Arthur Logan, director of the Upper Manhattan Medical Group, and George W. Goodman, executive director of the Harlem Neighborhood Association, with the announced intention of contesting Powell in the 1970 primaries because he was "not a full-time Congressman." On January 19, 1970, Powell said that after a successful battle with cancer, he intended to seek reelection. However, on June 23, 1970 he was defeated in the Democratic Primary by state assemblyman Charles Rangel.

Born in 1908 in New Haven, he grew up in New York City. (Has claimed that he had a Cherokee grandmother and that his mother was an illegitimate heiress of the Schaefer brewing fortune.) His father was in real estate and pastor of the Abyssinian Baptist Church. The family vacationed at Bar Harbor and exclusive Canadian resorts (always accepted as whites). Graduated from Colgate University, 1930, and Columbia University, 1932. D.D., Shaw University, 1935. In late 1930's Powell began devoting his time to black civic programs in Harlem. In 1941 was elected to the New York city council and three years later was elected to Congress. Has been married three times (his second wife was Hazel Scott, a singer and pianist). Two sons.

PRIDE, INC.

A labor department financed organization providing employment for ghetto youths in the District of Columbia. Started in 1967 by Rufus Mayfield, a convicted felon, who obtained a $300,000 labor department grant to employ 900 youths in a slum clean-up and rat-control program. Today has two divisions: Youth Pride Inc., which hires in-school and out-of-school youths to clean streets, etc., and Pride Economic Enterprises, which operates three service stations, and undertakes painting, landscaping, and other services for profit. Planned ventures include the development of a candy manufacturing company and a $2.5 million automotive center. By 1969, Pride Inc. had received more than six million dollars in grants from the labor department. The program has been attacked in Congress on the ground that federal funds should not be handled by persons with criminal records. Early in 1969, the General Accounting Office charged 269 cases of mismanagement, payroll padding and kickbacks, but GAO investigators eventually found only $2100 unaccounted for, less than one percent of Pride's budget. Nevertheless, in July 1969, the organization came under grand jury investigation, and in February 1970, some 17 former and present members were indicted on charges of irregularities involving the organization's funds. Executive director of operations: Marion Barry, Jr.: executive director of programs: Mary Treadwell; public relations director: William Minor. Headquarters: 1536 U Street, N.W., Washington, D.C.

PUERTO RICAN CIVIL RIGHTS, NATIONAL ASSOCIATION OF (NAPCR)

Founded in 1963 by Puerto Rican individuals and some 100 Puerto Rican organizations in the United States. Concerned with civil rights problems of Puerto Ricans in legislative, labor, police, legal, and housing matters, particularly in New York City (which has the highest concentration of Puerto Ricans in the country: 1.2 million). Sponsors community relations meetings with government and police officials and provides legal services. Claims to have 20,000 members. President: Mrs. Amalia Betanzos. Headquarters: 207 W. 106 Street, New York City.

A. PHILIP RANDOLPH

Considered the "elder statesman" of the civil rights movement. Has worked for 45 years to build an alliance between black Americans and the trade union movement. Opposing any form of strike-breaking by Negroes, he advocated instead full integration into the American trade union movement (today there are some two million black trade unionists). In 1925, began a long and backbreaking campaign to organize the Brotherhood of Sleeping Car Porters of the AFL which eventually won certification in 1937. Later became the first Negro vice-president of AFL-CIO. In 1941 organized and directed the first march on Washington which led President Roosevelt to establish the Commission of Fair Employment Practices. In 1963 was one of the major forces behind the march on Washington that year. Retired from AFL-CIO post in 1966 and is presently a member of its executive council. Born in Crescent City, Florida on April 15, 1889, he attended City College of New York and received a law degree from Howard University in 1941. Married to the former Lucille E. Campbell. *See also:* BAYARD RUSTIN.

CHARLES E. RANGEL

New York state assemblyman from central Harlem from 1966–70. Lawyer, former assistant United States attorney, and a former general counsel to the National Advisory Commission on Selective Service. In April 1969, Representative James H. Scheuer, one of the seven candidates running for the Democratic nomination for mayor of New York, picked Rangel to run on his ticket for city council president. Announced February 1970 he would run against Adam Clayton Powell for his congressional seat. He won the primary on June 23, 1970, by 203 votes. Born 1930, winner of Bronze Star, Korean War. Married, one child.

JOSEPH L. RAUH, JR.

One of the most prominent white lawyers identified with civil rights legislation and issues. As general counsel of the Leadership Conference on Civil Rights, he and Clarence Mitchell of the NAACP were the chief lobbyists for the Civil Rights Act of 1964, the Voting Rights Act

of 1965, and the Fair Housing Act of 1968. Also Washington counsel
of the United Auto Workers, the Brotherhood of Sleeping Car Porters,
Locomotive Firemen and Enginemen, and other labor groups. For 20
years was vice-chairman and chairman of the Democratic Central Committee for the District of Columbia. In 1946, helped form the liberal
Americans for Democratic Action, of which he was chairman from
1948–52, and currently vice-chairman. Born January 3, 1911 in Cin-
cinatti, Ohio, he graduated from Harvard University in 1932 and
Harvard Law School in 1935. Married, two sons.

THE REAL GREAT SOCIETY (RGS)
A predominantly Puerto Rican self-help organization for youths in New
York's Lower East Side and Spanish Harlem, it is funded by the Office
of Economic Opportunity (which in 1968 contributed $250,000). Or-
ganization's motto: "Nothing for Nothing." Started in 1964 as a
ghetto clean-up and renovation project for school dropouts, it developed
a University of the Streets (storefront schools where basic math and
reading are taught by volunteers), a leather goods store, night-club,
and the Town House, an educational and community center at 77 East
110th Street, the area known as "El Barrio." It received its first grant
in 1967 from the Vincent Astor Foundation. Directors: Carlos Garcia
and Angelo Giordani. See also: CARLOS (CHINO) GARCIA.

BENJAMIN REIFEL
Republican representative from South Dakota, is the only Indian currently serving in Congress. Elected to the House in 1960 from South
Dakota's First Congressional District. Has been active in promoting
congressional legislation to help the Indian population particularly in the
field of education. President of Arrow Inc., a nonprofit group which
provides funds for the schooling and training of Indian youth. Before
going into politics worked as an administrator for the Bureau of
Indian Affairs in the Department of Interior from 1930–60. Received
a B.S. from South Dakota State University (1932), and M.P.A. and
D.P.A. from Harvard University (1950, 1952). Was named Outstanding American Indian in 1956 by Amer-Indians, a national group based in
Chicago. Born September 19, 1906 in Parmelee, South Dakota. Married,
one child.

REPUBLIC OF NEW AFRICA
Detroit-based black separatist group that advocates the establishment
of an independent black nation in five Southern states. Involved in
Detroit ghetto gun battle, March 29, 1969, in which Patrolman Michael
Czapski was killed. Shooting followed meeting of the separatist group
at the New Bethel Baptist Church (whose pastor, Rev. C. L. Franklin,
is father of Aretha Franklin). After the shooting all 142 blacks inside
the church were arrested but within hours all but two of them had been
released through the intervention of Judge George Crockett, a black, on

the grounds that their rights had been violated. The judge's action led to storm of public and police protest. He defended himself at news conference April 3. Czapski's funeral, April 2, was attended by 2000 persons. The Republic of New Africa claims to have declared its "independence" from the United States, and is asking for $400 billion in "slavery damages" from the U.S. government. It has an armed guard which it calls the "Black Legion." Formed in March, 1968 by two brothers, Milton and Richard Henry, group's membership is believed to number in the hundreds. Milton, a lawyer known within the organization as Brother Gaidi, announced on August 23, 1969 at the group's national convention in Washington, that exiled black revolutionary Robert F. Williams had been appointed president of the group. At a meeting held in January 1970, group was reported split into two factions each headed by a founding brother: Milton leading original group and brother Richard (Brother Imari) leading the dissident faction. *See also:* GEORGE CROCKETT, ROBERT F. WILLIAMS.

JOSEPH RHODES, JR.

The only student member of President Nixon's commission on campus unrest, which is headed by former Pennsylvania Governor William W. Scranton. Appointed June 13, 1970, Rhodes caused an immediate stir by declaring to reporters that one thing he hoped to find out was whether "the President's and the Vice President's statements are killing people." On June 16, Vice President Agnew called for Rhodes' resignation. Born in Pittsburgh, Pennsylvania on August 14, 1947, the son of a black father and half-Chinese, half-Filipino mother, Rhodes graduated in 1969 from the California Institute of Technology, where as an undergraduate he had initiated a peaceful series of changes, subsequently called the "Rhodes Revolution," which placed students on the school's decision-making bodies. After graduation, received a three-year Junior Fellowship at Harvard.

GLORIA HAYS RICHARDSON

Formed Cambridge Nonviolent Action Committee in Cambridge, Maryland in 1963, to force acceptance of Negroes in white restaurants, bowling alleys, taverns, and other public accommodations. Also one of the founders of ACT Associates. Born in Baltimore, on May 6, 1922, she grew up in Cambridge, the daughter of a well-to-do druggist. A graduate of Howard University. Divorced, two children.

CLEVELAND ROBINSON

Succeeded A. Philip Randolph as president of the Negro American Labor Council, 1966. The council was formed in 1960 to promote employment equality and apprenticeship opportunity for black trade unionists. Robinson is also president of the National Council of Distributive Workers of America, and secretary-treasurer of its Local 65.

Active in several civil rights groups, he assisted in organization of 1963 Washington march. Born 1914 in Jamaica, West Indies.

ISAIAH ROBINSON

Vice President of New York City's reorganized Board of Education since July, 1970. Described as "a cool-headed militant" and a strong supporter of community control, he is an adviser to New York's IS 201 demonstration school district. A commercial artist, he has been involved in Harlem educational activities since 1955. Served as a second lieutenant and pilot in air force during World War II after graduating from Rosedale High School (Birmingham, Alabama), and attending Tuskegee Institute flying school. Also a graduate of Art Career School in New York. Served as consultant to several groups including Teachers Corps, Urban Coalition, the McGeorge Bundy panel on decentralization, and Fordham University's instructional administrators program. Married, one child. Born 1924.

JACKIE ROBINSON

The first Negro to break the color barrier in major league baseball (1947), he is currently chairman of the board of the Freedom National Bank, a New York bank with branches in Harlem and Brooklyn, and vice-president of the Proteus Company, a chain of seafood stands. After leaving professional baseball in 1956 became Chock Full o'Nuts (a New York restaurant chain) vice-president until 1964, when he became special assistant on community affairs to Governor Nelson Rockefeller. On August 14, 1968, endorsed Hubert Humphrey for president, left the Republican party and resigned from Rockefeller's staff, because "if Nixon wins, people will be so frustrated there will be horrible riots in all our major cities." Was one of the prime movers in campaign to block South Africa's admission to the 1968 Olympic games. Testified before the Senate Small Business subcommittee January 20, 1970, scoring the Nixon's Administration's efforts in black capitalism. Speaking of the commerce department's "Project Enterprise," he said it had failed so far because of bureaucratic inefficiency, red tape, and mistrust in the black community. He endorsed the franchise business however, saying it was a potential solution to black capitalism problems. Born in Cairo, Georgia on January 31, 1919, was a football, basketball, and track star in college. During World War II served in the army as a lieutenant. Played for the Brooklyn Dodgers 1947–56. Named to the Baseball Hall of Fame in 1962 both for his trailblazing and ballplaying. Married the former Rachel A. Isum (1946), three children.

CARL ROWAN

First Negro to sit in on National Security Council and cabinet meetings (1964), when he succeeded Edward R. Murrow as director of the U.S. Information Agency. Appointed by President Johnson, he resigned in July 1965, to return to journalism. Currently a nationally syndicated columnist for the *Chicago Daily News* and contributor to the *Reader's Digest*. In August 1967, he criticized Martin Luther King, Jr.'s opposition to the Vietnam war, declaring that this "created doubt about the Negro's loyalty to his country" and endangered civil rights advances. In August 1964, he declared that civil rights demonstrations "for the most part, serve only to becloud the real issues of the Negro's legitimate grievances" and called for "bold, uncompromising efforts to free the civil rights movement from the taint of street rioters." Rowan himself was the center of a civil rights incident in January 1962, when Washington's exclusive Cosmos Club refused him membership, leading to the resignation of several of its big name members, including John Kenneth Galbraith. After 13 years as an award-winning reporter for the *Minneapolis Tribune*, Rowan entered government service in 1961 when he was appointed deputy assistant secretary of state for public affairs in state department. He was a U.S. delegate to the U.N. in 1962 and ambassador to Finland in 1963. Author of two books on the race problem (*South of Freedom* and *Go South to Sorrow*), one on Southeast Asia (*The Pitiful and the Proud*), and the biography of Jackie Robinson (*Wait Till Next Year*). Born in Ravenscroft, Tennessee, August 11, 1925. During World War II became one of the first 15 Negroes to be raised to officer rank in the navy. Received B.A. at Oberlin College, Ohio in 1947 and M.A. in journalism at University of Minnesota in 1948. Married, with three children, he lives in Washington, D.C.

BAYARD RUSTIN

Executive director of the A. Philip Randolph Institute in New York. Rustin was the organizing genius behind the historic 1963 March on Washington (at its time the largest single protest demonstration in the nation's history) when, on August 28, more than 200,000 persons converged on the capital to dramatize Negro demands. A pacifist and former communist, Rustin was considered by many to be a dangerous radical. A civil rights activist since 1947, he helped to develop CORE and SCLC and also organized the first New York City school boycott in 1964. But recently, Rustin has criticized black revolutionaries, and attacked some of their most popular rallying cries—reparations, separatism, black studies, black capitalism—as "myths" which will only divide and isolate the black community and retard real progress. A firm believer in nonviolence, he has said that Negroes who choose violence can expect to end up in one of three ways: "in jail, in exile—or shot—and probably by Negroes." Born in West Chester, Pennsylvania, in 1910, one of 12 children, he was a track star, tennis champion and class valedictorian in high school. Attended City College of New York (1933–35), and joined the Young Communist League in 1936 but resigned in 1941 to become a pacifist. Was a conscientious objector during World War II and was jailed for 28 months. After the war he became active in civil rights and from 1941–54 was race relations director of Fellowship and Reconciliation, a pacifist organization that attempts to substitute nonviolence and reconciliation for violence through education and peaceful action. Office: 217 West 125th Street, New York, New York.

BUFFY SAINTE-MARIE

Successful Indian folksinger and songwriter ("Now That the Buffalo's Gone"), many of whose songs concern the plight of American Indians. In addition to frequent benefit performances and financial support, she has been an active spokesman for Indian rights. She supported the Indians in their bid for Alcatraz Island, and in April 1970 lobbied the California Legislature on behalf of the Pyramid Lake Indians. She also formed the Nihewan Foundation to provide scholarships and other aid to Indian students. Born a Plains Cree in Saskatchewan, Canada, February 20, 1941. Married to Dewane Bugbee, lives in Hawaii.

BEULAH SANDERS

Leader of New York City's dissident welfare recipients, who told House Ways and Means Committee, October 27, 1969, that the poor would "disrupt this country" if not given a share of the nation's wealth. "The middle class," she declared, "is getting it all." Mrs. Sanders appeared before the committee to urge higher guaranteed annual incomes. As chairman of New York's Citywide Coordinating Committee of Welfare Groups, which represents the city's predominantly black welfare recipients, she has led boycotts and other activities against cuts in relief payments and allowances. Born in New Bern, North Carolina, January 14, 1935, she settled in New York in 1955.

BOBBY SEALE

National chairman and titular head of the Black Panther party, which he helped found with Huey Newton in 1965, as well as chairman of the California Black Panthers. On August 19, 1969, Seale was arrested by FBI agents in Berkeley on a warrant issued in New Haven, Connecticut, charging him with kidnap, conspiracy to kidnap, murder, and conspiracy to murder Alex Rackley in a Panther building in New Haven in May 1969. Rackley, 24, who had been a member of the Panthers in New York, was found shot after apparent severe torture (his body showed multiple bruises, cigarette burns, ice-pick wounds, and rope marks around the wrists). Police linked his death with the earlier arrest of 21 Panthers in New York on charges of conspiring to bomb several large department stores, believing he was subjected to a kangaroo court and tortured because of suspected disloyalty to the Panthers. Seale was flown from California to Connecticut March 13, 1970 to stand trial on the charges. At a bail hearing, April 22, prosecution witness George Sams, Jr., who had pleaded guilty to second-degree murder in the case, testified that Seale had ordered Rackley's execution after concluding that he was a police informer.

In explaining Panther attitudes, Seale has said, "we realize that the white power structure's real power is military force and its police force. We can see our black communities being occupied by foreign troops. Now the man (white) can't afford to wage civil war on a full scale against us in this country and at the same time have wars going on throughout the world. We know this, and this is the basis for our power."

On March 20, 1969, Seale and seven others (the "Chicago Eight") became the first group indicted under the new anti-riot provision of the 1968 Civil Rights Act (which makes it a crime to cross state lines to incite riots or to teach the use of riot weapons) because of their involvement in the demonstrations during the Democratic National Convention in August 1968. The trial began September 24 and was marked from the beginning by dramatic confrontations between Seale and the 74-year-old judge, Julius J. Hoffman. Seale contended that his Constitutional rights were being violated because his own lawyer, who was recovering from an operation, was unable to be present. Seale frequently disrupted the trial with outbursts in which he called the judge a "racist," a "fascist," and "pig" and accused him of lying. On October 29, Seale was ordered gagged and chained to his chair in the courtoom. On November 5, Judge Hoffman convicted Seale on 16 counts of contempt of court and sentenced him to four years in prison, at the same time severing his case from that of the seven other defendants in the conspiracy trial, declaring an individual mistrial, and setting a new date (April 23, 1970) for Seale's trial on the conspiracy charges. Born 1937, Seale moved from Texas to Oakland as a child and later attended Merritt College in Oakland. After founding the Panthers, he traveled widely in the United States and also visited Western Europe and Scandinavia. In July 1969, he attended the Pan-African Cultural Festival in Algiers as a guest of the Algerian government. Author of *Seize the Time: The story of the Black Panther Party and Huey P. Newton* (Random House, 1970). *See also:* BLACK PANTHER PARTY, ELDRIDGE CLEAVER, HUEY P. NEWTON.

SEARCH FOR EDUCATION, ELEVATION AND KNOWLEDGE (SEEK)

Program providing special coaching and counseling for underprivileged students at City University of New York's colleges. Started in 1966, by 1969 the program was aiding more than 4,300 students at a cost of more than $10 million a year, with funds provided by the university, the city, and state. After student demonstrations in July 1969, the SEEK program was given the status of a department within the university. Current head is Dr. Leslie Berger. SEEK has eight units, one at each of the university's senior colleges.

BETTY SHABAZZ

Widow of Malcolm X. Currently lives in virtual seclusion with her six daughters in Mount Vernon, New York. In interview with *Look* magazine (March 4, 1969) said she believed that U.S. government was behind Malcolm X's murder, because "he learned some things the Government did not want him to know." An orthodox Muslim (former Black Muslim), after her husband's death (February 21, 1965), she made pilgrimage to Mecca, took name Hajj Bahiyah Betty Shabazz. Born 1937 in Detroit, attended Tuskegee Institute, and studied as nurse in New York, where she joined Black Muslims. Her daughters, who attend private schools, all have Arabic names: Attallah, Qubilah, Ilyasah, Gamilah, Lamumbah, Malikah, and Malaak.

FRED SHUTTLESWORTH

Veteran civil rights leader and former chief lieutenant to Martin Luther King, Jr. Led Birmingham, Alabama, integration movement, and was one of clergymen arrested with King for leading 1963 Birmingham demonstrations. Jailed more than 20 times. A founder of the SCLC, of which he is still a board and executive committee member, he is currently president of the Southern Conference Educational Fund, a 17-state interracial civil rights group focusing on integration, with headquarters in Louisville, Kentucky. But present residence is in Cincinnati, where he is pastor of Baptist Church of the Greater New Light, and works with a job-seeking program called the Valid Christian Improvement Association, modeled on Chicago's Operation Breadbasket. Says that ill health has curtailed his recent civil rights activities. Born March 18, 1922. Married, four children.

SAMUEL J. SIMMONS

Assistant secretary for equal opportunity in Department of Housing and Urban Development since February 1969, and leader of government team assigned by HUD Secretary Romney to work on "Detroit Plan" designed to end conflict between blacks and the building trades in that city. Director of Field Service Division, U.S. Commission on Civil Rights, 1964–68. Born April 13, 1927, in Flint, Michigan.

SOUTHERN CHRISTIAN LEADERSHIP CONFERENCE (SCLC)

Founded by Dr. Martin Luther King, Jr. after his successful Montgomery bus boycott in 1956, the SCLC rose to preeminence in the civil rights movement in the early sixties. Its stress was on nonviolent protest. Its first major campaign was in 1960, when King called on Negroes to begin "mass violation of immoral laws." In April and May 1963, King led the drive to desegregate facilities in Birmingham, Alabama, which became a landmark in the struggle to desegregate the South. In a major confrontation between marchers and the authorities, police dogs and fire-hoses were used against the marchers, and thousands of blacks were arrested—including hundreds of children—as well as Dr. King himself. In his now famous "Letter from a Birmingham Jail," King eloquently enunciated his principles. In August of the same year, he was a leading figure in the massive March on Washington, at which he delivered the most memorable of the day's addresses, "I have a dream . . ." In many Southern towns, King and his organization led boycotts, sit-ins, marches, voter registrations, and held lectures and forums. In October 1964, King's efforts were given international recognition when he was awarded the Nobel Peace Prize. He was then 35, the youngest recipient ever.

With the emergence of Stokely Carmichael and militant demands for "black power" in 1966, King's unquestioned leadership of the black cause began to wane. His efforts to widen the influence of his organization in the Northern cities were only partly successful. After his assassination in April 1968, the SCLC, under his successor Ralph Abernathy, organized the Poor People's March on Washington which took place in May of that year. But the march did not have the impact intended and it became increasingly evident that without the leadership of King SCLC would not play such a national role in the civil rights movement. It is still, however, the major civil rights force in the South that is currently working in political action campaigns and voter registration drives. On April 19, 1970, Abernathy announced that SCLC was seeking a new militancy: "We've got to lift Negroes to a new militancy of civil disobedience through which we can speak to the youth." The following month, the SCLC sponsored a 110-mile march from Perry, Georgia to Atlanta to focus attention on "general repression" by the Nixon Administration. SCLC maintains a staff of nearly 100 and has 300 affiliated groups across the nation. Financed by public and private donations, its income in recent years has been approximately a million dollars a year. Headquarters: 334 Auburn Avenue, N.W., Atlanta, Georgia. *See also:* RALPH D. ABERNATHY, JAMES BEVEL, JESSE JACKSON, CORETTA SCOTT KING, HOSEA WILLIAMS, ANDREW J. YOUNG.

SOUTHERN REGIONAL COUNCIL

Atlanta-based civil rights research agency. Since 1962, has conducted foundation-funded voter registration programs in the South which have added an estimated 1.5 million blacks to registration rolls in 11 Southern states. This program, known as the Voter Education Project, has included seminars, workshops, and conferences for candidates and officeholders. In October 1969, the council issued a report drawing attention to the rapid proliferation of all-white private schools in the South, which, it claimed, threatened to jeopardize public education throughout the region. In March 1970, published a survey (with Metropolitan Applied Research Center) showing almost 1,500 blacks were currently holding public office. The council was formed in 1918 by a group of Southern whites. In addition to special studies, publishes a quarterly review, *New South*. Executive director: Paul Anthony; president: John H. Wheeler; Voter Education Project director: John Lewis. Office: 5 Forsyth Street, N.W., Atlanta, Georgia.

DAVID SPENCER
Militant chairman of the school board of Harlem's Intermediate School 201 complex while it was focal point of decentralization struggle in 1968–69. In March 1969, was issued "strong reprimand" by New York City Board of Education for defying its orders on make-up classes following 1968 teachers' strike. (State supervisory committee had recommended his suspension.) However, on July 1, 1970, the complex was absorbed into District 5 according to New York's school redistricting program, with Spencer still heading school board. Spencer, who has become a hero figure in Harlem, is a former elevator operator-handyman, and is currently employed in the educational program of Chambers Memorial Baptist Church. Born February 14, 1931, in Hartford, Connecticut. Married, five children.

BISHOP STEPHEN G. SPOTTSWOOD
Chairman of the NAACP since 1961, whose outspoken keynote address at 1970 NAACP convention characterized Nixon Administration as "anti-Negro." A bishop of the African Methodist Episcopal Zion Church, and veteran of civil rights campaigns since 1919. Born Boston, Massachusetts, July 18, 1897. Graduated from Albright College, 1917, and Gordon College of Theology, 1919. Also studied at Yale Divinity School. Widower, five children.

CARL B. STOKES
Mayor of Cleveland and first Negro elected mayor of a major U.S. city (November 7, 1967), when he defeated Seth B. Taft (Republican, grandson of President Taft) in a close vote, 129,318 to 127,674. A moderate, Stokes had been opposed in the primary by the regular Democratic organization. He won reelection in November 1969, by a slightly wider margin (118,713 to 116,544) after a hard-fought campaign. As mayor, Stokes had received wide praise for efforts to maintain calm after the King assassination, but was criticized for his handling of the July 1968 rioting that followed a shootout between police and militants. After conferring with black leaders, Stokes had withdrawn national guardsmen and white policemen from ghetto areas of Hough and Glenville on July 24, and had turned over responsibility for law and order to 125 black policemen and hastily organized citizen patrols. After renewed violence and looting, however, he ordered guard units back into ghetto areas on July 25, a move widely interpreted both as surrender to pressure and admission of failure. On October 9, 1968,

Stokes dismissed Cleveland police chief, 68-year-old Michael Blackwell, saying the force needed modernizing and correction of "internal breakdown of morale." Named deputy inspector Patrick Gerity in his place. Stokes was prominent campaigner for Hubert Humphrey in 1968 presidential race. *Newsday*, April 2, 1969, commented: "In his appointments and actions, Stokes is hardly distinguishable from Mayor Lindsay or other liberal big city mayors. That would appear to be his goal. But many other politicians and voters won't settle for that. To them, Stokes is a Negro mayor and his race will still be the major issue, spoken or not, in the next mayoral election." Born June 21, 1927 in a Cleveland slum. After army service, graduated from University of Minnesota and Cleveland-Marshall Law School, and practiced law with his brother, Representative Louis Stokes, who was elected to Congress from Ohio in 1968. Elected to state legislature, 1962. Was leader of NAACP and Americans for Democratic Action in Cleveland. Married (second time), two children.

LOUIS STOKES

Democratic representative, and first black Congressman from Ohio. Brother of Carl Stokes, mayor of Cleveland. Represents Cleveland's Twenty-first Congressional District (largely the ghetto areas of Eastside, Garfield Heights, and Newberry Heights). Elected November 1968. Previously a lawyer with NAACP who gained a reputation for representing militants. "If a brother needed a lawyer, all he'd have to do was ask Louis," friends have said. Created his own image in spite of his brother Carl's achievements. Member of the all-black Congressional Ad Hoc Committee formed in December 1969 to investigate Panther/police clashes. Born in 1926, grew up in the Cleveland ghetto and raised by his mother (the boys' father died when they were infants). He worked as a shoeshine boy. Served with U.S. army in World War II, paid for his schooling at Western Reserve University and Cleveland-Marshall Law School, with the G.I. Bill. Married, four children.

STUDENT NATIONAL COORDINATING COMMITTEE (SNCC)

Since July 29, 1969 the new title of the Student Non-Violent Coordinating Committee. Formed in 1960 by a group of southern black college students, who felt that Martin Luther King's leadership was not sufficiently dynamic. Initiated voter registration drives in the south, later advocated the formation of a nationwide black political party with the black panther as its symbol. Became increasingly militant, particularly after Stokely Carmichael replaced John Lewis as chairman in 1966 and adopted the slogan and concept of black power. Membership at its height was estimated at 200, but by 1969 SNCC was disorganized, divided and flatly pronounced "dead" by William F. Haddad in *Man-*

hattan Tribune, June 14, 1969. Office: 360 Nelson Street, S.W., Atlanta, Georgia. *See also:* H. RAP BROWN, STOKELY CARMICHAEL, PHILIP HUTCHINGS, JAMES FORMAN, JOHN LEWIS.

REV. LEON H. SULLIVAN

Philadelphia civil rights leader whose practical job-training and self-help projects have become million-dollar operations and have spread throughout the country. A Baptist minister in the Negro ghetto of North Philadelphia, he began opening up job opportunities through a quiet consumers' boycott ("don't buy where you can't work") then found he could not find enough skilled Negroes to fill all the jobs. Deciding that "integration without preparation is frustration," in 1964 he set up his own job-training program in an abandoned police station, calling it the Opportunities Industrialization Center. By 1969, the center had trained more than 6,000 people and placed 5,000 of them in jobs in Philadelphia alone. And Federal agencies have financed similar centers in 90 cities. In 1969, 20,000 men and women went through OIC training. "My aim," Sullivan says, "is 100,000 by next year and by 1980 I hope . . . two million." OIC's budget across the country was $23 million in 1969. Sullivan's program stresses "attitude" and includes training in job interviews, grooming, and handling money. "You can't train someone by just putting him behind a machine," he says, "you've got to see that he is properly motivated and has a measure of self-respect." In 1968, when OIC centers became too numerous for Sullivan to handle alone, he set up the National Industrial Advisory Council to help guide and develop the operation with the late General Electric board chairman, Gerald Phillippe, as its first chairman. Currently, Sullivan is trying to get similar programs for the unskilled started abroad in such countries as Kenya, Ethiopia, Algeria, and the Dominican Republic. Sullivan also pioneered black capitalism with Zion Investment Associates, based on $10 contributions from members of his Zion Baptist Church. Since 1962 it has financed four major projects: a moderate-income apartment complex; a shopping center (the first in the United States to be owned and operated by blacks); a garment-making company; and Aerospace Enterprises, a subcontracting company started in May 1968 with more than $2.5 million worth of contracts from General Electric, for training hard-core unemployed as aerospace technicians. Meanwhile, his church congregation has grown from 600 to 5000, the largest in Philadelphia. Cited by U.S. Junior Chamber of Commerce as outstanding young man of Philadelphia, 1955. Named by *Life* magazine, as one of 100 outstanding young adults in United States, 1963. Born October 16, 1922, in Charleston, West Virginia. Ordained a Baptist minister at 17. Won athletic scholarship to West Virginia State College, later studied theology at Union Theological Seminary in New York. After going to Philadelphia in 1950, he set up programs to battle juvenile delinquency, and with other ministers, established effective city-wide organization for ending gang wars. Mar-

ried, three children. *See also:* OPPORTUNITIES INDUSTRIALIZA-
TION CENTER.

PERCY E. SUTTON
Lawyer and Manhattan borough president since 1966 when he replaced
Constance Baker Motley. Has served as president of the New York
branch of NAACP (1961) and was elected to the New York State Assembly in 1964. Also presided over the 1966 Democratic State Convention. Came into civil rights at 13 when he handed out leaflets for the
NAACP in San Antonio. Studied political science at Columbia University and received a law degree from Brooklyn Law School. Served
in army air corps intelligence during World War II, after which he continued his studies at Prairie View College, Tuskegee Institute, and Hampton Institute. Married twice (to the same woman), Leatrice O'Farrell,
first in 1942, and again in 1951, two children. Office: 200 West 135th
Street, New York City.

REIES LOPEZ TIJERINA
Mercurial former leader of New Mexico's militant Spanish-American land
claimants, the Alianza Federal de los Pueblos Libres (Federal Alliance
of Free City-States), founded by him in 1963. Alianza asserts historical
claim to about 2500 square miles of northern New Mexico, and in particular a 30-square-mile area they call the "San Joaquin Free City-State."
Born 1927, a former evangelist and migrant worker, Tijerina made headlines June 5, 1967, when he led an armed raid on the county courthouse
at Tierra Amarilla, in which two policemen were wounded. Tijerina
claimed his aim was to make a citizen's arrest of district attorney Al-
fonso Sanchez for his harassment of Alianza's activities. Arrested June
10 on charges of kidnapping and assault with intent to commit murder,
he was acquitted December 14, 1968, after conducting his own defense,
in which he claimed that his attempted citizen's arrest was justified.
Encouraged, in May and June 1969, he made unsuccessful attempts to
make a citizen's arrest of New Mexico Governor David F. Cargo, Chief-
Justice-designate Warren Burger, and scientists at the Los Alamos Lab-
oratory. Tijerina and his followers, mainly descendants of Spanish con-
quistadors and indigenous Indians, claim their ancestors received vast
land grants from the Spanish crown and Mexican government before
the 1848 Treaty of Guadalupe–Hidalgo which granted what is now
New Mexico to the United States. In 1969, Tijerina resigned abruptly
as Alianza's president because of a mystic experience directing him
to focus his energies on the Middle East crisis. He was succeeded by
Ramon Tijerina, one of his four brothers. In January 1970, Tijerina
was sentenced to a two-year jail sentence in Mo. for a 1966 attempt to
take over Carson National Forest. Alianza's membership is reputed to
be some 20,000 throughout New Mexico and the Southwest. Alianza's
headquarters: 1010 Third Street, Albuquerque, New Mexico.

TERENCE A. TODMAN
Ambassador to Chad, appointed July 16, 1969 by President Nixon. Career foreign service officer. After U.S. army service, 1945–49, he was graduated from the Inter-American University, P.R., 1951. Born in the Virgin Islands, March 13, 1926. Married, two sons, two daughters.

STERLING TUCKER
Executive director of Washington Urban League, the capital's major civil rights organization, since 1956. From July 1968, national director of the Urban League's new five million dollar "new thrust" program for the ghettos, described as a "constructive black power" project to develop black economic, social, and political power in ghetto areas. In February 1969, appointed by President Nixon as vice-chairman of District of Columbia municipal council. In June 1968, replaced Bayard Rustin as national coordinator of Poor People's March, after Rustin resigned over disagreement with SCLC leaders. Author of *Black Reflections on White Power* (published by Wm. B. Eerdmans), described as "a clear statement of the very important and growing position between the traditional civil rights movement and the violent revolutionary stance."
   Born Akron, Ohio, 1923. Graduated from the University of Akron (B.A., 1946, M.A., 1950) in social psychology. Began civil rights activity as a student, then as official of Urban League in Akron and Canton. Has lectured abroad with State Department. Married, two daughters. Office: 1424 16th Street, N.W., Washington, D.C.

UNITED NATIVE AMERICANS (UNA)
The most aggressive of the new Indian organizations, the UNA was formed in 1968 as a result of disenchantment with the policies of the Bureau of Indian Affairs and the "ultra-conservatism" of the National Congress of American Indians. UNA claims a membership of 12,000—mostly younger Indians and Eskimos living in urban centers. The group has also attacked Secretary of the Interior Walter Hickel for his policies toward the native population while he was governor of Alaska (1967–69) and circulates petitions and "Impeach Hickel" bumper stickers. President: Lehman Brightman, a Sioux-Creek Indian from South Dakota born in 1930. Has degrees from Oklahoma State University (1957) and University of California at Berkeley (1969) where he is currently working for his Ph.D. Also heads Berkeley's new School of Indian Studies. Married, one child. Mailing address: P.O. Box 26149, San Francisco, California.

URBAN COALITION, NATIONAL
On July 31, 1967, after the riots of Newark and Detroit, a group of 22 prominent Americans announced the formation of an urban coalition designed to focus attention on urban problems and to get "positive and progressive action" on them. The group, called together by Pittsburgh

Mayor Joseph Barr and New York Mayor John Lindsay, announced (August 7, 1969) that it planned to call a national convention of 1000 business, labor, religious, educational, civil rights, and city government leaders to seek solutions to pressing urban questions. The "emergency convocation," held in Washington, D.C., August 24, named Andrew Heiskell, chairman of the board of Time, Inc., and A. Philip Randolph, president of the Brotherhood of Sleeping Car Porters, as co-chairmen of coalition's steering committee. In February 1968, outgoing HEW Secretary John Gardner was named head of the organization, with the title of chairman. The coalition listed as its goals: an emergency federal program to provide jobs and training for urban poor; promotion of non-governmental efforts to train hardcore unemployed; and a long-range program for physical and social reconstruction of the cities. The group called upon "the nation and the Congress to reorder our national priorities, with a commitment of national resources equal to the dimension of the problems we face."

The national coalition merged with Urban America in early 1970. (Formed in 1965, Urban America was the first private national group which had focused on critical urban problems.) In March 1970, the coalition announced a two million dollar program to emphasize national issues involving housing, welfare, law reform, and helping minority contractors gain contracts. The coalition is financed by contributions from individuals, businesses and foundations, and its budget for 1969 was $4,394,000. There are also 47 local urban coalitions across the country of which all are financed independently. The local groups (which are separate and autonomous) can call upon the national staff for help in organizing programs and in finding sources of public and private support. Chairman: John W. Gardner. Steering Committee co-chairmen: William D. Eberle, Whitney M. Young, Jr., Andrew Heiskell, A. Philip Randolph. Headquarters: 1819 H. Street, N.W., Washington, D.C. *See also:* JOHN W. GARDNER, A. PHILIP RANDOLPH, WHITNEY M. YOUNG.

URBAN LEAGUE, NATIONAL

Founded in 1910 and known as one of the most affluent—and among the most effective—of all civil rights groups. Its national and 95 local leagues' resources in 1970 were estimated at over $45 million, including major federal and foundation grants, as well as support from commerce and industry. Emphasis is on furthering economic progress for the Negro. It operates training programs, helps find jobs, aids in health, education, and housing. In 1968 its 1,400 full-time workers found jobs for more than 60,000, upgraded workers in 10,000 jobs, and placed 20,000 in training programs.

Many new projects were begun in ghetto areas in 1968 and 1969 under the league's "new thrust" program. These were expanded in 1970. In 1968, the league officially embraced the concept of "black power." Executive Director Young said: "The words have caught the imagination; they come to convey, above all, pride and community solidarity and this is a positive and constructive concept." However, Young ruled out acceptance of black separatism. He said, "We do not intend to do the racists' job for them by accepting segregation, and we plan no one-way trips to Africa." Executive director: Whitney M. Young, Jr.; president: James A. Linen. Office: 55 East 52nd Street, New York City.

MARTA VALLE

Founder of a New York group called Amanece ("awaken"), which concerns itself primarily with self-help projects in the Puerto Rican community. Formed in 1967 by 25 Puerto Ricans in the city's municipal government who declared themselves frustrated over "lack of communication" between themselves and the higher echelons of Mayor John Lindsay's administration. The group began meeting to discuss better ways to help their people. Membership now includes most of the city's top Puerto Rican leaders. It is supported by membership dues. First major action was a voter-registration campaign in New York City in the summer of 1969. Mrs. Valle was appointed commissioner of New York City's Youth Services Agency November 28, 1967. Born 1934 in East Harlem, she was educated in public schools and graduated from Hunter College and Columbia University. Chairman of Amanece is José Morales, Jr., assistant administrator for health services, New York City.

ABRAHAM S. VENABLE

Director of the Office of Minority Business Enterprise in the Department of Commerce. Appointed October 28, 1969. Responsible for coordination of federal programs bearing on the development of new minority businesses. On November 6, Secretary of Commerce Maurice H. Stans announced that Venable would head Project Enterprise, the Nixon Administration's major program to aid black capitalism. Venable joined the commerce department in 1963, before which he was in private business. Born in Washington, D.C., on April 10, 1930, he has an M.A. in economics from Howard University, 1953. Married, three children. See also: PROJECT ENTERPRISE.

WYATT TEE WALKER

President of Educational Heritage, Inc., publishers of the Negro Heritage Library, and special assistant for urban affairs to New York Governor Rockefeller. Also active in anti-narcotic efforts in New York City. Had been executive director of SCLC from 1960–64, and is credited with laying the groundwork for the assault on racial segregation in Birmingham, Alabama in 1963. Also served briefly as interim pastor of Adam Clayton Powell's Abyssinian Baptist Church but was dismissed in September 1965, in a dispute over a visit by Martin Luther King, Jr.

Graduated from Virginia Union University in 1950. Married the former Theresa Edwards in 1950, four children. Office: 733 Yonkers Avenue, New York, New York.

WALTER E. WASHINGTON

First mayor of Washington, D.C., and first black mayor of any major city in the United States. Appointed by President Johnson after the capital's municipal government was reorganized in August, 1967, and reappointed for a four-year term by President Nixon, 1969. Early in his administration he was faced with the worst riots in the capital's history (for details, see chronology) following the assassination of Dr. Martin Luther King, Jr. in April, 1968. Received wide praise as a "moderating influence" during and after the riots, during which he made nightly television appeals for calm, mobilized the business community to provide emergency food and housing for victims, and organized vacation programs for thousands of young people. Later credited with easing tensions between police and black community and preventing major confrontations during anti-war and other demonstrations. Instituted a crackdown on slum landlords and stepped up efforts to combat the capital's high crime rate, for which he was held partly to blame by some critics. In June, 1970, visited the Soviet Union as guest of Moscow city council, as part of three-week State Department sponsored trip to Europe and Asia. A lawyer, Mayor Washington served 25 years with the capital's public housing authority before being appointed chairman of the New York City Housing Authority in 1966. Born in Dawson, Georgia in 1915, and graduate of Howard University Law School. Admitted to D.C. bar, 1948. His wife, Dr. Bennetta B. Washington, is director of the Women's Job Corps and a trustee of American Field Service. One daughter.

TED WATKINS

Chairman and project administrator of the Watts Labor Community Action Committee. Formed organization in 1965 before the Watts riots. Formerly worked as a fender specialist for the Ford Motor Company in Los Angeles for nearly 20 years. Born 1923 in Meridian, Mississippi. *See also:* WATTS LABOR COMMUNITY ACTION COMMITTEE.

BARBARA WATSON

Administrator of Bureau of Security and Consular Affairs, State Department, since 1968; the first woman and also the first Negro to hold position at this level in State Department. Joined the department in 1966 after serving as attorney with New York City government, latterly as head of the city's liaison with United Nations. Born New York City, November 5, 1918, daughter of Judge James S. Watson. Graduated Barnard College, 1943, and New York Law School, 1962, where she was named "most outstanding law student." Unmarried.

DANIEL WATTS

Editor of *Liberator* magazine (circulation 15,000) and a leading exponent of militant black nationalism. Born in New York City January 9, 1924, he was educated in the city's public schools and Columbia University (School of General Studies and School of Architecture, 1949–55). Gave up a career in architecture (at the firm of Skidmore, Owings and Merrill) to devote his time to the promotion of doctrines of militant black nationalism. Also founded the Afro-American Research Institute. Maintains that the city is the black man's land and that social disorder in urban areas, if organized around a carefully worked out ideology and programmed demands, will succeed in winning gains for Negroes. Lectures at colleges and universities across the country and teaches an accredited course in black journalism and literature at Fordham University. Divorced (from a white woman), one daughter. Office: 244 East 46th Street, New York City.

WATTS LABOR COMMUNITY ACTION COMMITTEE (WLCAC)

A Watts, Los Angeles, self-help organization reported to have been a major factor in keeping the ghetto cool during aftermath of Dr. Martin Luther King's assassination in 1968 and after defeat of Councilman Thomas Bradley in mayoralty race in 1969. Headed by former United Auto Workers official Ted Watkins, with UAW support, the organization is funded by the Department of Labor and supported by a number of labor union groups. It has initiated job training and employment projects ranging from gas stations to poultry farms. It converted barracks into dormitories for 50 underprivileged youths, and its 1969 summer program provided activities for 1,300 Watts youngsters. Total membership reportedly around 3,000. *See also:* TED WATKINS.

ROBERT C. WEAVER

First Negro cabinet member. Named by President Johnson, January 13, 1966, as cabinet-level secretary of the newly created Department of Housing and Urban Development (HUD) and sworn in five days later. Resigned November 1968, to become president of the projected Bernard M. Baruch College of New York University, which is to be built in an urban renewal area of Brooklyn to replace NYU's existing Baruch School of Business Administration. Weaver said he wanted to make the new school "a prototype of the urban university as an idea-generation and action-implementation center for meeting the paramount domestic challenge of our time." Headed the Housing and Home Finance Agency (HHFA), 1961–66. Born Washington, D.C., December 29, 1907. Dropped out of high school to work as an electrician, went on to graduate as an economist at Harvard, where he received his Ph.D. in 1934. Adviser on Negro affairs, Department of the Interior, 1933–37. Taught at Columbia and New York Universities, 1947–49. New York state rent administrator, 1955–59. Former chairman, NAACP. Author: *Dilemmas of Urban America*, 1965; *The Negro Ghetto*, 1948; and *Negro Labor: A National Problem*, 1946. His wife, Ella, is assistant professor of speech at Brooklyn College. One son.

SAMUEL Z. WESTERFIELD, JR.
Appointed ambassador to Liberia September 17, 1969, by President Nixon. He was deputy assistant secretary of state for African affairs, 1967–69. An economist, he was a professor of economics, Atlanta University, 1950–61. Joined state department, 1963. Educated Howard University (A.B., 1939) and Harvard (M.A., 1950, Ph.D., 1951). Born November 15, 1919 in Chicago. Married, two children.

GEORGE A. WILEY
Founder (1966) and director of the National Welfare Rights Organization. Former associate national director of CORE. An organic chemist with a Ph.D. from Cornell University, he taught at Syracuse University before joining CORE in the early 1960's. Subsequently squeezed out of office in a CORE leadership struggle, he deliberately limited the purpose of the new welfare rights organization to that of improving welfare benefits and distribution, avoiding issues which could be divisive. He has complained that the civil rights movement has "seriously impaired" its effectiveness through lack of agreement on objectives. Born February 26, 1931, and brought up in Rhode Island. Wiley is married with two children and lives in Washington, D.C. *See also:* NATIONAL WELFARE RIGHTS ORGANIZATION.

ROGER WILKINS
Director of studies in social development at the Ford Foundation in New York City. Nephew of Roy Wilkins, NAACP executive director. From 1966–68 was director of Community Relations Service in the Department of Justice and prior to that did welfare work in Cleveland, Ohio. Made headlines March 15, 1970, when he declined a White House invitation "out of conscience" because, he said, he felt that Nixon's policies were crushing Negro hopes. Office: 320 East 43rd Street, New York City.

ROY WILKINS
Executive director of the NAACP, which he has headed since 1955, and civil rights activist for 40 years. Wilkins has been one of the chief symbols of moderation in the turbulent civil rights scene of the 1960's. In firmly rejecting violence and the concepts of black power and black nationalism, and in voicing support for the use of troops to suppress racial riots, he has been a frequent target of criticism among the new generation of black militants. More recently, he has also voiced strong opposition to student demands for all-black departments on college campuses, describing this as a return to "segregation and Jim Crow." But his position as veteran leader of the nation's most influential civil

rights group has remained secure, according to *The New York Times*, because of "his mastery of the geography and mechanics of power in Washington." His ability to get action where others fail has earned him a reputation as "master strategist" and "statesman" in the cause of civil rights. With Arthur J. Goldberg, heads Commission of Inquiry into Black Panthers and Law Enforcement Officials which he helped form (December 16, 1969) to look into Panther/police clashes. Born in St. Louis on August 30, 1901, he graduated from the University of Minnesota in 1923. Became a newspaperman with the *Kansas City Call*, a Negro weekly, until joining the NAACP in 1931 as an assistant to Walter White. Married to the former Aminda Badeau of St. Louis.

HOSEA WILLIAMS
Vice president of SCLC and veteran of many of Dr. Martin Luther King's civil rights campaigns. Leader of May, 1970 "march against repression," from Perry, Georgia to Atlanta. March was seen as opening an active new phase in SCLC strategy. During the march, Williams called for "black power," a phrase attacked by the late Dr. King. But Williams explained that black power today meant self-respect, not violence. In June, 1970, Williams qualified as Republican primary candidate for secretary of state of Georgia. In 1968, ran unsuccessfully for Georgia House of Representatives as a Democrat. His wife, Juanita, qualified for 1970 Democratic primary for Controller General.

Born January 5, 1926, in Attapulgus, Georgia, Williams was a chemist with the U.S. Department of Agriculture before joining the civil rights movement, in which he soon became known for his skill in "grass roots" organization. Jailed more than 40 times during rights campaigns in the South.

JULIUS E. WILLIAMS
Midwest regional director for the NAACP. A long time NAACP worker, has served in various capacities in the organization—Youth Council president, branch secretary, branch executive committee member and vice-president of the Illinois State Conference. A native of Birmingham, Alabama, he was graduated from the Maywood, Illinois public schools. Has a B.A. in business administration from the University of Chicago and M.B.A. degree from the School of Commerce of Northwestern University. Office: 2704 Prospect Avenue, Kansas City, Missouri.

ROBERT F. WILLIAMS
Black revolutionary who returned to the United States September 12, 1969, after eight years' self-imposed exile in Cuba, North Vietnam, Communist China, and Tanzania. While abroad, published newsletter for American blacks urging revolution and advising on urban guerrilla-warfare techniques. Also called on blacks to refuse to serve in Vietnam—and

if they went, to kill white soldiers. Upon return, wearing Mao uniform, was taken into custody by FBI at Detroit airport. Later released. Told newsmen September 15 that United States today represented "the best chance ever for social changes and racial justice," and he was committed to developing a "selfless society."

In March 1970, he testified in secret before Senate Internal Security Subcommittee, answering questions on his travels abroad and meetings with Mao Tse-Tung, Fidel Castro and Ho Chi Minh. Some reports linked his activities with U.S. Intelligence but his lawyer denied it. Elected president of the Republic of New Africa at group's national convention in Washington, D.C., August 23, 1969, but was ousted from the office after internal party split, December, 1969.

Born 1925, Williams fled United States in August 1961, to avoid trial for allegedly kidnapping Mr. and Mrs. Bruce Stegall of Marshville, North Carolina, during a racial disturbance. Married, two sons. *See also:* REPUBLIC OF NEW AFRICA.

WOODLAWN ORGANIZATION
Formed in early 1961 as a community action group in the black Woodlawn area of Chicago's South Side. Led by Rev. Arthur Brazier, the organization has acted as arbiter between street gangs, led neighborhood improvement projects, and organized job-training and voter registration drives. Coordinated controversial Office of Economic Opportunity-funded job-training program for members of the Rangers and Disciples gangs, which was criticized at the Senate Government Operations Committee hearings in Washington, June 1968. Brazier was praised by Senator Charles H. Percy for his "courage, guts and determination." Brazier has charged that the Woodlawn area has been unfairly overlooked in the federal Model Cities program. He has told the story of his organization in *Black Self-Determination: The Story of the Woodlawn Organization,* published by Wm. B. Eerdmans, September 1969.

FRANK YERBY
Most commercially successful Negro writer. Has more than 20 novels to his credit—including the 1949 bestseller *Foxes of Harrow, Pride's Castle* (1948), *An Odor of Sanctity* (1965), *Goat Song* (1967)—which have grossed him over $10 million. Has lived abroad since 1952, for the past 10 years in Spain. Born in Augusta, Georgia, September 5, 1916. Graduated from Paine College (1937), receiving M.A. from Fisk University (1938). Married twice, four children.

ANDREW J. YOUNG
As executive vice-president of SCLC, Young is the official number-two man in the SCLC hierarchy and sometimes described as the "brains" of the organization. Like Ralph Abernathy, Young had been a friend of King's since the 1955 bus boycott in Montgomery, Alabama. He joined the SCLC in 1961 and was its executive director, 1964–67, when he be-

came executive vice-president. His forte is said to be community organization. Currently writing an analysis of both the history of the civil rights movement and the interrelated problems of racism, economic exploitation, war, and colonialism. In early 1970, Young announced he would run for Georgia's Fifth Congressional District as a Republican. Born March 12, 1932, in New Orleans, Louisiana, the son of Dr. A. J. Young, Sr. After studying at Dillard and Howard Universities, graduated from Hartford (Connecticut) Theological Seminary in 1955, was ordained a minister of the United Church of Christ and became a pastor in Marion, Alabama. Married to the former Jean Childs, three children.

WHITNEY M. YOUNG, JR.

Executive director of the National Urban League since 1961 and considered one of the nation's leading moderate leaders. Was outspoken critic of Nixon Administration's preventive detention proposals, calling them "an extreme reaction that could lead to a system of oppressive racial containment" (August 13, 1969). On the same date he told American Bar Association: "I sense a mood of repression slowly gathering force in this nation." Author of *Beyond Racism* (McGraw-Hill, 1969), in which he proposes creation of neighborhood development corporations, funded by a government-backed national economic development bank. Born in Lincoln Ridge, Kentucky, July 31, 1921. He grew up on the campus of Lincoln Institute where his father was a teacher and eventually president. Gained B.S. at Kentucky State College, 1941, and after war service as G.I. in Negro road construction company, graduated in social work at University of Minnesota and began to teach. Worked in Urban League groups, first in St. Paul and then in Omaha, while lecturing at colleges in both cities. Was dean of Atlanta University School of Social Work, 1954–60. In 1967, met with Pope Paul at the Vatican to discuss papal encyclical on racial justice. Married to former Margaret Buckner, two daughters. Lives in New Rochelle, New York.

YOUNG LORDS PARTY (YLP)

One of the newest of the militant civil rights organizations, the Young Lords started in 1960 as a Puerto Rican street gang in Chicago, shifted to a social-service club in 1964 and then to a political organization modeled on the Black Panther party in January 1969. Its proclaimed aim is to promote independence for all "Latinos" (Latin-Americans) through a brand of socialism based on a 13-point program which covers much of the same ground as the Panther's 10-point program. The Lords' philosophy has been described as a "grab-bag of just about every revolutionary statement in history." Their heroes are Pedro Albizu Campos, the late leftist leader who favored Puerto Rican independence, Che Guevara, Malcolm X, and Panther leaders Cleaver and Newton. In the summer of 1969, the Lords joined with the Panthers and the Appalachian Young Patriots, a group of poor-white revolutionaries and a former Chicago street gang, to form the Rainbow Coalition. The Lords are secretive about their membership but the *Black Panther* newspaper (February 17, 1970) listed Lord chapters in Puerto Rico, New York, Philadelphia, Newark, and Hayward, California. National headquarters: 836 W. Armitage Avenue, Chicago, Illinois. National chairman: Cha Cha Jiminez; minister of finance: Edwin Diaz; minister of information: Omar Lopez; minister of education: Polo.

The New York chapter, called the New York State Central Committee, joined the national organization in January 1969. But in May 1970 they split with the Chicago group because of organizational differences and became the Young Lords Party. It made headlines in December 1969 when it seized the First Spanish Methodist Church in East Harlem and held it for 11 days, seeking to force church authorities to provide space for a free breakfast program. On February 25, 1970 charges against the Lords were dropped after an agreement was reached calling for the city and East Harlem to establish a day care center in the church. The group claims income from the sale of its bi-monthly newspaper *Palante* (which means "right arm"), and from private sources. Membership, according to a 1969 *New York Times* estimate, is about 100. Headquarters: 1678 Madison Avenue, New York, New York. National chairman: Felipe Luciano.

Guide
to Acronyms

NOTE: This list constitutes the more familiar acronyms, and includes all those used in connection with civil rights organizations.

ABCD	Action for Boston Community Development	D & S	Bedford-Stuyvesant Development and Service Corporation
ACLU	American Civil Liberties Union	FIGHT	Freedom, Integration, God, Honor, Today
AIM	American Indian Movement	HAR-YOU-ACT	Harlem Youth-Action
AIO	Americans for Indian Opportunity	HUC	Harlem Unemployment Center
BEDC	Black Economic Development Conference	IAF	Industrial Areas Foundation
BEU	Black Economic Union	IFCO	Interreligious Foundation for Community Organization
BIA	Bureau of Indian Affairs		
BPP	Black Panther Party	JOBS	Job Opportunity in the Business Sector
BUF	Black United Front	LDF	Legal Defense and Education Fund, Inc. (NAACP)
CORE	Congress of Racial Equality		

MARC	Metropolitan Applied Research Center
MAYO	Mexican-American Youth Organization
NAACP	National Association for the Advancement of Colored People
NAPCR	National Association of Puerto Rican Civil Rights
NCAI	National Convention of American Indians
NEGRO	National Economic Growth and Recon-struction Organ.
OAAU	Organization of Afro-American Unity
OIC	Opportunities Industrial Center
ONAS	Organization of Native American Students
RGS	Real Great Society
SCLC	Southern Christian Leadership Conference
SEEK	Search for Education, Elevation and Knowl-edge
SNCC	Student National Co-ordinating Committee (formerly Student Non-Violent Coordinating Com-mittee)
UNA	United Native Americans
VEP	Voters Education Project
WLCAC	Watts Labor Com-munity Action Committee
YLP	Young Lords Party

Appendices

Appendix I

Congressional Voting Records on Civil Rights Acts from 1960 to 1968

1960 Civil Rights Act

(Contains penalties for obstructing school desegregation orders, requires preservation of voting records, provides for court referees, strengthens 1957 Civil Rights Act.)

SENATE
(Vote Total: 71 for, 18 against)

VOTES FOR

Anderson (D–NM)	Capehart (R–Ind)	Douglas (D–Ill)
Bartlett (D–Alaska)	Carroll (D–Colo)	Engle (D–Cal)
Beall (R–Md)	Case (R–NJ)	Fong (R–Hawaii)
Bennett (R–Utah)	Case (D–SDak)	Frear (D–Del)
Bible (D–Nev)	Chavez (D–NM)	Gore (D–Tenn)
Bridges (R–NH)	Church (D–Idaho)	Green (D–RI)
Brunsdale (R–NDak)	Clark (D–Pa)	Gruening (D–Alaska)
Bush (R–Conn)	Cooper (R–Ky)	Hart (D–Mich)
Butler (R–Md)	Cotton (R–NH)	Hartke (D–Ind)
Byrd (D–WVa)	Curtis (R–Nebr)	Hayden (D–Ariz)
Cannon (D–Nev)	Dirksen (R–Ill)	Hennings (D–Mo)

Hickenlooper (R–Iowa)   Martin (R–Iowa)   Proxmire (D–Wisc)
Hruska (R–Nebr)   McCarthy (D–Minn)   Randolph (D–Wva)
Jackson (D–Wash)   McGee (D–Wyo)   Saltonstall (D–Mass)
Javits (R–NY)   McNamara (D–Mich)   Scott (R–Pa)
Johnson (D–Tex)   Monroney (D–Okla)   Smith (R–Me)
Keating (R–NY)   Morse (D–Ore)   Symington (D–Mo)
Kefauver (D–Tenn)   Morton (R–Ky)   Wiley (R–Wisc)
Kennedy (D–Mass)   Moss (D–Utah)   Williams (R–Del)
Kuchel (R–Cal)   Mundt (R–SDak)   Williams (D–NJ)
Lausche (D–Ohio)   Murray (D–Mont)   Yarborough (D–Tex)
Long (D–Hawaii)   Muskie (D–Me)   Young (D–Ohio)
Lusk (D–Ore)   Pastore (D–RI)   Young (R–NDak)
Magnuson (D–Wash)   Prouty (R–Vt)

                                                 Total: 71

VOTES AGAINST

Byrd (D–Va)   Johnston (D–SC)   Sparkman (D–Ala)
Eastland (D–Miss)   Jordan (D–NC)   Stennis (D–Miss)
Ellender (D–La)   Long (D–La)   Talmadge (D–Ga)
Ervin (D–NC)   McClellan (D–Ark)   Thurmond (D–SC)
Fulbright (D–Ark)   Robertson (D–Va)
Hill (D–Ala)   Russell (D–Ga)   Total: 18
Holland (D–Fla)   Smathers (D–Fla)

HOUSE OF REPRESENTATIVES
(Vote Total: 311 for, 119 against)

VOTES FOR

Adair (R–Ind)   Becker (R–NY)   Burdick (D–NDak)
Addonizio (D–NJ)   Belcher (R–Okla)   Burke (D–Ky)
Albert (D–Okla)   Bentley (R–Mich)   Burke (D–Mass)
Allen (R–Ill)   Berry (R–SDak)   Byrne (D–Pa)
Andersen (D–Minn)   Betts (R–Ohio)   Byrnes (R–Wisc)
Anfuso (D–NY)   Blatnik (D–Minn)   Cahill (R–NJ)
Ashley (D–Ohio)   Boland (D–Mass)   Canfield (R–NJ)
Aspinall (D–Colo)   Boling (D–Mo)   Cannon (D–Mo)
Auchincloss (R–NJ)   Bolton (R–Ohio)   Carnahan (D–Mo)
Avery (R–Kans)   Bosch (R–NY)   Cederberg (R–Mich)
Ayers (R–Ohio)   Bow (R–Ohio)   Celler (D–NY)
Bailey (D–WVa)   Bowles (D–Conn)   Chamberlain (R–Mich)
Baker (R–Tenn)   Brademas (D–Ind)   Chelf (D–Ky)
Baldwin (R–Cal)   Bray (R–Ind)   Chenoweth (R–Colo)
Baring (D–Nev)   Breeding (D–Kans)   Church (R–Ill)
Barr (D–Ind)   Brewster (D–Md)   Clark (D–Pa)
Barrett (D–Pa)   Brock (D–Nebr)   Coad (D–Iowa)
Barry (R–NY)   Broomfield (R–Mich)   Coffin (D–Me)
Bass (R–NH)   Brown (D–Mo)   Cohelan (D–Cal)
Bates (R–Mass)   Brown (R–Ohio)   Collier (R–Ill)
Baumhart (R–Ohio)   Buckley (D–NY)   Conte (R–Mass)

Cook (D–Ohio)
Corbett (R–Pa)
Cunningham (R–Nebr)
Curtin (R–Pa)
Curtis (R–Mo)
Curtis (R–Mass)
Daddario (D–Conn)
Dague (R–Pa)
Daniels (D–NJ)
Dawson (D–Ill)
Delaney (D–NY)
Dent (D–Pa)
Denton (D–Ind)
Derounian (R–NY)
Derwinski (R–Ill)
Devine (R–Ohio)
Diggs (D–Mich)
Dingell (D–Mich)
Dixon (R–Utah)
Donohue (D–Mass)
Dooley (R–NY)
Dorn (R–NY)
Doyle (D–Cal)
Dulski (D–NY)
Dwyer (R–NJ)
Edmondson (D–Okla)
Fallon (D–Md)
Farbstein (D–NY)
Fascell (D–Fla)
Feighan (D–Ohio)
Fenton (R–Pa)
Fino (R–NY)
Flood (D–Pa)
Flynn (D–Wisc)
Fogarty (D–RI)
Foley (D–Md)
Forand (D–RI)
Ford (R–Mich)
Frelinghuysen (R–NJ)
Friedel (D–Md)
Fulton (R–Pa)
Gallagher (D–NJ)
Garmatz (D–Md)
Gavin (R–Pa)
George (D–Kans)
Giaimo (D–Conn)
Gilbert (D–NY)
Glenn (R–NJ)
Goodell (R–NY)
Granahan (D–Pa)

Gray (D–Ill)
Green (D–Ore)
Green (D–Pa)
Griffen (R–Mich)
Gross (R–Iowa)
Gubser (R–Cal)
Hagen (D–Cal)
Halleck (R–Ind)
Halpern (R–NY)
Hargis (D–Kans)
Hays (D–Ohio)
Healey (D–NY)
Hechler (D–Wva)
Henderson (R–Ohio)
Hess (R–Ohio)
Hiestand (R–Cal)
Hoeven (R–Iowa)
Hoffman (R–Ill)
Hogan (D–Ind)
Holifield (D–Cal)
Holland (D–Pa)
Holt (R–Cal)
Holtzman (D–NY)
Horan (R–Wash)
Hosmer (R–Cal)
Hull (D–Mo)
Inouye (D–Hawaii)
Irwin (D–Conn)
Jarman (D–Okla)
Johnson (D–Cal)
Johnson (D–Colo)
Johnson (D–Md)
Johnson (D–Wisc)
Judd (R–Minn)
Karsten (D–Mo)
Karth (D–Minn)
Kasem (D–Cal)
Kastenmeier (D–Wisc)
Kearns (R–Pa)
Kee (D–WVa)
Keith (R–Mass)
Kelly (D–NY)
Keogh (D–NY)
Kilday (D–Tex)
Kilgore (D–Tex)
King (D–Cal)
King (D–Utah)
Kluczynski (D–Ill)
Knox (R–Mich)
Kowalski (D–Conn)

Kyl (R–Iowa)
Lafore (R–Pa)
Laird (R–Wisc)
Lane (D–Mass)
Langen (R–Minn)
Lankford (D–Md)
Latta (R–Ohio)
Lesinski (D–Mich)
Levering (D–Ohio)
Lindsay (R–NY)
Libonati (D–Ill)
Lipscomb (R–Cal)
McCormack (D–Mass)
McCulloch (R–Ohio)
McDonogh (R–Cal)
McDowell (D–Del)
McFall (D–Cal)
McGinley (D–Nebr)
McGovern (D–SDak)
McIntire (R–Me)
Macdonald (D–Mass)
Machrowicz (D–Mich)
Mack (D–Ill)
Mack (R–Wash)
Madden (D–Ind)
Magnuson (D–Wisc)
Mailliard (R–Cal)
Marshall (D–Minn)
Martin (R–Mass)
May (R–Wash)
Merrow (R–NH)
Metcalf (D–Mont)
Meyer (D–Vt)
Michel (R–Ill)
Miller, C. (D–Cal)
Miller, G. (D–Cal)
Miller (R–NY)
Milliken (R–Pa)
Moeller (D–Ohio)
Monagan (D–Conn)
Montoya (D–NMex)
Moore (R–WVa)
Moorhead (D–Pa)
Morgan (D–Pa)
Morris (D–NMex)
Moss (D–Cal)
Moulder (D–Mo)
Multer (D–NY)
Mumma (R–Pa)
Murphy (D–Ill)

Natcher (D–Ky)
Nelson (R–Minn)
Nix (D–Pa)
Norblad (R–Ore)
O'Brien (D–NY)
O'Brien (D–Ill)
O'Hara (D–Ill)
O'Hara (D–Mich)
O'Konski (R–Wisc)
Oliver (D–Me)
O'Neill (D–Mass)
Osmers (R–NJ)
Ostertag (R–NY)
Pelly (R–Wash)
Perkins (D–Ky)
Pfost (D–Idaho)
Philbin (D–Mass)
Pillion (R–NY)
Pirnie (R–NY)
Porter (D–Ore)
Price (D–Ill)
Prokop (D–Pa)
Pucinski (D–Ill)
Quie (R–Minn)
Quigley (D–Pa)
Rabaut (D–Mich)
Randall (D–Mo)
Ray (R–NY)
Reece (R–Tenn)
Rees (R–Kans)
Reuss (D–Wisc)
Rhodes (R–Ariz)
Rhodes (D–Pa)
Riehlman (R–NY)
Rivers (D–Alaska)
Robison (R–NY)

Rodino (D–NJ)
Rogers (D–Colo)
Rogers (R–Mass)
Rooney (D–NY)
Roosevelt (D–Cal)
Rostenkowski (D–Ill)
Roush (D–Ind)
St. George (R–NY)
Santangelo (D–NY)
Saund (D–Cal)
Saylor (R–Pa)
Schenck (R–Ohio)
Scherer (R–Ohio)
Schwengel (R–Iowa)
Shelley (D–Cal)
Sheppard (D–Cal)
Shipley (D–Ill)
Short (R–NDak)
Siler (R–Ky)
Simpson (R–Ill)
Sisk (D–Cal)
Slack (D–WVa)
Smith (R–Cal)
Smith (D–Iowa)
Springer (R–Ill)
Staggers (D–WVa)
Steed (D–Okla)
Stratton (D–NY)
Stubblefield (D–Ky)
Sullivan (D–Mo)
Taylor (R–NY)
Teague (R–Cal)
Teller (D–NY)
Thompson (D–NJ)
Thomson (R–Wyo)
Thornberry (D–Tex)

Toll (D–Pa)
Tollefson (R–Wash)
Udall (D–Ariz)
Ullman (D–Ore)
Vanik (D–Ohio)
Van Pelt (R–Wisc)
Van Zandt (R–Pa)
Wainwright (R–NY)
Wallhauser (R–NJ)
Walter (D–Pa)
Wampler (D–Ind)
Watts (D–Ky)
Weaver (R–Nebr)
Weis (R–NY)
Westland (R–Wash)
Wharton (R–NY)
Widnall (R–NJ)
Wier (D–Minn)
Wilson (R–Cal)
Withrow (R–Wisc)
Wolf (D–Iowa)
Wright (D–Tex)
Yates (D–Ill)
Younger (R–Cal)
Zablocki (D–Wisc)
Zelenko (D–NY)

Total: 311

Paired For
Arends (R–Ill)
Chipperfield (R–Ill)
Griffiths (D–Mich)
Kirwan (D–Ohio)

VOTES AGAINST

Abbitt (D–Va)
Abernethy (D–Miss)
Alexander (D–NC)
Alford (D–Ark)
Alger (R–Tex)
Andrews (D–Ala)
Ashmore (D–SC)
Bass (D–Tenn)
Beckworth (D–Tex)
Bennett (D–Fla)
Bennett (R–Mich)
Boggs (D–La)

Bonner (D–NC)
Boykin (D–Ala)
Brooks (D–La)
Brooks (D–Tex)
Brown (D–Ga)
Broyhill (R–Va)
Budge (R–Idaho)
Burleson (D–Tex)
Casey (D–Tex)
Colmer (D–Miss)
Cooley (D–NC)
Cramer (R–Fla)

Davis (D–Ga)
Davis (D–Tenn)
Dorn (D–SC)
Dowdy (D–Tex)
Downing (D–Va)
Durham (D–NC)
Elliott (D–Ala)
Everett (D–Tenn)
Evins (D–Tenn)
Fisher (D–Tex)
Flynt (D–Ga)
Forrester (D–Ga)

Fountain (D–NC)
Frazier (D–Tenn)
Gary (D–Va)
Gathings (D–Ark)
Grant (D–Ala)
Haley (D–Fla)
Hardy (D–Va)
Harmon (D–Ind)
Harris (D–Ark)
Harrison (D–Va)
Hebert (D–La)
Hemphill (D–SC)
Herlong (D–Fla)
Hoffman (R–Mich)
Huddleston (D–Ala)
Ikard (D–Tex)
Jennings (D–Va)
Jensen (R–Iowa)
Johansen (R–Mich)
Jonas (R–NC)
Jones (D–Ala)
Jones (D–Mo)
Kitchin (D–NC)
Landrum (D–Ga)
Lennon (D–NC)
Loser (D–Tenn)
McMillan (D–SC)

McSween (D–La)
Mahon (D–Tex)
Mason (R–Ill)
Matthews (D–Fla)
Meader (R–Mich)
Mills (D–Ark)
Mitchell (D–Ga)
Morris (D–Okla)
Morrison (D–La)
Murray (D–Tenn)
Norrell (D–Ark)
Passman (D–La)
Patman (D–Tex)
Pilcher (D–Ga)
Poage (D–Tex)
Poff (R–Va)
Preston (D–Ga)
Rains (D–Ala)
Riley (D–SC)
Rivers (D–SC)
Roberts (D–Ala)
Rogers (D–Fla)
Rogers (D–Tex)
Rutherford (D–Tex)
Scott (D–NC)
Selden (D–Ala)
Sikes (D–Fla)

Smith (R–Kans)
Smith (D–Miss)
Smith (D–Va)
Spence (D–Ky)
Taber (R–NY)
Teague (D–Tex)
Thomas (D–Tex)
Thompson (D–La)
Thompson (D–Tex)
Trimble (D–Ark)
Tuck (D–Va)
Utt (R–Cal)
Vinson (D–Ga)
Whitener (D–NC)
Whitten (D–Miss)
Williams (D–Miss)
Willis (D–La)
Winstead (D–Miss)
Young (D–Tex)

Total: 109

Paired Against
Barden (D–NC)
Blitch (D–Ga)
Jackson (R–Cal)
Kilburn (R–NY)

1964 Civil Rights Act

(Voting rights, equal access to public accommodations, desegregation of public facilities and schools, equal employment, and non-discrimination in federally assisted programs.)

SENATE
(Vote Total: 73 for, 27 against)

VOTES FOR

Aiken (R–Vt)
Allott (R–Colo)
Anderson (D–NM)
Bartlett (D–Alaska)
Bayh (D–Ind)
Beall (R–Md)
Bennett (R–Utah)
Bible (D–Nev)
Boggs (R–Del)

Brewster (D–Md)
Burdick (D–ND)
Cannon (D–Nev)
Carlson (R–Kans)
Case (R–NJ)
Church (D–Idaho)
Clark (D–Pa)
Cooper (R–Ky)
Curtis (R–Nebr)

Dirksen (R–Ill)
Dodd (D–Conn)
Dominick (R–Colo)
Douglas (D–Ill)
Edmondson (D–Okla)
Engle (D–Cal)
Fong (R–Hawaii)
Gruening (D–Alaska)
Hart (D–Mich)

Hartke (D–Ind)
Hayden (D–Ariz)
Hruska (R–Nebr)
Humphrey (D–Minn)
Inouye (D–Hawaii)
Jackson (D–Wash)
Javits (R–NY)
Jordan (R–Idaho)
Keating (R–NY)
Kennedy (D–Mass)
Kuchel (R–Cal)
Lausche (D–Ohio)
Long (D–Mo)
McCarthy (D–Minn)
McGee (D–Wyo)
McGovern (D–SDak)

McIntyre (D–NH)
McNamara (D–Mich)
Magnuson (D–Wash)
Mansfield (D–Mont)
Metcalf (D–Mont)
Miller (R–Iowa)
Monroney (D–Okla)
Morse (D–Ore)
Morton (R–Ky)
Moss (D–Utah)
Mundt (R–SDak)
Muskie (D–Me)
Nelson (D–Wisc)
Neuberger (D–Ore)
Pastore (D–RI)
Pearson (R–Kans)

Pell (D–RI)
Prouty (R–Vt)
Proxmire (D–Wisc)
Randolph (D–WVa)
Ribicoff (D–Conn)
Saltonstall (R–Mass)
Scott (R–Pa)
Smith (R–Me)
Symington (D–Mo)
Williams (R–Del)
Williams (D–NJ)
Yarborough (D–Tex)
Young (D–Ohio)
Young (R–NDak)

Total: 73

VOTES AGAINST

Byrd (D–Va)
Byrd (D–WVa)
Cotton (R–NH)
Eastland (D–Miss)
Ellender (D–Ky)
Ervin (D–NC)
Fulbright (D–Ark)
Goldwater (R–Ariz)
Gore (D–Tenn)

Hill (D–Ala)
Hickenlooper (R–Iowa)
Holland (D–Fla)
Johnston (D–SC)
Jordan (D–NC)
Long (D–La)
McClellan (D–Ark)
Mechem (R–NMex)
Robertson (D–Va)

Russell (D–Ga)
Simpson (R–Wyo)
Smathers (D–Fla)
Sparkman (D–Ala)
Stennis (D–Miss)
Talmadge (D–Ga)
Thurmond (D–SC)
Tower (R–Tex)
Walters (D–Tenn)

Total: 27

HOUSE OF REPRESENTATIVES
(Vote Total: 289 for, 126 against)

VOTES FOR

Abele (R–Ohio)
Adair (R–Ind)
Addabbo (D–NY)
Albert (D–Okla)
Anderson (R–Ill)
Andrews (R–NDak)
Arends (R–Ill)
Ashley (D–Ohio)
Aspinall (D–Colo)
Auchincloss (R–NJ)
Ayers (R–Ohio)
Baldwin (R–Cal)
Barrett (D–Pa)
Barry (R–NY)
Bass (D–Tenn)

Bates (R–Mass)
Becker (R–NY)
Bell (R–Cal)
Betts (R–Ohio)
Blatnik (D–Minn)
Boland (D–Mass)
Bolling (D–Mo)
Bolton, F. (R–Ohio)
Bolton, O. (R–Ohio)
Bow (R–Ohio)
Brademas (D–Ind)
Bray (R–Ind)
Bromwell (R–Iowa)
Brooks (D–Tex)
Broomfield (R–Mich)

Brotzman (R–Colo)
Brown (R–Ohio)
Brown (D–Cal)
Bruce (R–Ind)
Buckley (D–NY)
Burke (D–Mass)
Burkhalter (D–Cal)
Burton (R–Utah)
Burton (D–Cal)
Byrne (D–Pa)
Byrnes (R–Wisc)
Cahill (R–NJ)
Cameron (D–Cal)
Carey (D–NY)
Cederberg (R–Mich)

Celler (D–NY)
Chamberlain (R–Mich)
Chenoweth (R–Colo)
Clancy (R–Ohio)
Clausen (R–Cal)
Cleveland (D–NH)
Cohelan (D–Cal)
Collier (R–Ill)
Conte (R–Mass)
Corbett (R–Pa)
Corman (D–Cal)
Cunningham (R–Nebr)
Curtin (R–Pa)
Curtis (R–Mo)
Daddario (D–Conn)
Dague (R–Pa)
Daniels (D–NJ)
Dawson (D–Ill)
Delaney (D–NY)
Dent (D–Pa)
Denton (D–Ind)
Derounian (R–NY)
Derwinski (R–Ill)
Devine (R–Ohio)
Diggs (D–Mich)
Dingell (D–Mich)
Dole (R–Kans)
Donohue (D–Mass)
Dulski (D–NY)
Duncan (D–Ore)
Dwyer (R–NJ)
Edmondson (D–Okla)
Edwards (D–Cal)
Ellsworth (R–Kans)
Fallon (D–Md)
Farbstein (D–NY)
Feighan (D–Ohio)
Findley (R–Ill)
Finnegan (D–Ill)
Fino (R–NY)
Flood (D–Pa)
Fogarty (D–RI)
Ford (R–Mich)
Fraser (D–Minn)
Frelinghuysen (R–NJ)
Friedel (D–Md)
Fulton (R–Pa)
Fulton (D–Tenn)
Gallagher (D–NJ)
Garmatz (D–Md)

Giaimo (D–Conn)
Gilbert (D–NY)
Gill (D–Hawaii)
Glenn (R–NJ)
Gonzalez (D–Tex)
Goodell (R–NY)
Goodling (R–Pa)
Grabowski (D–Conn)
Gray (D–Ill)
Green (D–Ore)
Green (D–Pa)
Griffen (R–Mich)
Griffiths (D–Mich)
Grover (R–NY)
Gubser (R–Cal)
Hagen (D–Cal)
Halleck (R–Ind)
Halpern (R–NY)
Hays (D–Ohio)
Healey (D–NY)
Hechler (D–WVa)
Hoeven (R–Iowa)
Hoffman (R–Ill)
Holifield (D–Cal)
Holland (D–Pa)
Horan (R–Wash)
Horton (D–NY)
Hosmer (R–Cal)
Hutchinson (R–Mich)
Ichord (D–Mo)
Joelson (D–NJ)
Johnson (D–Cal)
Johnson (R–Pa)
Johnson (D–Wisc)
Karsten (D–Mo)
Kastenmeier (D–Wisc)
Hanna (D–Cal)
Hansen (D–Wash)
Harding (D–Idaho)
Harsha (R–Ohio)
Harvey (R–Mich)
Harvey (R–Ind)
Hawkins (D–Cal)
Kee (D–WVa)
Keith (R–Mass)
Kelly (D–NY)
Keogh (D–NY)
King (R–NY)
King (D–Cal)
Kirwan (D–Ohio)

Klucyznski (D–Ill)
Kunkel (R–Pa)
Kyl (R–Iowa)
Laird (R–Wisc)
Langen (R–Minn)
Latta (R–Ohio)
Leggett (D–Cal)
Libonati (D–Ill)
Lindsay (R–NY)
Long (D–Md)
McClory (R–Ill)
McCulloch (R–Ohio)
McDade (R–Pa)
McDowell (D–Del)
McFall (D–Cal)
McIntire (R–Me)
McLoskey (R–Ill)
Macdonald (D–Mass)
MacGregor (R–Minn)
Madden (D–Ind)
Mailliard (R–Cal)
Martin (R–Mass)
Martin (R–Nebr)
Mathias (R–Md)
Matsunaga (D–Hawaii)
May (R–Wash)
Michel (R–Ill)
Miller (D–Cal)
Milliken (R–Pa)
Minish (D–NJ)
Minshall (R–Ohio)
Monagan (D–Conn)
Montoya (D–NMex)
Moore (R–WVa)
Moorhead (D–Pa)
Morgan (D–Pa)
Morris (D–NMex)
Morse (R–Mass)
Morton (R–Md)
Mosher (R–Ohio)
Moss (D–Cal)
Multer (D–NY)
Murphy (D–Ill)
Murphy (D–NY)
Nedzi (D–Mich)
Nelson (R–Minn)
Nix (D–Pa)
O'Brien (D–NY)
O'Hara (D–Ill)
O'Hara (D–Mich)

O'Konski (R–Wisc)
Olsen (D–Mont)
Olson (D–Minn)
O'Neill (D–Mass)
Osmers (R–NJ)
Ostertag (R–NY)
Patten (D–NJ)
Pelly (R–Wash)
Pepper (D–Fla)
Perkins (D–Ky)
Philbin (D–Mass)
Pickle (D–Tex)
Pike (D–NY)
Pillion (R–NY)
Pirnie (R–NY)
Price (D–Ill)
Pucinski (D–Ill)
Quie (R–Minn)
Randall (D–Mo)
Reid (R–NY)
Reifel (D–SDak)
Reuss (D–Wisc)
Rhodes (R–Ariz)
Rhodes (D–Pa)
Rich (R–Ohio)
Riehlman (R–NY)
Rivers (D–Alaska)
Robison (R–NY)
Rodino (D–NJ)
Rogers (D–Colo)
Rooney (D–Pa)
Roosevelt (D–Cal)
Rosenthal (D–NY)
Rostenkowski (D–Ill)
Rotney (D–NY)

Roudebush (R–Ind)
Roush (D–Ind)
Roybel (D–Cal)
Rumsfeld (R–Ill)
Ryan (D–Mich)
Ryan (D–NY)
St. George (R–NY)
St. Germain (D–RI)
St. Onge (D–Conn)
Saylor (R–Pa)
Schadeberg (R–Wisc)
Schenck (R–Ohio)
Schenecbeli (R–Pa)
Schweiker (R–Iowa)
Schwengel (R–Iowa)
Secrest (D–Ohio)
Senner (D–Ariz)
Sheppard (D–Cal)
Shipley (D–Ill)
Shriver (R–Kans)
Sibal (R–Conn)
Sickles (D–Md)
Sisk (D–Cal)
Skubitz (R–Kans)
Slack (D–WVa)
Smith (D–Iowa)
Springer (R–Ill)
Staebler (D–Mich)
Stafford (R–Vt)
Staggers (D–WVa)
Steed (D–Okla)
Stinson (R–Wash)
Stratton (D–NY)
Sullivan (D–Mo)
Taft (R–Ohio)

Talcott (R–Cal)
Teague (R–Cal)
Thomas (D–Tex)
Thompson (D–NJ)
Thomson (R–Wisc)
Toll (D–Pa)
Tollefson (R–Wash)
Tupper (R–Me)
Udall (D–Ariz)
Ullman (D–Ore)
Van Deerlin (D–Cal)
Vanik (D–Ohio)
Wallhauser (R–NJ)
Weaver (R–Pa)
Weltner (D–Ga)
Westland (R–Wash)
Whalley (R–Pa)
Wharton (R–NY)
White (D–Idaho)
Widnall (R–NJ)
Wilson (D–Cal)
Wydler (R–NY)
Younger (R–Cal)
Zablocki (D–Wisc)

Total: 289

Paired For
Clark (D–Pa)
Karth (D–Minn)
Lloyd (R–Utah)
Miller (R–NY)
Norblad (R–Ore)
Powell (D–NY)

VOTES AGAINST

Abbitt (D–Va)
Abernethy (D–Miss)
Alger (R–Tex)
Andrews (D–Ala)
Ashbrook (R–Ohio)
Ashmore (D–SC)
Baker (R–Tenn)
Baring (D–Nev)
Battin (R–Mont)
Beckworth (D–Tex)
Beermann (R–Nebr)
Belcher (R–Okla)
Bennett (D–Fla)

Berry (R–SDak)
Boggs (D–La)
Bonner (D–NC)
Brock (R–Tenn)
Broyhill (R–NC)
Broyhill (R–Va)
Burleson (D–Tex)
Casey (D–Tex)
Chelf (D–Ky)
Clawson (R–Cal)
Colmer (D–Miss)
Cooley (D–NC)
Cramer (R–Fla)

Davis (D–Ga)
Davis (D–Tenn)
Dorn (D–SC)
Dowdy (D–Tex)
Downing (D–Va)
Elliott (D–Ala)
Everett (D–Tenn)
Evins (D–Tenn)
Fascell (D–Fla)
Fisher (D–Tex)
Flynt (D–Ga)
Foreman (R–Tex)
Forrester (D–Ga)

Fountain (D–NC)
Fuqua (D–Fla)
Gary (D–Va)
Gathings (D–Ark)
Gibbons (D–Fla)
Grant (D–Ala)
Gross (R–Iowa)
Gurney (R–Fla)
Hagen (D–Ga)
Haley (D–Fla)
Hall (R–Mo)
Hardy (D–Va)
Harris (D–Ark)
Harrison (R–Wyo)
Henderson (D–NC)
Herlong (D–Fla)
Huddleston (D–Ala)
Hull (D–Mo)
Jarman (D–Okla)
Jennings (D–Va)
Jensen (R–Iowa)
Johansen (R–Mich)
Jonas (R–NC)
Jones (D–Ala)
Jones (D–Mo)
Kilgore (D–Tex)
Knox (R–Mich)
Kornegay (R–NC)
Landrum (D–Ga)
Lennon (D–NC)
Lipscomb (R–Cal)
Long (D–La)

McMillan (D–SC)
Mahon (D–Tex)
Marsh (D–Va)
Martin (R–Cal)
Matthews (D–Fla)
Meader (R–Mich)
Mills (D–Ark)
Morrison (D–La)
Murray (D–Tenn)
Natcher (D–Ky)
Passman (D–La)
Patman (D–Tex)
Poage (D–Tex)
Poff (R–Va)
Pool (D–Tex)
Purcell (D–Tex)
Quillen (R–Tenn)
Rains (D–Ala)
Reid (R–Ill)
Rivers (D–SC)
Roberts (D–Ala)
Roberts (D–Tex)
Rogers (D–Fla)
Scott (D–NC)
Selden (D–Ala)
Short (R–NDak)
Sikes (D–Fla)
Siler (R–Ky)
Smith (R–Cal)
Smith (D–Va)
Snyder (R–Ky)
Stephens (D–Ga)

Stubblefield (D–Ky)
Taylor (D–NC)
Teague (D–Tex)
Thompson (D–La)
Thompson (D–Tex)
Trimble (D–Ark)
Tuck (D–Va)
Tuten (D–Ga)
Van Pelt (R–Wisc)
Vinson (D–Ga)
Waggonner (D–La)
Watson (D–SC)
Watts (D–Ky)
Whitener (D–NC)
Whitten (D–Miss)
Williams (D–Miss)
Willis (D–La)
Wilson (R–Cal)
Wilson (R–Ind)
Winstead (D–Miss)
Wright (D–Tex)
Wyman (R–NH)
Young (D–Tex)

Total: 126

Paired Against
Hebert (D–La)
Kilburn (R–NY)
Pilcher (D–Ga)
Rogers (D–Tex)
Utt (R–Cal)
Wickersham (D–Okla)

1965 Voting Rights Act

(Authorizes federal examiners to register Negro voters at state level.)

SENATE
(Vote Total: 77 for, 19 against)

VOTES FOR

Aiken (R–Vt)
Allott (R–Colo)
Anderson (D–NMex)
Bartlett (D–Alaska)
Bass (D–Tenn)
Bayh (D–Ind)

Bennett (R–Utah)
Boggs (R–Del)
Brewster (D–Md)
Burdick (D–NDak)
Carlson (R–Kans)
Case (R–NJ)

Clark (D–Pa)
Cooper (R–Ky)
Cotton (R–NH)
Curtis (R–Nebr)
Dirksen (R–Ill)
Dodd (D–Conn)

Dominick (R–Colo)
Douglas (D–Ill)
Fannin (R–Ariz)
Fong (R–Hawaii)
Gore (D–Tenn)
Gruening (D–Alaska)
Harris (D–Okla)
Hart (D–Mich)
Hartke (D–Ind)
Hayden (D–Ariz)
Hickenlooper (R–Iowa)
Hruska (R–Nebr)
Inouye (D–Hawaii)
Jackson (D–Wash)
Javits (R–NY)
Jordan (R–Idaho)
Kennedy, E. (D–Mass)
Kennedy, R (D–NY)
Kuchel (R–Cal)
Lausche (D–Ohio)
Long (D–Mo)

McCarthy (D–Minn)
McGee (D–Wyo)
McGovern (D–SDak)
McIntyre (D–NH)
McNamara (D–Mich)
Magnuson (D–Wash)
Mansfield (D–Mont)
Metcalf (D–Mont)
Miller (R–Iowa)
Mondale (D–Minn)
Monroney (D–Okla)
Montoya (D–NMex)
Morse (D–Ore)
Morton (R–Ky)
Moss (D–Utah)
Mundt (R–SDak)
Murphy (R–Cal)
Muskie (D–Me)
Nelson (D–Wisc)
Neuberger (D–Ore)
Pastore (D–RI)

Pell (D–RI)
Prouty (R–Vt)
Proxmire (D–Wisc)
Randolph (D–WVa)
Ribicoff (D–Conn)
Saltonstall (R–Mass)
Scott (R–Pa)
Simpson (R–Wyo)
Smith (R–Me)
Symington (D–Mo)
Tydings (D–Md)
Williams (R–Del)
Williams (D–NJ)
Yarborough (D–Tex)
Young (D–Ohio)
Young (R–NDak)

Total: 77

Paired For
Cannon (D–Nev)

VOTES AGAINST

Byrd (D–Va)
Eastland (D–Miss)
Ellender (D–La)
Ervin (D–NC)
Fulbright (D–Ark)
Hill (D–Ala)
Holland (D–Fla)
Jordan (D–NC)

Long (D–La)
McClellan (D–Ark)
Robertson (D–Va)
Russell (D–Ga)
Russell (D–SC)
Smathers (D–Fla)
Sparkman (D–Ala)
Stennis (D–Miss)

Talmadge (D–Ga)
Thurmond (R–SC)
Tower (R–Tex)

Total: 19

Paired Against
Byrd (D–WVa)

HOUSE OF REPRESENTATIVES
(Vote Total: 333 for, 85 against)

VOTES FOR

Adair (R–Ind)
Adams (D–Wash)
Addabbo (D–NY)
Albert (D–Okla)
Anderson (R–Ill)
Anderson (D–Tenn)
Andrews (R–NDak)
Annunzio (D–Ill)
Arends (R–Ill)
Ashbrook (**R–Ohio**)
Ashley (D–Ohio)

Aspinall (D–Colo)
Ayers (R–Ohio)
Baldwin (R–Cal)
Bandstra (D–Iowa)
Barrett (D–Pa)
Bates (R–Mass)
Battin (R–Mont)
Belcher (R–Okla)
Bell (R–Cal)
Bennett (D–Fla)
Berry (R–SDak)

Betts (R–Ohio)
Bingham (D–NY)
Blatnik (D–Minn)
Boggs (D–La)
Boland (D–Miss)
Bolling (D–Mo)
Bolton (R–Ohio)
Brademas (D–Ind)
Bray (R–Ind)
Brooks (D–Tex)
Broomfield (R–Mich)

Brown (D–Cal)
Brown (R–Ohio)
Burke (D–Mass)
Burton (R–Utah)
Burton (D–Cal)
Byrne (D–Pa)
Byrnes (R–Wisc)
Cabell (D–Tex)
Cahill (R–NJ)
Callan (D–Nebr)
Cameron (D–Cal)
Carey (D–NY)
Carter (R–Ky)
Cederberg (R–Mich)
Celler (D–NY)
Chamberlain (R–Mich)
Chelf (D–Ky)
Clancy (R–Ohio)
Clark (D–Pa)
Clausen (R–Cal)
Clawson (R–Cal)
Cleveland (R–NH)
Clevenger (D–Mich)
Cohelan (D–Cal)
Conable (R–NY)
Conte (R–Mass)
Conyers (D–Mich)
Corbett (R–Pa)
Corman (D–Cal)
Craley (D–Pa)
Cramer (R–Fla)
Culver (D–Iowa)
Cunningham (R–Nebr)
Curtin (R–Pa)
Curtis (R–Mo)
Daddario (D–Conn)
Dague (R–Pa)
Daniels (D–NJ)
Davis (R–Wisc)
Dawson (D–Ill)
de la Garza (D–Tex)
Delaney (D–NY)
Dent (D–Pa)
Denton (D–Pa)
Derwinski (R–Ill)
Devine (R–Ohio)
Diggs (D–Mich)
Dingell (D–Mich)
Dole (R–Kans)

Donohue (D–Mass)
Dow (D–NY)
Dulski (D–NY)
Duncan (D–Ore)
Dwyer (R–NJ)
Dyal (D–Cal)
Edmondson (D–Okla)
Edwards (D–Cal)
Ellsworth (R–Kans)
Evans (D–Colo)
Evins (D–Tenn)
Fallon (D–Md)
Farbstein (D–NY)
Farnsley (D–Ky)
Farnum (D–Mich)
Fascell (D–Fla)
Feighan (D–Ohio)
Findley (R–Ill)
Fino (R–NY)
Flood (D–Pa)
Fogarty (D–RI)
Foley (D–Wash)
Ford (D–Mich)
Ford (R–Mich)
Fraser (D–Minn)
Frelinghuysen (R–NJ)
Friedel (D–Md)
Fulton (R–Pa)
Fulton (D–Tenn)
Gallagher (D–NJ)
Garmatz (D–Md)
Giaimo (D–Conn)
Gibbons (D–Fla)
Gilbert (D–NY)
Gilligan (D–Ohio)
Gonzalez (D–Tex)
Goodell (R–NY)
Grabowski (D–Conn)
Gray (D–Ill)
Green (D–Ore)
Green (D–Pa)
Greigg (D–Iowa)
Grider (D–Tenn)
Griffen (R–Mich)
Griffiths (D–Mich)
Grover (R–NY)
Gubser (R–Cal)
Hagen (D–Cal)
Halleck (R–Ind)

Halpern (R–NY)
Hamilton (D–Ind)
Hanley (D–NY)
Hanna (D–Cal)
Hansen (D–Iowa)
Hansen (D–Wash)
Harsha (R–Ohio)
Harvey (R–Mich)
Hathaway (D–Me)
Hawkins (D–Cal)
Hays (D–Ohio)
Hechler (D–WVa)
Helstoski (D–NJ)
Hicks (D–Wash)
Holifield (D–Cal)
Holland (D–Pa)
Horton (R–NY)
Howard (D–NJ)
Hull (D–Mo)
Hungate (D–Mo)
Huot (D–NH)
Hutchinson (R–Mich)
Ichord (D–Mo)
Irwin (D–Conn)
Jacobs (D–Ind)
Jarman (D–Okla)
Jennings (D–Va)
Joelson (D–NJ)
Johnson (D–Cal)
Johnson (D–Pa)
Johnson (D–Okla)
Karsten (D–Mo)
Karth (D–Minn)
Kastenmeier (D–Wisc)
Kee (D–WVa)
Keith (R–Mass)
Kelly (D–NY)
King (D–Cal)
King (R–NY)
King (D–Utah)
Kirwan (D–Ohio)
Kluczynski (D–Ill)
Krebs (D–NJ)
Kunkel (R–Pa)
Laird (R–Wisc)
Langen (R–Minn)
Latta (R–Ohio)
Leggett (D–Cal)
Lindsay (R–NY)

Lipscomb (R–Cal)
Long (D–Md)
Love (D–Ohio)
McCarthy (D–NY)
McClory (R–Ill)
McCulloch (R–Ohio)
McDade (R–Pa)
McDowell (D–Del)
McFall (D–Cal)
McGarth (D–NJ)
McVicker (D–Colo)
Macdonald (D–Mass)
MacGregor (R–Minn)
Machen (D–Md)
Mackay (D–Ga)
Mackie (D–Mich)
Madden (D–Ind)
Mailliard (R–Cal)
Martin (R–Nebr)
Martin (R–Mass)
Mathias (R–Md)
Matsunaga (D–Hawaii)
Meeds (D–Wash)
Michel (R–Ill)
Miller (D–Cal)
Minish (D–NJ)
Mink (D–Hawaii)
Minshall (R–Ohio)
Mize (R–Kans)
Moeller (D–Ohio)
Monagan (D–Conn)
Moore (R–WVa)
Moorhead (D–Pa)
Morgan (D–Pa)
Morris (D–NMex)
Morrison (D–La)
Morse (R–Mass)
Mosher (R–Ohio)
Moss (D–Cal)
Multer (D–NY)
Murphy (D–NY)
Murphy (D–Ill)
Natcher (D–Ky)
Nedzi (D–Mich)
Nelsen (R–Minn)
Nix (D–Pa)
O'Brien (D–NY)
O'Hara (D–Ill)
O'Hara (D–Mich)

O'Konski (R–Wisc)
Olsen (D–Mont)
Olson (D–Minn)
O'Neill (D–Mass)
Ottinger (D–NY)
Patten (D–NJ)
Pelly (R–Wash)
Pepper (D–Fla)
Perkins (D–Ky)
Philbin (D–Mass)
Pickle (D–Tex)
Pike (D–NY)
Pirnie (R–NY)
Price (D–Ill)
Pucinski (D–Ill)
Quie (R–Minn)
Race (D–Wisc)
Randall (D–Mo)
Redlin (D–NDak)
Reid (R–Ill)
Reid (R–NY)
Reifel (R–SDak)
Reinecke (R–Cal)
Resnick (D–NY)
Reuss (D–Wisc)
Rhodes (R–Ariz)
Rhodes (D–Pa)
Rivers (D–Alaska)
Robison (R–NY)
Rodino (D–NJ)
Rogers (D–Colo)
Rogers (D–Fla)
Rogers (D–Tex)
Ronan (D–Ill)
Roncalio (D–Wyo)
Rooney (D–NY)
Rooney (D–Pa)
Roosevelt (D–Cal)
Rosenthal (D–NY)
Rostenkowski (D–Ill)
Roudebush (R–Ind)
Roush (D–Ind)
Roybal (D–Cal)
Rumsfeld (R–Ill)
Ryan (D–NY)
St. Germain (D–RI)
St. Onge (D–Conn)
Saylor (R–Pa)
Scheuer (D–NY)

Schisler (D–Ill)
Schmidhauser (D–Iowa)
Schneebeli (R–Pa)
Schweiker (R–Pa)
Secrest (D–Ohio)
Senner (D–Ariz)
Shipley (D–Ill)
Shriver (R–Kans)
Sickles (D–Md)
Sisk (D–Cal)
Skubitz (R–Kans)
Slack (D–WVa)
Smith (R–NY)
Smith (D–Iowa)
Springer (R–Ill)
Stafford (R–Vt)
Staggers (D–WVa)
Stalbaum (D–Wisc)
Stanton (R–Ohio)
Steed (D–Okla)
Stratton (D–NY)
Stubblefield (D–Ky)
Sullivan (D–Mo)
Sweeney (D–Ohio)
Talcott (R–Cal)
Teague (R–Cal)
Tenzer (D–NY)
Thompson (D–NY)
Thomson (D–Wisc)
Todd (D–Mich)
Tunney (D–Cal)
Tupper (R–Me)
Udall (D–Ariz)
Ullman (D–Ore)
Van Deerlin (D–Cal)
Vanik (D–Ohio)
Vigorito (D–Pa)
Vivian (D–Mich)
Walker (D–NMex)
Watkins (R–Pa)
Watts (D–Ky)
Weltner (D–Ga)
Whalley (R–Pa)
White (D–Idaho)
White (D–Tex)
Widnall (R–NJ)
Wilson, B. (R–Cal)
Wilson, C. (D–Cal)
Wolff (D–NY)
Wright (D–Tex)

Wyatt (R–Ore)
Wydler (R–NY)
Yates (D–Ill)
Young (D–Tex)

Younger (R–Cal)
Zablocki (D–Wisc)

Total: 333

Paired For
Keogh (D–NY)
Thomas (D–Tex)
Toll (D–Pa)

VOTES AGAINST

Abbitt (D–Va)
Abernethy (D–Miss)
Andrews (D–Ala)
Andrews (R–Ala)
Ashmore (D–SC)
Beckworth (D–Tex)
Brock (R–Tenn)
Broyhill (R–NC)
Broyhill (R–Va)
Buchanan (R–Ala)
Burleson (D–Tex)
Callaway (R–Ga)
Casey (D–Tex)
Collier (R–Ill)
Colmer (D–Miss)
Cooley (D–NC)
Davis (D–Ga)
Dickinson (R–Ala)
Dorn (D–SC)
Dowdy (D–Tex)
Downing (D–Va)
Duncan (R–Tenn)
Edwards (R–Ala)
Erlenborn (R–Ill)
Everett (D–Tenn)
Fisher (D–Tex)
Flynt (D–Ga)
Fountain (D–NC)
Fuqua (D–Fla)
Gathings (D–Ark)
Gettys (D–SC)

Gross (R–Iowa)
Gurney (R–Fla)
Hagen (D–Ga)
Haley (D–Fla)
Hall (R–Mo)
Hansen (R–Idaho)
Hardy (D–Va)
Harris (D–Ark)
Hebert (D–La)
Henderson (D–NC)
Herlong (D–Fla)
Jonas (R–NC)
Jones (D–Ala)
Jones (D–Mo)
Kornegay (D–NC)
Landrum (D–Ga)
Lennon (D–NC)
Long (D–La)
McEwen (R–NY)
McMillan (D–SC)
Mahon (D–Tex)
Martin (R–Ala)
Marsh (D–Va)
Matthews (D–Fla)
Murray (D–Tenn)
O'Neal (D–Ga)
Patman (D–Tex)
Poage (D–Tex)
Poff (R–Va)
Pool (D–Tex)

Quillen (R–Tenn)
Rivers (D–SC)
Roberts (D–Tex)
Satterfield (D–Va)
Scott (D–NC)
Selden (D–Ala)
Sikes (D–Fla)
Smith (R–Cal)
Smith (D–Va)
Stephens (D–Ga)
Taylor (D–NC)
Teague (D–Tex)
Trimble (D–Ark)
Tuck (D–Va)
Tuten (D–Ga)
Utt (R–Cal)
Waggonner (D–La)
Walker (R–Miss)
Watson (R–SC)
Whitener (D–NC)
Whitten (D–Miss)
Williams (D–Miss)
Willis (D–La)

Total: 85

Paired Against
Bonner (D–NC)
Mills (D–Ark)
Passman (D–La)

1966 Civil Rights Bill

(Included provision to ban racial discrimination in sale or rental of housing. Bill laid aside after Senate filibuster.)

SENATE
(Vote Total: 52 for, 41 against)

NOTE: This was the final vote to invoke cloture. It failed to obtain two-thirds majority to stop filibuster and therefore ended consideration of bill by Congress. It was later reintroduced and became the 1968 Civil Rights Act.

VOTES FOR

Aiken (R–Vt)
Bartlett (D–Alaska)
Bass (D–Tenn)
Bayh (D–Ind)
Boggs (R–Del)
Brewster (D–Md)
Burdick (D–NDak)
Case (R–NJ)
Church (D–Idaho)
Clark (D–Pa)
Dodd (D–Conn)
Douglas (D–Ill)
Fong (R–Hawaii)
Gore (D–Tenn)
Griffin (R–Mich)
Gruening (D–Alaska)
Hart (D–Mich)
Hartke (D–Ind)
Inouye (D–Hawaii)
Jackson (D–Wash)

Javits (R–NY)
Kennedy, E. (D–Mass)
Kennedy, R. (D–NY)
Kuchel (R–Cal)
Long (D–Mo)
McCarthy (D–Minn)
McGee (D–Wyo)
McGovern (D–SDak)
McIntyre (D–NH)
Mansfield (D–Mont)
Metcalf (D–Mont)
Mondale (D–Minn)
Monroney (D–Okla)
Montoya (D–NMex)
Morse (D–Ore)
Moss (D–Utah)
Muskie (D–Me)
Nelson (R–Wisc)
Neuberger (D–Ore)
Pastore (D–RI)

Pell (D–RI)
Proxmire (D–Wisc)
Randolph (D–WVa)
Ribicoff (D–Conn)
Saltonstall (R–Mass)
Scott (R–Pa)
Smith (R–Me)
Symington (D–Mo)
Tydings (D–Md)
Williams (D–NJ)
Yarborough (D–Tex)
Young (D–Ohio)

Total: 52

Paired For
Allott (R–Colo)
Dominick (R–Colo)
Harris (D–Okla)
Magnuson (D–Wash)

VOTES AGAINST

Bennett (R–Utah)
Bible (D–Nev)
Byrd (D–Va)
Byrd (D–WVa)
Cannon (D–Nev)
Carlson (R–Kans)
Cotton (R–NH)
Curtis (R–Nebr)
Dirksen (R–Ill)
Eastland (D–Miss)
Ellender (D–La)
Ervin (D–NC)
Fannin (R–Ariz)
Fulbright (D–Ark)
Hickenlooper (R–Iowa)
Hill (D–Ala)

Holland (D–Fla)
Hruska (R–Nebr)
Jordan (R–Idaho)
Jordan (D–NC)
Lausche (D–Ohio)
Long (D–La)
McClellan (D–Ark)
Miller (R–Iowa)
Morton (R–Ky)
Mundt (R–SDak)
Murphy (R–Cal)
Pearson (R–Kans)
Prouty (R–Vt)
Robertson (D–Va)
Russell (D–Ga)
Russell (D–SC)

Simpson (R–Wyo)
Smathers (D–Fla)
Sparkman (D–Ala)
Stennis (D–Miss)
Talmadge (D–Ga)
Thurmond (R–SC)
Tower (R–Tex)
Williams (R–Del)
Young (D–Ohio)
Young (R–NDak)

Total: 41

Paired Against
Cooper (R–Ky)
Hayden (D–Ariz)

HOUSE OF REPRESENTATIVES
(Vote Total: 259 for, 157 against)

VOTES FOR

Adair (R–Ind)
Adams (D–Wash)
Addabbo (D–NY)
Albert (D–Okla)
Andrews (R–NDak)

Annunzio (D–Ill)
Arends (R–Ill)
Ashley (D–Ohio)
Ayers (R–Ohio)
Bandstra (D–Iowa)

Barrett (D–Pa)
Bates (R–Mass)
Bell (R–Cal)
Bingham (D–NY)
Boland (D–Mass)

Bolling (D–Mo)
Bow (R–Ohio)
Brademas (D–Ind)
Brooks (D–Tex)
Broomfield (R–Mich)
Brown (D–Cal)
Brown (R–Ohio)
Burke (D–Mass)
Burton (R–Utah)
Burton (D–Cal)
Byrne (D–Pa)
Byrnes (R–Wisc)
Cahill (R–NJ)
Callan (D–Nebr)
Carey (D–NY)
Cederberg (R–Mich)
Celler (D–NY)
Chamberlain (R–Mich)
Clark (D–Pa)
Cleveland (R–NH)
Clevenger (D–Mich)
Cohelan (D–Cal)
Conable (R–NY)
Conte (R–Mass)
Conyers (D–Mich)
Corbett (D–Pa)
Corman (D–Cal)
Craley (D–Pa)
Culver (D–Iowa)
Cunningham (R–Nebr)
Curtis (R–Mo)
Daddario (D–Conn)
Dague (R–Pa)
Daniels (D–NJ)
Davis (R–Wisc)
Dawson (D–Ill)
de la Garza (D–Tex)
Delaney (D–NY)
Dent (D–Pa)
Denton (D–Ind)
Derwinski (R–Ill)
Diggs (D–Mich)
Dingell (D–Mich)
Donohue (D–Mass)
Dow (D–NY)
Dulski (D–NY)
Duncan (D–Ore)
Dwyer (R–NJ)
Dyal (D–Cal)
Ellsworth (R–Kans)

Erlenborn (R–Ill)
Evans (D–Colo)
Farbstein (D–NY)
Farnsley (D–Ky)
Farnum (D–Mich)
Fascell (D–Fla)
Feighan (D–Ohio)
Findley (R–Ill)
Fino (R–NY)
Flood (D–Pa)
Fogarty (D–RI)
Ford (D–Mich)
Ford (R–Mich)
Fraser (D–Minn)
Frelinghuysen (R–NJ)
Friedel (D–Md)
Fulton (R–Pa)
Fulton (D–Tenn)
Gallagher (D–NJ)
Giaimo (D–Conn)
Gibbons (D–Fla)
Gilbert (D–NY)
Gilligan (D–Ohio)
Gonzalez (D–Tex)
Goodell (R–NY)
Grabowski (D–Conn)
Gray (D–Ill)
Green (D–Ore)
Green (D–Pa)
Greigg (D–Iowa)
Grider (D–Tenn)
Griffiths (D–Mich)
Grover (R–NY)
Halleck (R–Ind)
Halpern (R–NY)
Hamilton (D–Ind)
Hanley (D–NY)
Hansen (D–Iowa)
Hansen (D–Wash)
Harvey (R–Mich)
Hathaway (D–Me)
Hays (D–Ohio)
Hechler (D–WVa)
Helstoski (D–NJ)
Hicks (D–Wash)
Holifield (D–Cal)
Holland (D–Pa)
Horton (R–NY)
Howard (D–NJ)
Huot (D–NH)

Hutchinson (R–Mich)
Irwin (D–Conn)
Jacobs (D–Ind)
Joelson (D–NJ)
Johnson (D–Cal)
Johnson (R–Pa)
Johnson (D–Okla)
Karsten (D–Mo)
Karth (D–Minn)
Kastenmeier (D–Wisc)
Kee (D–WVa)
Keith (R–Mass)
Kelly (D–NY)
Keogh (D–NY)
King (D–Cal)
King (D–Utah)
Kirwin (D–Ohio)
Kluczynski (D–Ill)
Krebs (D–NJ)
Kunkel (R–Pa)
Kupferman (R–NY)
Laird (R–Wisc)
Langen (R–Minn)
Leggett (D–Cal)
Long (D–Md)
Love (D–Ohio)
McCarthy (D–NY)
McClory (R–Ill)
McCulloch (R–Ohio)
McDade (R–Pa)
McDowell (D–Del)
McEwen (R–NY)
McFall (D–Cal)
McGarth (D–NJ)
McVicker (D–Colo)
Macdonald (D–Mass)
MacGregor (R–Minn)
Mackie (D–Mich)
Madden (D–Ind)
Mailliard (R–Cal)
Martin (R–Mass)
Mathias (R–Md)
Matsunaga (D–Hawaii)
Meeds (D–Wash)
Michel (R–Ill)
Miller, G. (D–Cal)
Minish (D–NJ)
Mink (D–Hawaii)
Moeller (D–Ohio)
Monagan (D–Conn)

Moorhead (D–Pa)
Morgan (D–Pa)
Morse (R–Mass)
Mosher (R–Ohio)
Moss (D–Cal)
Multer (D–NY)
Murphy (D–NY)
Murphy (D–Ill)
Nedzi (D–Mich)
Nelsen (R–Minn)
Nix (D–Pa)
O'Brien (D–NY)
O'Hara (D–Ill)
O'Hara (D–Mich)
O'Konski (R–Wisc)
Olsen (D–Mont)
Olson (D–Minn)
O'Neill (D–Mass)
Ottinger (D–NY)
Patten (D–NJ)
Pepper (D–Fla)
Perkins (D–Ky)
Philbin (D–Mass)
Pike (D–NY)
Pirnie (R–NY)
Price (D–Ill)
Pucinski (D–Ill)
Quie (R–Minn)
Redlin (D–NDak)
Rees (D–Cal)
Reid (R–NY)
Reifel (R–SDak)
Resnick (D–NY)
Reuss (D–Wisc)
Rhodes (D–Pa)

Rivers (D–Alaska)
Robison (R–NY)
Rodino (D–NJ)
Rogers (D–Colo)
Ronan (D–Ill)
Roncalio (D–Wyo)
Rooney (D–NY)
Rooney (D–Pa)
Rosenthal (D–NY)
Rostenkowski (D–Ill)
Roush (D–Ind)
Roybal (D–Cal)
Rumsfeld (R–Ill)
Ryan (D–NY)
St. Germain (R–RI)
St. Onge (D–Conn)
Saylor (R–Pa)
Scheuer (D–NY)
Schisler (D–Ill)
Schmidhauser (D–Iowa)
Schneebeli (R–Pa)
Schweiker (R–Pa)
Senner (D–Ariz)
Shipley (D–Ill)
Shriver (R–Kans)
Sickles (D–Md)
Sisk (D–Cal)
Slack (D–WVa)
Smith (R–NY)
Smith (D–Iowa)
Springer (R–Ill)
Stafford (R–Vt)
Staggers (D–WVa)
Stalbaum (D–Wisc)
Stanton (R–Ohio)

Stratton (D–NY)
Sullivan (D–Mo)
Sweeney (D–Ohio)
Tenzer (D–NY)
Thompson (D–NJ)
Thomson (R–Wisc)
Todd (D–Mich)
Tunney (D–Cal)
Tupper (R–Me)
Udall (D–Ariz)
Vanik (D–Ohio)
Vigorito (D–Pa)
Vivian (D–Mich)
Waldie (D–Cal)
Weltner (D–Ga)
Whalley (R–Pa)
White (D–Idaho)
Widnall (R–NJ)
Wilson (D–Cal)
Wolff (D–NY)
Wydler (R–NY)
Yates (D–Ill)
Young (D–Tex)
Zablocki (D–Wisc)

Total: 259

Paired For
Blatnik (D–Minn)
Edwards (D–Cal)
Hawkins (D–Cal)
Powell (D–NY)
Ullman (D–Ore)
Van Deerlin (D–Cal)

VOTES AGAINST

Abbitt (D–Va)
Abernethy (D–Miss)
Anderson (D–Ill)
Anderson (D–Tenn)
Andrews (R–Ala)
Ashbrook (R–Ohio)
Ashmore (D–SC)
Aspinall (D–Colo)
Baring (D–Nev)
Battin (R–Mont)
Beckworth (D–Tex)
Belcher (R–Okla)
Bennett (D–Fla)

Berry (R–SDak)
Betts (R–Ohio)
Boggs (D–La)
Bolton (R–Ohio)
Bray (R–Ind)
Brock (R–Tenn)
Broyhill (R–NC)
Broyhill (R–Va)
Buchanan (R–Ala)
Burleson (D–Tex)
Cabell (D–Tex)
Callaway (R–Ga)
Cameron (D–Cal)

Carter (R–Ky)
Casey (D–Tex)
Chelf (D–Ky)
Clancy (R–Ohio)
Clausen (R–Cal)
Clawson (R–Cal)
Collier (R–Ill)
Colmer (D–Miss)
Cooley (D–NC)
Cramer (R–Fla)
Curtin (R–Pa)
Davis (D–Ga)
Devine (R–Ohio)

Dickinson (R–Ala)
Dole (R–Kans)
Dorn (R–SC)
Dowdy (D–Tex)
Downing (D–Va)
Duncan (R–Tenn)
Edmondson (D–Okla)
Edwards (R–Ala)
Everett (D–Tenn)
Evins (D–Tenn)
Fallon (D–Md)
Fisher (D–Tex)
Flynt (D–Ga)
Foley (D–Wash)
Fountain (D–NC)
Fuqua (D–Fla)
Garmatz (D–Md)
Gathings (D–Ark)
Gettys (D–SC)
Gross (R–Iowa)
Gubser (R–Cal)
Gurney (R–Fla)
Hagan (D–Ga)
Hagen (D–Cal)
Haley (D–Fla)
Hall (R–Mo)
Hansen (R–Idaho)
Hardy (D–Va)
Harsha (R–Ohio)
Harvey (R–Ind)
Hebert (D–La)
Henderson (D–NC)
Herlong (D–Fla)
Hosmer (R–Cal)
Hull (D–Mo)
Hungate (D–Mo)
Ichord (D–Mo)
Jarman (D–Okla)
Jennings (D–Va)
Jonas (R–NC)
Jones (D–Ala)
Jones (D–Mo)
Jones (D–NC)

Kornegay (D–NC)
Landrum (D–Ga)
Latta (R–Ohio)
Lennon (D–NC)
Lipscomb (R–Cal)
Long (D–La)
McMillan (D–SC)
Machen (D–Md)
Mackay (D–Ga)
Mahon (D–Tex)
Marsh (D–Va)
Martin (R–Ala)
Martin (R–Neb)
Matthews (D–Fla)
May (R–Wash)
Mills (D–Ark)
Minshall (R–Ohio)
Mize (R–Kans)
Moore (R–WVa)
Morris (D–NMex)
Morton (R–Md)
Natcher (D–Ky)
O'Neal (D–Ga)
Passman (D–La)
Patman (D–Tex)
Pelly (R–Wash)
Pickle (D–Tex)
Poage (D–Tex)
Poff (R–Va)
Pool (D–Tex)
Purcell (D–Tex)
Quillen (R–Tenn)
Race (D–Wisc)
Randall (D–Mo)
Reid (R–Ill)
Reinecke (R–Cal)
Rhodes (R–Ariz)
Rivers (D–SC)
Roberts (D–Tex)
Rogers (D–Fla)
Roudebush (R–Ind)
Satterfield (D–Va)
Scott (D–NC)

Secrest (D–Ohio)
Selden (D–Ala)
Sikes (D–Fla)
Skubitz (R–Kans)
Smith (R–Cal)
Smith (D–Va)
Steed (D–Okla)
Stephens (D–Ga)
Stubblefield (D–Ky)
Talcott (R–Cal)
Taylor (D–NC)
Teague (R–Cal)
Teague (D–Tex)
Thompson (D–Tex)
Trimble (D–Ark)
Tuck (D–Va)
Tuten (D–Ga)
Ullman (D–Ore)
Utt (R–Cal)
Waggonner (D–La)
Walker (R–Miss)
Walker (D–NMex)
Watkins (R–Pa)
Watson (R–SC)
Watts (D–Ky)
White (D–Tex)
Whitener (D–NC)
Whitten (D–Miss)
Williams (D–Miss)
Wilson (R–Cal)
Wright (D–Tex)
Wyatt (R–Ore)
Younger (R–Cal)

Total: 157

Paired Against
Andrews (D–Ala)
Edwards (D–La)
Hanna (D–Cal)
Murray (D–Tenn)
Rogers (D–Tex)
Willis (D–La)

1968 Civil Rights Act

(Federal ban on housing discrimination.)

SENATE
(Vote Total: 71 for, 20 against)

VOTES FOR

Aiken (R–Vt)	Griffin (R–Mich)	Mundt (R–SDak)
Allott (R–Colo)	Greuning (D–Alaska)	Murphy (R–Cal)
Anderson (D–NMex)	Hansen (R–Wyo)	Muskie (D–Me)
Baker (R–Tenn)	Hart (D–Mich)	Nelson (R–Wisc)
Bartlett (D–Alaska)	Hartke (D–Ind)	Pearson (R–Kans)
Bayh (D–Ind)	Hatfield (R–Ore)	Pell (D–RI)
Bennett (R–Utah)	Hayden (D–Ariz)	Percy (R–Ill)
Bible (D–Nev)	Hruska (R–Nebr)	Prouty (R–Vt)
Brewster (D–Md)	Inouye (D–Hawaii)	Proxmire (D–Wisc)
Boggs (R–Del)	Jackson (D–Wash)	Randolph (D–WVa)
Brooke (R–Mass)	Javits (R–NY)	Ribicoff (D–Conn)
Burdick (D–WVa)	Jordan (R–Idaho)	Scott (R–Pa)
Byrd (D–WVa)	Kennedy, E. (D–Mass)	Smith (R–Me)
Cannon (D–Nev)	Kennedy, R. (D–NY)	Symington (D–Mo)
Carlson (R–Kans)	Lausche (D–Ohio)	Tydings (D–Md)
Case (R–NJ)	Long (D–Mo)	Williams (D–NJ)
Church (D–Idaho)	McGee (D–Wyo)	Yarborough (D–Tex)
Clark (D–Pa)	McGovern (D–SDak)	Young (R–NDak)
Cooper (R–Ky)	Magnuson (D–Wash)	Young (D–Ohio)
Cotton (R–NH)	Mansfield (D–Mont)	
Curtis (R–Nebr)	Mondale (D–Minn)	Total: 71
Dirksen (R–Ill)	Monroney (D–Okla)	
Dodd (D–Conn)	Montoya (D–NMex)	*Paired For*
Dominick (R–Colo)	Morse (D–Ore)	Harris (D–Okla)
Fong (R–Hawaii)	Morton (R–Ky)	Kuchel (R–Cal)
Gore (D–Tenn)	Moss (D–Utah)	Pastore (D–RI)

VOTES AGAINST

Byrd (D–Va)	Jordan (D–NC)	Thurmond (R–SC)
Eastland (D–Miss)	Long (D–La)	Williams (R–Del)
Ellender (D–La)	McClellan (D–Ark)	
Ervin (D–NC)	Russell (D–Ga)	Total: 20
Fannin (R–Ariz)	Smathers (D–Fla)	
Fulbright (D–Ark)	Sparkman (D–Ala)	*Paired Against*
Hill (D–Ala)	Spong (R–Va)	Hickenlooper (R–Iowa)
Holland (D–Fla)	Stennis (D–Miss)	Miller (R–Iowa)
Hollings (R–SC)	Talmadge (D–Ga)	Tower (R–Tex)

HOUSE OF REPRESENTATIVES
(Vote Total: 250 for, 172 against)

VOTES FOR

Adams (D–Wash)
Addabbo (D–NY)
Albert (D–Okla)
Anderson (R–Ill)
Andrew (R–NDak)
Annunzio (D–Ill)
Ashley (D–Ohio)
Ayers (R–Ohio)
Barrett (D–Pa)
Bates (R–Mass)
Bell (R–Cal
Berry (R–SDak)
Betts (R–Ohio)
Biester (R–Pa)
Bingham (D–NY)
Blatnik (D–Minn)
Boland (D–Mass)
Boggs (D–La)
Bolling (D–Mo)
Brademas (D–Ind)
Brasco (D–NY)
Brooks (D–Tex)
Broomfield (R–Mich)
Brotzman (R–Colo)
Brown (R–Mich)
Brown (D–Cal)
Brown (R–Ohio)
Burke (D–Mass)
Burton (D–Cal)
Bush (R–Tex)
Button (R–NY)
Byrne (D–Pa)
Byrnes (R–Wisc)
Cahill (R–NJ)
Carey (D–NY)
Cederberg (R–Mich)
Celler (D–NY)
Chamberlain (R–Mich)
Clark (D–Pa)
Cleveland (R–NH)
Cohelan (D–Cal)
Conable (R–NY)
Conte (R–Mass)
Conyers (D–Mich)
Corbett (R–Pa)

Corman (D–Cal)
Cowger (R–Ky)
Culver (D–Iowa)
Cunningham (R–Nebr)
Daddario (D–Conn)
Daniels (D–NJ)
Dawson (D–Ill)
de la Garza (D–Tex)
Dellenback (R–Ore)
Denney (R–Nebr)
Dent (D–Pa)
Diggs (D–Mich)
Dingell (D–Mich)
Dole (R–Kans)
Donohue (D–Mass)
Dow (D–NY)
Dulski (D–NY)
Dwyer (R–NJ)
Eckhardt (D–Tex)
Edwards (D–Cal)
Eilberg (D–Pa)
Erlenborn (R–Ill)
Esch (R–Mich)
Eshleman (R–Pa)
Evans (D–Colo)
Farbstein (D–NY)
Fascell (D–Fla)
Feighan (D–Ohio)
Findley (R–Ill)
Flood (D–Pa)
Foley (D–Wash)
Ford (D–Mich)
Ford (R–Mich)
Fraser (D–Minn)
Frelinghuysen (R–NJ)
Friedel (D–Md)
Fulton (R–Pa)
Fulton (D–Tenn)
Gallagher (D–NJ)
Giaimo (D–Conn)
Gilbert (D–NY)
Gonzalez (D–Tex)
Goodell (R–NY)
Green (D–Ore)
Green (D–Pa)

Griffiths (D–Mich)
Grover (R–NY)
Gude (R–Md)
Halpern (R–NY)
Hamilton (D–Ind)
Hanley (D–NY)
Hanna (D–Cal)
Hansen (D–Wash)
Harvey (R–Mich)
Hathaway (D–Me)
Hawkins (D–Cal)
Hays (D–Ohio)
Hechler (D–WVa)
Heckler (R–Mass)
Helstoski (D–NJ)
Hicks (D–Wash)
Holifield (D–Cal)
Holland (D–Pa)
Horton (R–NY)
Howard (D–NJ)
Hunt (R–NJ)
Hutchinson (R–Mich)
Irwin (D–Conn)
Jacobs (D–Ind)
Joelson (D–NJ)
Johnson (D–Cal)
Karth (D–Minn)
Kastenmeier (D–Wisc)
Kazen (D–Tex)
Kee (D–WVa)
Keith (R–Mass)
Kelly (D–NY)
Kirwin (D–Ohio)
Kleppe (R–NDak)
Kupferman (R–NY)
Kyros (D–Me)
Laird (R–Wisc)
Langen (R–Minn)
Leggett (D–Cal)
Lloyd (R–Utah)
Long (D–Md)
Lukens (R–Ohio)
McCarthy (D–NY)
McClosky (R–Cal)
McClory (R–Ill)

McCulloch (R–Ohio)
McDade (R–Pa)
McDonald (R–Mich)
McEwen (R–NY)
McFall (D–Cal)
Macdonald (D–Mass)
MacGregor (R–Minn)
Madden (D–Ind)
Mailliard (R–Cal)
Mathias (R–Md)
Matsunaga (D–Hawaii)
May (R–Wash)
Mayne (R–Iowa)
Meeds (D–Wash)
Meskill (R–Conn)
Michel (R–Ill)
Miller (D–Cal)
Minish (D–NJ)
Mink (D–Hawaii)
Mize (R–Kans)
Monagan (D–Conn)
Moore (R–WVa)
Moorhead (D–Pa)
Morgan (D–Pa)
Morris (D–NMex)
Morse (R–Mass)
Mosher (R–Ohio)
Moss (D–Cal)
Murphy (D–NY)
Murphy (D–Ill)
Nedzi (D–Mich)
Nelsen (R–Minn)
Nix (D–Pa)
O'Hara (D–Ill)
O'Hara (D–Mich)
O'Konski (R–Wisc)
Olsen (D–Mont)
O'Neill (D–Mass)
Ottinger (D–NY)
Patten (D–NJ)

Pelly (R–Wash)
Pepper (D–Fla)
Perkins (D–Ky)
Philbin (D–Mass)
Pike (D–NY)
Pirnie (R–NY)
Pollock (R–Alaska)
Price (D–Ill)
Quie (R–Minn)
Railsback (R–Ill)
Rees (D–Cal)
Reid (R–NY)
Reifel (R–SDak)
Reuss (D–Wisc)
Rhodes (D–Pa)
Riegle (R–Mich)
Robison (R–NY)
Rodino (D–NJ)
Rogers (D–Colo)
Ronan (D–Ill)
Rooney (D–NY)
Rooney (D–Pa)
Rosenthal (D–NY)
Rostenkowski (D–Ill)
Roush (D–Ind)
Roybal (D–Cal)
Rumsfeld (R–Ill)
Ruppe (R–Mich)
Ryan (D–NY)
St. Germain (R–RI)
St. Onge (D–Conn)
Sandman (R–NJ)
Scheuer (D–NY)
Schneebeli (R–Pa)
Schweiker (R–Pa)
Schwengel (R–Iowa)
Shipley (D–Ill)
Sisk (D–Cal)
Slack (D–WVa)
Smith (R–NY)

Smith (D–Iowa)
Springer (R–Ill)
Stafford (R–Vt)
Staggers D–WVa)
Stanton (R–Ohio)
Steiger (R–Wisc)
Stratton (D–NY)
Sullivan (D–Mo)
Taft (R–Ohio)
Tenzer (D–NY)
Thompson (D–NJ)
Thomson (R–Wisc)
Tiernan (D–RI)
Tunney (D–Cal)
Udall (D–Ariz)
Ullman (D–Ore)
Van Deerlin (D–Cal)
Vander Jagt (R–Mich)
Vanik (D–Ohio)
Vigorito (D–Pa)
Waldie (R–Cal)
Whalen (R–Ohio)
Widnall (R–NJ)
Wilson (D–Cal)
Winn (R–Kans)
Wolff (D–NY)
Wright (D–Tex)
Wyatt (R–Ore)
Wydler (R–NY)
Wyman (R–NH)
Yates (D–Ill)
Young (D–Tex)
Zablocki (D–Wisc)
Zwach (R–Minn)

Total: 250

Paired For
King (D–Cal)

VOTES AGAINST

Abbitt (D–Va)
Abernethy (D–Miss)
Adair (R–Ind)
Anderson (D–Tenn)
Andrews (D–Ala)
Arends (R–Ill)
Ashbrook (R–Ohio)
Aspinall (D–Colo)

Baring (D–Nev)
Battin (R–Mont)
Belcher (R–Okla)
Bennett (D–Fla)
Bevill (D–Ala)
Blackburn (R–Ga)
Blanton (D–Tenn)
Bolton (R–Ohio)

Bow (R–Ohio)
Bray (R–Ind)
Brinkey (D–Ga)
Brock (R–Tenn)
Broyhill (R–NC)
Broyhill (R–Va)
Buchanan (R–Ala)
Burke (R–Fla)

Burleson (D–Tex)
Burton (R–Utah)
Cabell (D–Tex)
Carter (R–Ky)
Casey (D–Tex)
Clancy (R–Ohio)
Clausen (R–Cal)
Clawson (R–Cal)
Collier (R–Ill)
Colmer (D–Miss)
Cramer (R–Fla)
Curtis (R–Mo)
Davis (R–Wisc)
Davis (D–Ga)
Delaney (D–NY)
Derwinski (R–Ill)
Devine (R–Ohio)
Dickinson (R–Ala)
Dorn (R–SC)
Dowdy (D–Tex)
Downing (D–Va)
Duncan (R–Tenn)
Edmondson (D–Okla)
Edwards (D–La)
Edwards (R–Ala)
Everett (D–Tenn)
Evins (D–Tenn)
Fallon (D–Md)
Fisher (D–Tex)
Flynt (D–Ga)
Fountain (D–NC)
Fuqua (D–Fla)
Galifanakis (D–NC)
Gardner (R–NC)
Garmatz (D–Md)
Gathings (D–Ark)
Gettys (D–SC)
Gibbons (D–Fla)
Goodling (R–Pa)
Gray (D–Ill)
Griffin (D–Miss)
Gross (R–Iowa)
Gubser (R–Cal)
Gurney (R–Fla)
Hagan (D–Ga)
Haley (D–Fla)
Hall (R–Mo)
Halleck (R–Ind)
Hammerschmitt
    (R–Ark)
Hansen (R–Idaho)

Hardy (D–Va)
Harrison (R–Wyo)
Harsha (R–Ohio)
Hebert (D–La)
Henderson (D–NC)
Hosmer (R–Cal)
Hull (D–Mo)
Ichord (D–Mo)
Jarman (D–Okla)
Johnson (R–Pa)
Jonas (R–NC)
Jones (D–Ala)
Jones (D–NC)
Kluczynski (D–Ill)
Kornegay (D–NC)
Kuykendall (R–Tenn)
Kyl (R–Iowa)
Landrum (D–Ga)
Latta (R–Ohio)
Lennon (D–NC)
Lipscomb (R–Cal)
Long (D–La)
McClure (R–Idaho)
McMillan (D–SC)
Machen (D–Md)
Mahon (D–Tex)
Marsh (D–Va)
Martin (R–Neb)
Mathias (R–Cal)
Miller (R–Ohio)
Mills (D–Ark)
Minshall (D–Ohio)
Montgomery (D–Miss)
Morton (R–Md)
Myers (R–Ind)
Natcher (D–Ky)
Nichols (D–Ala)
O'Neal (D–Ga)
Passman (D–La)
Patman (D–Tex)
Pettis (R–Cal)
Pickle (D–Tex)
Poff (R–Va)
Pool (D–Tex)
Price (R–Tex)
Pryor (D–Ark)
Pucinski (D–Ill)
Purcell (D–Tex)
Quillen (R–Tenn)
Randall (D–Mo)
Rarick (D–La)

Reid (R–Ill)
Reinecke (R–Cal)
Rhodes (R–Ariz)
Rivers (D–SC)
Roberts (D–Tex)
Rogers (D–Fla)
Roudebush (R–Ind)
Satterfield (D–Va)
Saylor (R–Pa)
Schadeberg (R–Wisc)
Scherle (R–Iowa)
Scott (R–Va)
Selden (D–Ala)
Shriver (R–Kans)
Sikes (D–Fla)
Skubitz (R–Kans)
Smith (R–Cal)
Smith (R–Okla)
Snyder (R–Ky)
Steed (D–Okla)
Steiger (R–Ariz)
Stephens (D–Ga)
Stubblefield (D–Ky)
Stuckey (D–Ga)
Talcott (R–Cal)
Taylor (D–NC)
Teague (D–Cal)
Teague (D–Tex)
Thompson (R–Ga)
Tuck (D–Va)
Utt (R–Cal)
Waggonner (D–La)
Walker (D–NMex)
Wampler (R–Va)
Watson (R–SC)
Watkins (R–Pa)
Watts (D–Ky)
Whalley (R–Pa)
White (D–Tex)
Whitener (D–NC)
Whitten (D–Miss)
Wiggins (R–Cal)
Williams (R–Pa)
Willis (D–La)
Wilson (R–Cal)
Wylie (R–Ohio)
Zion (R–Ind)

Total: 172

Paired Against
Ashmore (D–SC)

Appendix II

States with Civil Rights Laws and Agencies with Civil Rights Responsibilities

STATE	TOTAL POPULATION	NON-WHITE POPULATION	LAWS*	NAME OF AGENCY	EXECUTIVE OFFICER	ADDRESS AND TELEPHONE
ALASKA	273,000	55,000 [23.7%]	E H A	Alaska State Commission for Human Rights	Willard L. Bowman	520 MacKay Building 338 Denali St., Anchorage 99501 Tel: 272–9504
ARIZONA	1,302,161	325,540 [25%]	E A	Arizona Civil Rights Commission	Wilbur R. Johnson	1623 W. Washington St. Phoenix 85007 Tel: (602) 271–5263
CALIFORNIA	18,815,000 (as of 1965)	3,438,023 [18.2%]	E H A	California Fair Employment Practices Commission	Peter R. Johnson	455 Golden Gate Ave. San Francisco 94102 Tel: (415) 557–2000
COLORADO	2,072,000	87,821 [4.2%]	E H A	Colorado Civil Rights Commission	James F. Reynolds	312 State Services Bldg. 1525 Sherman St. Denver 80203 Tel: (303) 892–2621
CONNECTICUT	2,975,000	190,000 [15.65%]	E H A	Commission on Human Right & Opportunities	Arthur L. Green	90 Washington St. Hartford 06106 Tel: (203) 566–3350
DELAWARE	589,810	89,180 [15.1%]	E A	Department of Labor and Industrial Relations Division Against Discrimination	Ernest J. Camoirano, Jr.	506 West 10th St. Wilmington 19801 Tel: (302) 658–9251
DISTRICT OF COLUMBIA	808,000	509,040 [63%]	E H A	District of Columbia Human Relations Commission	James C. Slaughter	Room 5, District Bldg. 14th and E Streets N.W. 20004 Tel: (202) 629–4723

* This column indicates if state has a law against discrimination in employment (E), private schools and colleges (S), housing not receiving public funds (H), public accommodations (A).

STATE	TOTAL POPULATION	NON-WHITE POPULA-TION	LAWS*	NAME OF AGENCY	EXECUTIVE OFFICER	ADDRESS AND TELEPHONE
HAWAII	792,444	571,828 [72.2%]	E H	Department of Labor and Industrial Relations	Robert K. Hasegawa	825 Mililani St. Honolulu 96813 Tel: 548–2211
IDAHO	667,191 (1960 census)	9,808 [.014%]	E A	Department of Labor	W. L. Robison	Industrial Administration Building 317 Main Street, Boise 83702 Tel: (208) 344–5811
ILLINOIS	10,893,000	1,070,906 [10%]	E A	Illinois Commission on Human Relations	Roger W. Nathan	160 North LaSalle St. Chicago 60601 Tel: (312) FI6–2000 ext. 583
INDIANA	5,000,000	375,000 [7%]	E S H A	Indiana Civil Rights Commission	C. Lee Crean, Jr.	1004 State Office Bldg. Indianapolis 46204 Tel: (317) 633–4855
IOWA	2,757,537	28,828 [1.05%]	E H A	Iowa Civil Rights Commission	Alvin Hays, Jr.	State Capitol Bldg. Des Moines 50319 Tel: (515) 281–5129
KANSAS	2,178,611	99,945 [4.12%]	E A	Kansas Commission on Civil Rights	Homer C. Floyd	Rm. 1155 W, State Office Bldg. Topeka 66612 Tel: (913) 296–3206
KENTUCKY	3,038,156	215,949 [7.3%]	E A	Kentucky Commission on Human Rights	Galen Martin	Mammoth Life Bldg. 600 West Walnut St. Louisville 40203 Tel: (502) 564–3550

* This column indicates if state has a law against discrimination in employment (E), private schools and colleges (S), housing not receiving public funds (H), public accommodations (A).

STATE	TOTAL POPULATION	NON-WHITE POPULA-TION	LAWS*	NAME OF AGENCY	EXECUTIVE OFFICER	ADDRESS AND TELEPHONE
MAINE	969,265 (1960 census)	6,056 [.62%]	E H A	Department of Labor and Industry	Miss Marion E. Martin	Rm. 413, State Office Bldg. Augusta 04330 Tel: (207) 289–3331
MARYLAND	3,100,689 (1960 census)	526,770 [17%]	E H A	Maryland Commission on Human Relations	Treadwell O. Phillips	301 West Preston St. Baltimore 21201 Tel: (301) 383–3010
MASSACHU-SETTS	5,295,281	150,209 [2.87%]	E S H A	Massachusetts Commission Against Discrimination	Walter H. Nolan	120 Tremont St. Boston 02108 Tel: (617) 727–3990
MICHIGAN	8,584,000	891,000 [10.4%]	E S H A	Michigan Civil Rights Commission	Burton I. Gordin	1000 Cadillac Square Bldg. Detroit 48226 Tel: (313) 222–1810
MINNESOTA	3,413,864 (1960 census)	42,261 [1.2%]	E S H A	Department of Human Rights	Thomas J. Donaldson	60 State Office Bldg. St. Paul 55101 Tel: (612) 221–2931
MISSOURI	4,319,813	396,846 [9%]	E A	Missouri Commission on Human Rights	Richard E. Risk	Box 1129 314 East High St. Jefferson City 65101 Tel: (314) 635–7961

* This column indicates if state has a law against discrimination in employment (E), private schools and colleges (S), housing not receiving public funds (H), public accommodations (A).

STATE	TOTAL POPULATION	NON-WHITE POPULATION	LAWS*	NAME OF AGENCY	EXECUTIVE OFFICER	ADDRESS AND TELEPHONE
MONTANA	694,000	unavailable	E A	Department of Labor and Industry	Sidney G. Smith	1336 Helena Ave. Helena 59601 Tel: (406) 449-3472
NEBRASKA	1,416,000	53,000 [2.6%]	E A	Nebraska Equal Opportunity Commission	Emmet J. Dennis, Jr.	P.O. Box 4862 State Capitol Bldg. Lincoln 68502 Tel: (314) 473-1624
NEVADA	500,000	40,000 [11.5%]	E A	Nevada Commission on Equal Rights of Citizens	Tyrone K. Leiv	Rm. 100-B, State Bldg. 215 East Bonanza Las Vegas 89101 Tel: (702) 385-0104
NEW HAMPSHIRE	607,000 (1960 census)	2,600 [.4%]	E H A	Commission for Human Rights	Marsha Macey	State House Concord 03301 Tel: (630) 271-2767
NEW JERSEY	7,000,000	700,000 [10%]	E S H A	New Jersey Division of Civil Rights, Department of Law and Public Safety	James H. Blair	1100 Raymond Blvd. Newark 07102 Tel: (201) 648-2700
NEW MEXICO	951,023	344,382 [36.2%]	E A	Human Rights Commission of New Mexico	Byron L. Stewart	1015 Tijeras, N.W. Albuquerque, 87501 Tel: (505) 842-3122

* This column indicates if state has a law against discrimination in employment (E), private schools and colleges (S), housing not receiving public funds (H), public accommodations (A).

STATE	TOTAL POPULATION	NON-WHITE POPULA-TION	LAWS*	NAME OF AGENCY	EXECUTIVE OFFICER	ADDRESS AND TELEPHONE
NEW YORK	18,072,089	1,834,026 [10.1%]	E SHA	New York State Division of Human Rights	John C. Clancy	270 Broadway New York City 10007 Tel: (212) 488–7610
NORTH CAROLINA	5,000,000	1,250,000 [25%]	none	North Carolina Good Neighbor Council	D. S. Coltrane	P.O. Box 12525 Raleigh, N.C. 27205 Tel: (919) 829–7996/3354
OHIO	10,749,221	879,861 [8.2%]	E H A	Ohio Civil Rights Commission	Ellis L. Ross	240 Parsons Avenue Columbus 43215 Tel: (614) 469–2785
OKLAHOMA	2,328,284 (1960 census)	220,384 [9.5%]	none	Oklahoma Human Rights Commission	William Y. Rose	P.O. Box 53004 Oklahoma City 73105 Tel: (405) 521–2360
OREGON	1,768,687 (1960 census)	36,650 [2.1%]	E H A	Civil Rights Division, Oregon Bureau of Labor	Russell O. Rogers	466 State Office Bldg. Portland 97201 Tel: (503) 226–2161 ext. 557
PENNSYLVANIA	11,319,366 (1960 census)	865,362 [7.6%]	E SHA	Pennsylvania Human Relations Commission	Milo A. Manly	100 North Cameron St. Harrisburg 17001 Tel: (717) 787–5010
RHODE ISLAND	859,488 (1960 census)	20,776 [2.4%]	E H A	Rhode Island Commission for Human Rights	Donald D. Taylor	244 Broad St. Providence 02903 Tel: (401) 521–7100 ext. 6612 or 6613

* This column indicates if state has a law against discrimination in employment (E), private schools and colleges (S), housing not receiving public funds (H), public accommodations (A).

STATE	TOTAL POPULATION	NON-WHITE POPULATION	LAWS*	NAME OF AGENCY	EXECUTIVE OFFICER	ADDRESS AND TELEPHONE
TENNESSEE	4,000,000	600,000 [15%]	none	Tennessee Commission for Human Development	Cornelius Jones	C3-305 Cordell Hull Bldg. Nashville 37219 Tel: (615) 741-2424
TEXAS	9,579,677 (1960 census)	2,836,584 [29.6%]	none	Good Neighbor Commission of Texas	Glenn E. Garrett	P.O. Drawer E Austin 78711 Tel: (512) 475-3581
UTAH	1,000,000	10,000 [1%]	E A	Anti-Discrimination Division, Industrial Commission of Utah	John R. Schone	Rm. 418, State Capitol Bldg. Salt Lake City 84114 Tel: (801) 328-5552
VERMONT	439,000	500 [0.1%]	E H A	State Attorney General's Office	James Jeffords	State House Montpelier 05602 Tel: (802) 223-2311
WASHINGTON	3,000,000	16,000 [5.33%]	E S A	Washington State Board Against Discrimination	Alfred E. Cowles	1411 Fourth Avenue Bldg. Seattle 98101 Tel: (206) MU2-4594
WEST VIRGINIA	1,860,421 (1960 census)	89,378 [4.8%]	E A	West Virginia Human Rights Commission	Carl W. Glatt	P & G Bldg. 2019 E. Washington St. Charleston 25305 Tel: (304) 348-2616

* This column indicates if state has a law against discrimination in employment (E), private schools and colleges (S), housing not receiving public funds (H), public accommodations (A).

STATE	TOTAL POPULATION	NON-WHITE POPULA-TION*	LAWS*	NAME OF AGENCY	EXECUTIVE OFFICER	ADDRESS AND TELEPHONE
WISCONSIN	4,000,000	117,127 [2.9%]	E H A	Equal Rights Division, Department of Industry, Labor and Human Relations	Clifton H. Lee	4802 Sheboygan Ave. Madison 53702 Tel: (608) 266-3131
WYOMING	318,000	6,900 [2.16%]	E A	Department of Labor and Statistics	Paul H. Bachman	304 State Capitol Bldg. Cheyenne 82001 Tel: (307) 777-7261/7262

* This column indicates if state has a law against discrimination in employment (E), private schools and colleges (S), housing not receiving public funds (H), public accommodations (A).

Appendix III

Civil Rights Chronology from 1954 to 1970

1954

MAY 17

BROWN VS. BOARD OF EDUCATION decision paved the way for school desegregation as Supreme Court unanimously ruled racial segregation in public schools unconstitutional. Decision affected 17 states with compulsory public school segregation. Did not affect "separate but equal" doctrine when applied in other areas and does not apply to private schools.

1955

DEC. 5

MONTGOMERY BUS BOYCOTT began, after Mrs. Rosa Parks, a seamstress, arrested and fined $10 for refusing to give up seat to white person. Dr. Martin Luther King, Jr., then a Montgomery pastor, took over leadership of 381-day boycott, was arrested and his home was bombed. Boycott ended Nov. 1956, when federal court injunction prohibited segregation on buses. King gained national prominence.

1956

FEB. 3

UNIVERSITY OF ALABAMA IN TUSCALOOSA ordered by Supreme Court to admit first Negro student, Autherine Lucy. Students demonstrated. Miss Lucy suspended Feb. 7 for "safety." Ordered reinstated by federal district judge, she was "expelled" Feb. 29 for accusations she had made in court. She made no further attempt to reenter. (University remained segregated until 1963.)

1957
MAY 17
PRAYER PILGRIMAGE to Washington. On steps of Lincoln Memorial, Dr. King delivered first major address, calling for Negro voting rights. "Give us the ballot. . . ."

SEPTEMBER
LITTLE ROCK CENTRAL HIGH. Pres. Eisenhower federalized Arkansas National Guard, and sent in 1,000 paratroopers to restore order and escort nine Negro students to previously all-white high school. Troops remained on call for entire school year. When Supreme Court refused to delay integration, Little Rock schools closed for 1958–59 school year; reopened on desegregated basis.

SEPT. 9
1957 CIVIL RIGHTS ACT signed. First civil rights legislation passed by Congress since Reconstruction. It empowered federal government to seek court injunctions against obstruction or deprivation of voting rights. Act created Civil Rights Commission, and established Civil Rights Division in Department of Justice.

FEB. 1
SIT-IN MOVEMENT began with sit-in at a Woolworth store lunch counter in Greensboro, N.C. and spread rapidly throughout nation. By end of year, many hotels, movie theatres, libraries, supermarkets, and amusement parks had lowered barriers against Negroes.

MAY 6
1960 CIVIL RIGHTS ACT signed, strengthening 1957 act by authorizing judges to appoint "referees" to help Negroes register and vote. The 1960 act also provided criminal penalties for bombings, bomb threats, and mob action designed to obstruct court orders.

NOVEMBER
NEW ORLEANS. Desegregation of two elementary schools led to white boycott, picketing, and violence.

1960
DEC. 5
U.S. SUPREME COURT in a 7–2 decision held that discrimination in bus-terminal restaurants operated primarily for the service of interstate passengers is a violation of the Interstate Commerce Act.

1961

JAN. 10
PEACEFUL GEORGIA DESEGREGATION. First desegregation in public education in Georgia was peaceful, as Negro students Charlayne Hunter and Hamilton Holmes enrolled at University of Georgia in Athens.

MAY 4
FREEDOM RIDES began from Washington, D.C., with New Orleans as goal. Bus stoned and burned in Anniston, Ala., May 14. Riders also attacked in Birmingham May 14, and Montgomery May 20, where riots led to martial law. In Jackson, Miss., riders arrested.

1962

SUMMER
ALBANY, GEORGIA. Several civil rights groups combined to force desegregation of all public facilities, but failed. Division among leaders. Dr. King arrested for "parading without a permit," released after anonymous donor paid fine.

SEPT. 30–OCT. 1
MEREDITH ENTERS "OLE MISS." Two killed, many injured in riots, as 29-year-old air force veteran, James Meredith, enrolled at University of Mississippi, Oxford. Meredith blocked in school doorway by Gov. Ross Barnett. Pres. Kennedy federalized National Guard, sent in army troops. Former Maj. Gen. Edwin A. Walker arrested for "inciting rebellion." Note: Meredith was graduated Aug. 18, 1963.

1963

APR. 23
WHITE POSTMAN SLAIN. White Baltimore postman, William Moore, shot to death on road in northeastern Alabama during walk from Tennessee to Mississippi, carrying sign urging "Equal Rights for All."

APRIL–MAY
BIRMINGHAM MASS DEMONSTRATIONS began Apr. 3. Dr. King and other ministers arrested Apr. 12 by Police Commissioner "Bull" Connor. Fire hoses and police dogs used on marchers, including school children, May 2–7. On May 10, biracial agreement announced to desegregate public accommodations, increase job opportunities, and free those arrested.

MAY 11
BIRMINGHAM NEGROES RIOT after bombs thrown at home of Dr. King's younger brother, Rev. A. D. King, and at King's motel room.

In three-hour riot, houses and stores burned, and police vehicles smashed.

JUNE 11
GOV. WALLACE IN SCHOOLHOUSE DOOR. Alabama Gov. George Wallace carried out 1962 campaign pledge to "stand in the schoolhouse door" to prevent integration of Alabama's schools. Confronted Deputy Attorney General Nicholas Katzenbach and other officials at door of University of Alabama's Foster Hall, where Negro students Vivian Malone and James Hood were to register. Katzenbach brought proclamation from Pres. Kennedy. Wallace read long statement on "oppression of state's rights." But at second confrontation later same day, Wallace withdrew and Negro students registered.

JUNE 12
MEDGAR EVERS MURDERED. NAACP State Chairman Medgar Evers shot to death as he entered his home in Jackson, Miss. Byron de la Beckwith of Greenwood, Miss., charged with the murder, but two trials resulted in mistrials (Feb. 7 and Apr. 17, 1964).

JUNE 14
CAMBRIDGE, MARYLAND. Gov. Tawes called in National Guard after weeks of racial demonstrations and riots. Attorney General Robert Kennedy called both sides to his office for intensive negotiations, and July 23 announced agreement reached on desegregation, low-rent housing, new biracial committee. Oct. 1, Cambridge voters defeated amendment requiring equal accommodations in restaurants and motels.

AUG. 28
MARCH ON WASHINGTON. Largest, most dramatic, and among most peaceful of all civil rights demonstrations. Marchers numbering 250,000, 60,000 of them white, filled the mall from Lincoln Memorial to Washington Monument, and urged support for pending civil rights legislation. Highlighted by Martin Luther King speech: "I have a dream . . ." Chief organizer of march was Bayard Rustin.

SEPT. 15
BIRMINGHAM CHILDREN KILLED. Four girls (ages 11 to 14) were killed, and many other Negro children injured when bomb exploded during Bible class at Birmingham's Sixteenth Street Baptist Church. This was twenty-first bombing incident against Birmingham Negroes in eight years—all "unsolved." Pres. Kennedy (on September 16), expressed Americans' "deep sense of outrage and grief."

1964
JUNE 21
RIGHTS WORKERS MURDERED. Three young civil rights workers, Michael Schwerner and Andrew Goodman, both whites from New

York City, and James Chaney, a Negro from Meridian, Miss., missing while working on summer voter registration project. Search joined by more than 400 servicemen before bodies found August 4 in shallow grave. Fifty FBI agents had also joined the search. Grave was six miles southwest of Philadelphia, Miss. All three had been shot, and Chaney brutally beaten. On Dec. 4, the FBI arrested 21 white men, including sheriff and deputy cheriff of Neshoba County, Miss. on federal charges of conspiracy to violate Civil Rights Code. At preliminary hearing, Dec. 10, charges were dismissed by U.S. Commissioner of the Justice Department Esther Carter, who termed government's evidence "hearsay." (At Meridian, Miss., Oct. 20, 1967, after a new trial, an all-white federal court jury convicted seven on charges of conspiracy to murder, including chief deputy sheriff of Neshoba County, Cecil Price, and Klan imperial wizard, Sam Bowers. Neshoba Sheriff Lawrence Rainey was found not guilty. Convictions described as first-ever for civil rights slayings in Mississippi. Dec. 30, Bowers given maximum ten-year sentence; Price, six years; others three to ten years.)

JULY 2
1964 CIVIL RIGHTS ACT signed by Pres. Johnson. Most far-reaching civil rights legislation since Reconstruction contained new provisions to help guarantee Negroes the right to vote and access to public accommodations such as hotels, motels, restaurants, and places of amusement; authorized the federal government to sue to desegregate public facilities and schools; extended life of Civil Rights Commission and gave it new powers; provided for cut-off of federal funds where programs administered discriminatorily; required most companies and labor unions to grant equal employment opportunity; established Community Relations Service in Department of Justice to help solve rights problems; required Census Bureau to gather voting statistics by race; and authorized justice department to enter into a pending civil rights case. (Senate, for first time in its history, voted to end a filibuster over civil rights.)

JULY 18–23
NEW YORK CITY RIOTS. Rioting in Harlem followed shooting of 15-year-old Negro school boy, James Powell, by off-duty police officer, Lt. Thomas Gilligan, whom boy allegedly attacked with knife. After charges of police brutality at CORE rally July 18, crowd marched on police station, demanding Gilligan's ouster. In subsequent rioting, one Negro killed, 81 civilians and 35 police injured, widespread damage and looting occurred. July 19, battle between Negroes and Puerto Ricans in Brownsville section of Brooklyn. July 20–22, riots in Bedford-Stuyvesant. Acting Mayor Paul Screvane announced July 20 an investigation of Powell death and charges against police; also promised more Negro policemen in Harlem.

JULY 24–26
ROCHESTER, NEW YORK, RIOTS. Gov. Rockefeller mobilized National Guard. Three hundred guardsmen, 200 state troopers sent into city. One white man killed, 300 persons reported injured, including 22 policemen.

JULY 29
CALL FOR MORATORIUM. Expressing concern over "white backlash," leaders of several civil rights organizations called for "broad curtailment, if not total moratorium" on all mass marches, picketing, and other demonstrations until after November 3 presidential election.

AUGUST
OTHER RIOTS: Jersey City, N.J., August 2–4, 56 persons injured including 22 police; Paterson, N.J., August 11–12; Elizabeth, N.J., August 12–13; Dixmoor suburb of Chicago, August 16; Philadelphia, August 28. 28.

SEPT. 14
NEW YORK SCHOOL BUSSING. New York City began controversial program to end segregation by "bussing" pupils of 10 "paired" schools, five mostly Negro, five mostly white. White parent groups organized school boycott, September 14–15.

DEC. 10
1964 NOBEL PEACE PRIZE awarded to Dr. Martin Luther King, Jr., in Oslo, Norway. King became fourteenth American, third Negro, and, at 35 years of age, the youngest person to win the Nobel Peace Prize. Other Negro recipients were: Dr. Ralph Bunche in 1950, and South African Zulu chief, Albert Luthuli, in 1960.

1965

JANUARY–FEBRUARY
SELMA, ALABAMA VOTING DRIVE, led by Dr. King. During height of demonstrations, Feb. 1–4, more than 3,000 arrested, including King. Feb. 4, federal court bans literacy test and other technicalities used against voter applicants. Feb. 9, King met with Pres. Johnson at White House on voting right guarantees.

FEB. 21
MALCOLM X MURDERED. Shot to death at rally of his followers in Audubon Ballroom, New York City, at age 39. Black Muslim headquarters in New York and San Francisco burned. (Mar. 10, 1966, three Negroes—Talmadge Hayer, Norman 3X Butler, and Thomas 15X Johnson—convicted of first degree murder, sentenced to life imprisonment.)

MAR. 11
REV. JAMES REEB DIES after he and two other white Unitarian ministers beaten by white men while assisting Selma vote drive, Mar. 9.

(Three white men indicted for Reeb's murder, Apr. 13; acquitted by Selma jury, Dec. 10.)

MAR. 13
PRES. JOHNSON meets with Gov. Wallace on Selma situation. Mar. 15, president addresses joint session of Congress, appeals for passage of legislation to guarantee voting rights, condemns "crippling legacy of bigotry and injustice." Mar. 17, submits draft voting rights bill.

MAR. 21–25
SELMA-MONTGOMERY MARCH. After two earlier attempts turned back by state troopers, King and Ralph Bunche led 54-mile march to Alabama state capitol, the 300 marchers (limited by agreement) protected by hundreds of army troops and National Guardsmen. In Montgomery, crowd grew to estimated 25,000. Gov. Wallace twice refused to receive delegation, finally did so Mar. 30.

MAR. 25
MRS. VIOLA LIUZZO KILLED. A white civil rights worker from Detroit, who operated auto shuttle-service for the Selma-Montgomery march, shot to death while driving on U.S. Highway 80 near Selma. (See later entries, *re* Collie Leroy Wilkins.)

MAR. 26
PRES. JOHNSON DENOUNCES KKK, announced arrest of four Klan members in connection with Mrs. Liuzzo's murder. (See later entries.)

MAR. 30
HOUSE UN-AMERICAN ACTIVITIES COMMITTEE voted to open full investigation of Klan and its "shocking crimes."

MAY 3
KLANSMAN COLLIE LEROY WILKINS tried for murder of Mrs. Liuzzo. Trial resulted in hung jury. At later trial, Oct. 22, jury acquitted Wilkins. But Dec. 3, Wilkins and two others, Eugene Thomas and William Eaton, were convicted on charges of conspiracy (1870 law) and sentenced to 10 years. Apr. 27, U.S. Court of Appeals upheld convictions. (Meantime, Eaton had died.)

MAY 30
FIRST NEGRO GRADUATES from University of Alabama—Vivian Malone.

JULY 1–22
MARCHES IN BOGALUSA, La., led by James Farmer of CORE. July 19, justice department filed criminal and civil contempt actions against Bogalusa officials. July 22, Gov. McKeithen announced formation of biracial committee.

JULY 13
THURGOOD MARSHALL nominated solicitor general, first Negro to hold the office.

AUG. 6
1965 VOTING RIGHTS ACT signed by Pres. Johnson. Provided for registration by federal examiners of Negro voters turned away by state officials.

AUG. 11–16
WATTS RIOTS. For six days, anarchy raged in black ghetto of Los Angeles, one of the worst riots in the nation's history. Thirty-five dead (28 Negroes), nearly 900 injured, more than 3,500 arrests. More than 12,500 National Guardsmen called in. Entire city blocks burned to the ground, buses and ambulances stoned, snipers fired at policemen, firemen, and airplanes. Damage in millions of dollars.

OCTOBER
"IMPERIAL WIZARD" ROBERT SHELTON refused to answer any questions at House Un-American Activities Committee hearing, invoking his constitutional rights.

1966

JAN. 3
FLOYD McKISSICK succeeded James Farmer as national director of CORE.

JAN. 10
JULIAN BOND, elected to Georgia legislature, denied seat on grounds of disloyalty, for opposing U.S. Vietnam policy.

JAN. 13
ROBERT WEAVER named head of Department of Housing and Urban Development, became first Negro to serve in presidential cabinet.

JAN. 25
CONSTANCE BAKER MOTLEY, former NAACP lawyer and Manhattan borough president, became first Negro woman to be named a federal judge.

MAR. 25
SUPREME COURT BARS POLL TAX for all elections.

MAY 4
MORE THAN 80 PER CENT of Alabama's registered Negroes vote in Democratic primary. Sheriffs James Clark (Selma) and Al Lingo (Birmingham) fail to get renominated.

MAY 16
STOKELY CARMICHAEL named new head of SNCC, replacing John Lewis.

JUNE 6

JAMES MEREDITH shot soon after beginning his 220-mile "march against fear" from Memphis, Tenn. to Jackson, Miss. March then continued by assortment of civil rights groups, and ended June 26 with rally in Jackson addressed by Martin Luther King, Stokely Carmichael, and Meredith himself. During march, about 4,000 Negroes registered.

JUNE 6–26

"BLACK POWER" is first enunciated by Stokely Carmichael during Meredith march. Concept is endorsed by CORE at its national convention (July 1–4), but condemned by King, Wilkins, and other moderates.

JULY 10

KING LAUNCHED CHICAGO DRIVE to make Chicago an "open city," demanding end to discrimination in housing, schools, and employment, and a civilian review board for police. July 12–15, three nights of rioting sweep Chicago's West Side black district, two Negroes killed, scores of police and civilians injured, more than 350 arrests. King met with Mayor Daley, announced four-point agreement to ease tensions in city.

JULY 18–23

HOUGH RIOTS IN CLEVELAND. Four killed, 50 injured as shooting, fire-bombing, and looting sweep black area of Hough, on Cleveland's East Side.

AUG. 5

KING STONED IN CHICAGO as he led march through crowds of angry whites in Gage Park section of Chicago's Southwest Side. A near-riot ensued as whites battled police. King left Chicago August 6.

1967

JANUARY–APRIL

ADAM CLAYTON POWELL OUSTED as chairman of House Education and Labor Committee, Jan. 9, and barred from taking seat in House, Jan. 10, pending "investigation of his qualifications." House committee recommended Feb. 23, that Powell be seated, but with loss of seniority and public censure, by speaker, after finding he "wrongfully and willfully appropriated to his own use" public funds totaling $46,226. Powell assessed to pay House $40,000 at $1,000 a month. On Mar. 1, House voted to exclude Powell from Ninetieth Congress. Powell's suit to reverse House decision was dismissed Apr. 7. Powell reelected in special election Apr. 11, with 86 percent of the vote.

JAN. 12–13

ALABAMA FEDERAL AID CRISIS. Alabama was warned that federal support for welfare programs and public health service would be cut off because of refusal to comply with 1964 Civil Rights Act.

FEB. 15
1967 CIVIL RIGHTS ACT, with "open housing" provision, proposed
by Pres. Johnson in special message to Congress. Bill also aimed at
strengthening laws against interference with federal action, preventing
discrimination in selection of juries, and almost doubling appropria-
tions for Community Relations Service. (Bill not passed in 1967; still
pending at time of Martin Luther King's death, April 4, 1968.)

FEB. 28
RAMSEY CLARK named attorney general at age 39.

MAR. 22
ALABAMA ORDERED TO DESEGREGATE all public schools at
start of fall semester. Federal court order marked first time since 1954
Supreme Court desegregation ruling that entire state was placed under
single injunction to end discrimination.

MAR. 25
KING ATTACKS VIETNAM POLICY. Led Chicago march of 5,000
white and Negro antiwar demonstrators. At Coliseum, King branded
war "a blasphemy against all that America stands for," charged that U.S.
forces "committing atrocities equal to any perpetrated by the Vietcong,"
and war "seeks to perpetrate white colonialism." At New York press
conference, April 4, King calls on young whites and Negroes to boycott the war by declaring themselves to be conscientious objectors.
King position assailed by NAACP and others.

APR. 16
KING WARNS "TEN CITIES WILL EXPLODE." At impromptu
news conference in New York, King warned that at least 10 cities "could
explode in racial violence this summer." Described the cities as "powder
kegs" and said "the intolerable conditions which brought about racial
violence last summer still exist." Cities he named: Cleveland, Chicago,
Los Angeles, Oakland, Calif., Washington, Newark, and New York.
Other cities not named.

MAY 3
ALABAMA STATUTE "UNCONSTITUTIONAL." Alabama stat-
ute countering federal guidelines for school desegregation declared "unconstitutional" by federal court in Montgomery.

MAY 10–11
NEGRO STUDENT RIOT. One Negro killed, two wounded in rioting
on campus of all-Negro Jackson State College, Miss.

MAY 12
H. RAP BROWN succeeded Stokely Carmichael as chairman of SNCC.

MAY 17
RENT SUBSIDIES INCREASE voted down by House, 232 to 171.

MAY 29
CALIFORNIA HOUSING RULING. Supreme Court declared "unconstitutional" the state's voter-approved amendment to constitution which gave property owners "absolute discretion" in resale and rental of housing.

JUNE 2–5
BOSTON (ROXBURY) experienced first large-scale rioting in many years. Over 60 injured, nearly 100 arrested.

JUNE 11–13
TAMPA, FLORIDA RIOT after police killed Negro robbery suspect. At NAACP suggestion, Negro youth patrol replaced National Guard in Negro section, successfully kept order.

JUNE 12
KING CONVICTION UPHELD. Supreme Court upheld contempt-of-court convictions of King and seven other Negro leaders who led 1963 marches in Birmingham, Ala., in defiance of a temporary restraining order. King and aides entered jail October 30 to serve out four-day sentence.

JUNE 12–15
CINCINNATI RIOT. Over 60 injured, 404 arrested.

JUNE 16–17
NEGRO STUDENTS RIOT AT TEXAS STATE UNIVERSITY. One policeman killed, two wounded. One student wounded, 488 students arrested.

JUNE 17
ATLANTA INCIDENTS. Stokely Carmichael provoked police, arrested. Negro youth patrol formed, poverty workers and Mayor Allen active, rioting averted.

JUNE 19
DE FACTO SEGREGATION RULING. Federal judge ordered schools in Washington, D.C., to end de facto segregation by fall semester. Ruling viewed as historic extension of Supreme Court ban on intentional school segregation to include segregation resulting from segregated population patterns.

JUNE 23
KODAK AND "FIGHT" REACHED ACCORD in Rochester, N.Y. Ended bitter six-month struggle between the company and the militant civil rights group ("Freedom, Independence, God, Honor, Today"). Accord provided for cooperation in job training and placement for hard-core unemployed.

JULY 6
MORE THAN 50 PERCENT OF NEGROES REGISTERED. Department of Justice reported that more than 50 percent of all eligible Negro voters were registered in states of Mississippi, Georgia, Alabama, Louisiana, and South Carolina.

JULY 12–17
NEWARK RIOTS. Twenty-three die, 725 injured (revised figures), and more than 1,000 persons arrested in six days of rioting, burning, looting, and street battles. Damage in millions of dollars. Rioting triggered by arrest and rumored death of Negro cab driver John Smith.

JULY 16
MOB KILLS PLAINFIELD POLICEMAN. A white policeman shot and beaten to death by mob of Negro youths in Plainfield, N.J., in racial outbreak which began July 14 and continued for four days of looting and vandalism. National Guard called in.

JULY 20
RAT EXTERMINATION BILL DEFEATED in House, 207 to 176. Pres. Johnson termed action "a cruel blow to the poor children of America."

JULY 20–23
BLACK POWER CONFERENCE IN NEWARK. Largest and most diverse group of American Negro leaders ever assembled. Militant and separatist mood dominated. Press barred.

JULY 23–30
DETROIT RIOTS. Forty-three die, 324 injured (revised figures) in nation's worst riot of the century. Five thousand persons lost homes as fires gutted large parts of city's ghetto areas. Nearly 1,500 separate fires reported. Damage in millions of dollars. July 24, Gov. Romney requested federal troops, and nearly 5,000 paratroopers flown to nearby Selfridge Air Force Base; moved into city July 25. Total of more than 15,000 troops, National Guardsmen, and police on duty. First time in 24 years that U.S. troops used to quell civil strife.

JULY 25
CAMBRIDGE, MARYLAND VIOLENCE, nearly 20 buildings destroyed, mostly in Negro business section. National Guard called in. Outbreak followed speech by H. Rap Brown in which he called on crowd of young Negroes to "burn this town down."

JULY 26
H. RAP BROWN ARRESTED at Washington airport for "inciting to riot."

JULY 26
MODERATE NEGRO LEADERS DEPLORE RIOTS. In a joint statement, four moderate Negro leaders, Martin Luther King, Jr., A. Philip Randolph, Roy Wilkins, and Whitney Young appeal for end to riots which, they say, "have proved ineffective, disruptive, and highly damaging to the Negro population, to the civil rights cause and to the entire nation. . . . Killing, arson and looting are criminal acts and should be dealt with as such. Equally guilty are those who incite, provoke and call specifically for such action."

JULY 27
PRESIDENT APPOINTS RIOT COMMISSION. Gov. Kerner of Illinois named chairman, and Mayor Lindsay of New York vice-chairman of National Advisory Commission on Civil Disorders, "to investigate origins of recent disorders" and make recommendations "to prevent or contain such disorders in the future."

JULY 30
MILWAUKEE RIOTS. Four killed.

OTHER RIOTS DURING JULY. Michigan: Lansing, Kalamazoo, Saginaw, Grand Rapids. *California:* San Francisco, San Bernardino, Long Beach, Fresno, Marin City. *New York:* Rochester, Mt. Vernon, Poughkeepsie, Peekskill, Nyack. *Connecticut:* Hartford. *New Jersey:* Englewood, Paterson, Elizabeth, New Brunswick, Jersey City, Palmyra, Passaic. Also: Philadelphia, Pa.; Providence, R.I.; Phoenix, Ariz.; Portland, Ore.; Wichita, Kan.; South Bend, Ind.; Memphis, Tenn.; and Wilmington, Del.

JULY 31
"URBAN COALITION," organization of business, civic, labor, religious, and civil rights leaders, headed by John Gardner, called on nation to revise priorities, bring more resources to bear on domestic problems.

AUG. 10
MORE NEGROES IN NATIONAL GUARD urged by president's riot commission.

AUG. 14
ANTI-SEMITIC issue of SNCC newsletter caused storm, resignations. Harry Golden resigns from SNCC Aug. 24.

AUG. 28
FATHER GROPPI began series of night marches for open housing in Milwaukee. Led more than 100 marches before sentenced to six-months imprisonment February 13, 1968 for resisting arrest. Sentence stayed for two-year probation, $500 fine.

SEPT. 7
McNAMARA ANNOUNCED that Pentagon would extend campaign to end housing discrimination against Negro servicemen.

OCT. 2
"BIG-BUSINESS" PROGRAM announced by Pres. Johnson to attract firms to build or expand in ghetto communities.

NOV. 2
REPORT ON NEGRO CONDITIONS said more Negroes in middle-income bracket, but living conditions in hard-core city slums unchanged or deteriorating.

DEC. 9
RURAL POVERTY REPORT called widespread rural poverty "acute" and "national disgrace."

1968

JAN. 4
LEROI JONES, Negro poet and playwright, sentenced to two and a half to three years and fined $1,000 for illegal possession of firearms during Newark riots. Jan. 9 granted $25,000 bail, freed. February 7, headed advisory group at ghetto elementary school in Newark.

JAN. 9
ADAM CLAYTON POWELL in Watts declared: "History is going to record that the Second Civil War and the beginning of the black revolution was born here." At UCLA Jan. 10 urged white students to join "black revolution."

BLACK UNITED FRONT formed at secret meeting in Washington, D.C.

JAN. 17
PRES. JOHNSON, in State of Union address, called for programs to train and hire hard-core unemployed, rebuild cities, and immediately build 300,000 housing units for low and middle income families. Jan. 24, sent special message to Congress on civil rights.

JAN. 18
EARTHA KITT OUTBURST at White House meeting of white and Negro women. Miss Kitt told Mrs. Lyndon Johnson that young Negroes rebel and "take pot" because "they're going to be shot and maimed in Vietnam."

FEB. 8
ORANGEBURG, S.C. VIOLENCE. Three Negro youths shot to death, 34 persons wounded in outbreak at South Carolina State College,

Orangeburg, triggered by protest over segregated bowling alley. Alley was desegregated.

FEB. 10
NEW JERSEY RIOT REPORT charged that National Guardsmen and police used "excessive and unjustified force" against Negroes during Newark riots.

FEB. 27
CHARLES EVERS led six white segregationists in special Congressional election, Mississippi's third District. Defeated in run-off.

FEB. 29
PRESIDENT'S NATIONAL ADVISORY COMMISSION ON CIVIL DISORDERS issued report, warning that nation "is moving toward two societies, one black, one white—separate and unequal." Commission called for "massive and sustained commitment to action," recommended sweeping reforms in federal and local law enforcement, welfare, employment, housing, education, and news-reporting. "There can be no higher priority for national action . . ."

MAR. 4
MARTIN LUTHER KING, JR. praised riot commission for "wisdom to perceive the truth and courage to state it," and described report as "a physician's warning of approaching death (of American society) with a prescription to life. The duty of every American is to administer the remedy without regard for the cost and without delay."

MAR. 28
KING led 6,000-strong protest march through downtown Memphis, Tenn., in support of city's striking sanitation workers, mostly Negroes. Disorders broke out, Negro youths looted stores, one 16-year-old Negro killed, 50 persons injured.

APR. 4
KING ASSASSINATED as he stood talking on balcony of his second-floor room at Lorraine Motel in Memphis. Died in St. Joseph's Hospital from gunshot wound in neck.

APR. 5–8
VIOLENCE, LOOTING AND ARSON flared up in Washington, Chicago, Pittsburgh, Baltimore. Rioting in Washington's Negro section worst in capital's history. Four P.M. curfew imposed. More than 9,000 U.S. army troops called in to guard White House, Capitol, etc. Forty-eight hour toll reached eight dead, 987 injured, more than 700 fires, hundreds homeless. Over 4,000 arrests (most for breaking curfew).

APR. 7
NATIONAL DAY OF MOURNING for Dr. Martin Luther King, Jr.

APR. 8
MRS. MARTIN LUTHER KING took husband's place in leading massive, silent, and orderly march through streets of Memphis. Marchers estimated between 20,000 and 40,000 including sympathizers from all parts of nation. At City Hall Plaza, Mrs. King said: "We must carry on" and asked: "How many men must die before we can really have a free and true and peaceful society? How long will it take?"

APR. 9
KING FUNERAL IN ATLANTA

APR. 11
REPORTED FIGURES OF RIOTING aftermath resulting from King's assassination recorded in 125 cities in 28 states. National figures were: 46 dead (mainly blacks); 2,600 injured (half in Washington, D.C. and mainly blacks); 21,270 arrested (mostly for looting); property damage put at $45 million as estimated by insurance companies; 55,000 troops involved (34,000 National Guard, 21,000 federal).

1968 CIVIL RIGHTS ACT prohibiting racial discrimination in the sale or rental of housing passed by Congress. Affects approximately 80 percent of nation's housing.

MAY 11
POOR PEOPLE'S CAMPAIGN, headed by Rev. Ralph Abernathy, Martin Luther King's successor and SCLC president, got underway in Washington, D.C. Purpose of month-long campaign was to pressure Congress and administration for legislation to alleviate poverty. Resurrection City USA, a canvas and plywood encampment built near Lincoln Memorial, housed some 3,000 who participated.

JUNE 5
SENATOR ROBERT KENNEDY SHOT IN LOS ANGELES, after winning California Democratic nomination for president, by Sirhan Bishara Sirhan, a 24-year-old Jordanian Arab. Kennedy died the next day.

JUNE 19
SOLIDARITY DAY MARCH climax of Poor People's Campaign. More than 50,000 marched the mile-long route from Washington Monument to Lincoln Memorial. Half of the participants were white and included Vice-President Hubert Humphrey.

JUNE 24
RESURRECTION CITY CLOSED by Washington police after demonstration permit expired. Abernathy and 300 demonstrators staged march to Capitol and Abernathy sent to jail. Released July 16, an-

nouncing Washington phase of campaign over. Said Congress had "failed to move meaningfully against problems of poverty."

AUG. 6

POOR PEOPLE'S CAMPAIGN moved to Miami Beach, Republican National Convention site, to demonstrate to GOP delegates the aims of campaign against poverty.

1969

MAY 4

JAMES FORMAN, director of Black Economic Development Conference, presented his "Black Manifesto" at New York's Riverside Church. Document set forth demands for $500 million in reparations from white churches and synagogues to be paid to blacks.

JUNE–SEPTEMBER

INTEGRATION OF CONSTRUCTION INDUSTRY. Most vociferous civil rights action of 1969 was aimed at nation's highly paid construction industry whose tightly-knit union organizations continued to resist employment of minorities throughout the 1960's. Cities where important action took place: Chicago, Pittsburgh, Seattle, Buffalo, Detroit, Philadelphia, and New York.

SEPT. 23

THE PHILADELPHIA PLAN, a pilot program setting guidelines for hiring minorities on all federally assisted construction projects in Philadelphia, ordered into effect by Secretary of Labor George P. Schultz. He announced on September 29 that similar plans were to be extended to New York, Boston, Chicago, Detroit, Los Angeles, Pittsburgh, St. Louis, San Francisco, and Seattle. Plan seen as signal that Nixon Administration planned to concentrate its civil rights activity in area of equal job opportunity.

OCT. 30

SUPREME COURT HANDS DOWN UNANIMOUS DECISION ordering that segregation in schools must end "at once." Court replaced its 1954 decision of "all deliberate speed" with the more rigorous standard of immediate compliance. The decision, upheld also by the Fifth Circuit Court of New Orleans, was result of delaying actions in 33 Mississippi school districts.

NOV. 4

CARL STOKES reelected mayor of Cleveland, Ohio.

NOV. 20

ALCATRAZ ISLAND seized by a group of 89 Indians and held by them.

DEC. 4–8
A PRE-DAWN RAID BY CHICAGO POLICE on the apartment of
Fred Hampton, Illinois Panther leader, results in his death, the death of
Panther Mark Clark, and the arrest of seven other Panthers. Four days
later, Los Angeles police raid Panther headquarters there killing three
Panthers and wounding four in a four-hour gun battle. Both incidents
bring cries from concerned citizen groups as well as militants. By the
end of the month, eight official inquiries are instituted to determine if
there is a national conspiracy against Panthers which is out to destroy
their organization, as Panthers claim. Among those investigating other
than governmental, are the all black Ad Hoc Committee of U.S. Congressmen, headed by Rep. Charles Diggs of Michigan, and the Commission of Inquiry into the Black Panthers and Law Enforcement Officials,
headed by Arthur J. Goldberg and Roy Wilkins.

1970

FEB. 2
PRE-TRIAL HEARINGS START IN NEW YORK CITY for 13
Black Panthers charged with conspiring to bomb public places in 1969,
after spending a year in jail because they were unable to post the
$100,000 bail set on them.

MAR. 8
H. RAP BROWN DISAPPEARS the day before his trial is to begin
in Bel Air, Maryland for a 1967 indictment for inciting a riot in Cambridge, Maryland. He was subsequently placed on the F.B.I.'s "ten most
wanted" list.

MAR. 18
STOKELY CARMICHAEL RETURNS TO U.S. saying he intends to
wage "a relentless struggle against the poison of drugs in the black community."

MAR. 21
HIGHEST RANKING BLACK in government, Andrew F. Brimmer,
board member of the Federal Reserve System, criticizes Nixon Administration's approach to black capitalism, saying that although blacks have
made significant progress as a group in 1960's, gains were so unevenly
distributed there was a "deepening schism in the black community."

MAR. 24
PRESIDENT NIXON MAKES A POLICY STATEMENT on school
desegregation, saying the administration would not abandon or under-
mine gains made since 1954 Supreme Court ruling of "separate but
equal." Maintains that while applying all government resources toward
eliminating *de jure* segregation in South's public schools, he could not
require elimination of *de facto* segregation in North or South (resulting

from residential housing patterns), until the courts provided further guidance.

APR. 11

THE COMMISSION ON CIVIL RIGHTS, an independent six-member federal agency, criticizes President Nixon's March 24 statement on school desegregation calling it inadequate, over-cautious and possibly signaling a major retreat on the issue of school integration.

MAY 1–3

A PEACEFUL MAY DAY RALLY is held at Yale University in New Haven in which 12,000 demonstrators, watched over by 2,500 National Guardsmen, massed in support of Black Panthers on trial for the 1969 murder of Alex Rackley. The rally climaxed a week of student protest which caused the closing down of the University and produced the controversial statement by Yale's president, Kingman Brewster, saying "I am skeptical of the ability of black revolutionaries to achieve a fair trial anywhere in the U.S."

MAY 8

SEVEN BLACK PANTHERS FREED of all criminal charges stemming from Chicago shootout (Dec. 1969). According to Illinois State Attorney Edward V. Hanrahan, the methods used to gather evidence might have prevented "our satisfying judicial standards of proof."

MAY 11

SIX NEGRO MEN WERE KILLED in Augusta, Ga. when rioting flared up during a peaceful demonstration by the black community protesting the death of a 16 year-old boy who was murdered in prison.

MAY 15

A STUDENT AT JACKSON STATE COLLEGE in Jackson, Miss., and a high school senior, both blacks, were killed in a barrage of gun fire that riddled a Jackson State College dormitory. The incident reportedly started when bottles and stones were thrown at cars driven by whites. Police claim they fired in response to sniper fire.

MAY 20

A 100-MILE MARCH THROUGH GEORGIA'S BLACK BELT started from Perry to Atlanta. Organized by Southern Christian Leadership Conference and mastermined by Hosea Williams, SCLC vice-president, the purpose was to protest the "growing repressions of blacks and students in the state and the nation."

MAY 22

H. RAP BROWN IN ALGIERS, reports the Washington Star, "according to government sources."

MAY 29
THE CALIFORNIA COURT OF APPEALS REVERSES its 1968 decision which sentenced Huey P. Newton to 2–15 years in prison for a 1967 Oakland shooting. Released Aug. 5th on $50,000 bail.

JUNE 16
KENNETH A. GIBSON, an engineer turned politician, decisively defeated incumbent Hugh J. Addonizio by 11,000 votes in a bitterly fought mayoral runoff-election in Newark, N.J. Gibson became the first black mayor in any major city on the Eastern Seaboard.

JUNE 29
NAACP CHAIRMAN BISHOP SPOTTSWOOD labeled Nixon administration "anti-Negro" in keynote address to NAACP's 61st Annual Convention in Cincinnati.

JUNE 30
WHITE HOUSE RESPONDS TO "ANTI-NEGRO" CHARGE in telegram to NAACP Chairman Spottswood, from Nixon aide Leonard Garment, detailing civil rights achievements and calling charge "unfair" and "disheartening."

JULY 5–8
ASBURY PARK RIOTING. More than 165 injured and 100 arrested in four nights of disturbances in N.J. seaside resort, where black leaders demanded jobs, better housing, youth programs and removal of certain city officials.

JULY 8
PRESIDENT NIXON MEETS INDIAN LEADERS at White House and endorses bill to restore 48,000 acres of New Mexico to the Taos Pueblos, and signs message to Congress urging better health and economic programs for Indians.

JULY 9
SCHOOL DESEGREGATION SUITS brought by Department of Justice against state of Mississippi and school districts in Arkansas, Florida, and South Carolina which had failed to produce acceptable desegregation plans.

PHILADELPHIA CONTRACTORS who failed to hire sufficient blacks under the Philadelphia Plan receive show-cause orders in administration's "first overt enforcement action" to ensure compliance with the plan, which set minority hiring standards as condition of federal contracts.

JULY 10
SEGREGATED PRIVATE SCHOOLS warned by Internal Revenue Commissioner Randolph Thrower that their tax-exempt status would be revoked. Move seen aimed particularly at many new private schools established in South to evade public school desegregation.

JULY 13
POLITICAL ANALYST SAMUEL LUBELL, in new book, *The Hidden Crisis in American Politics,* says "Polarization of racial feeling has become probably the strongest political force agitating New York City's voters."

BLACK ACADEMY OF ARTS AND LETTERS institutes a black "Hall of Fame," naming as first members the late W. E. B. DuBois, historian Carter G. Woodson, and artist Henry O. Tanner.

JULY 15
U.S. SENATE BACKS ALASKAN NATIVES. In overwhelming vote, 76–8, U.S. Senate passed bill granting Alaskan natives ten million acres and one billion dollars cash compensation in settlement of century-old claims. Bill would establish Alaska Native Commission and two native corporations to handle economic and social services.

FIRST BLACK MAYOR OF DAYTON, OHIO. City commissioner James Howell McGee appointed first black mayor of Dayton, Ohio following resignation of previous mayor. Born in West Virginia, November 8, 1918, McGee graduated from Ohio State law school and became known as a militant civil rights lawyer. Married, two daughters.

JULY 17
SENATOR STROM THURMOND (R–SC) denounces Nixon administration's school desegregation policies as "breach of faith" which "could cost the President reelection in 1972."

JULY 19
BLACK COALITION URGED by Whitney M. Young, Jr., executive director, at National Urban League's 60th Annual Convention in New York. Young denies Nixon administration is anti-black, as charged at NAACP convention, and says a coalition of black forces could more effectively negotiate with the government.

JULY 20
NATIONAL URBAN COALITION announces 2.9 million dollar project to help black contractors compete for large construction jobs in big cities.

JULY 29
MAJORITY OF GRAPE GROWERS in California (65%) sign with Cesar Chavez's farm workers union, making it the first successful union in the history of agriculture.

AUG. 1970
CHICAGO BLACKS DISILLUSIONED. Chicago black coalition is reported breaking up, due in part to, disappointment over job program which had provided only 75 instead of promised 4000 openings accord-

ing to *Washington Post*. Gang violence resumed. To protect black community from gangs, Rev. Jesse Jackson forms new group called Black Men Moving, headed by Rev. John Barber.

AUG. 8
ROBERT J. BROWN, only black aide in White House, praises Nixon policies against critics such as NAACP Chairman Bishop G. Spottswood saying that the President was "becoming much more sensitive to the problems of blacks."

AUG. 15
ANGELA DAVIS, controversial assistant professor of philosophy at U.C.L.A. who was dismissed on June 19 from her $10,000 a-year faculty post by California's Board of Regents for membership in the Communist Party (Miss Davis claimed it was because of her race), was sought in the August 7 shootout at Marin County courthouse in which 4 were killed including a judge. Local authorities claimed they had evidence that 3 guns used in the killing belonged to Miss Davis. Panther leader, Huey Newton, recently released from jail, called the incident "more significant than either Watts or Detriot."

AUG. 18
PANTHER   MINISTER   OF   INFORMATION,   ELDRIDGE CLEAVER, arrives in Hanoi with Panther delegation for "Solidarity Day" between North Vietnam and American blacks.

SEPT. 3–7
CONGRESS OF AFRICAN PEOPLE in Atlanta, Georgia. Goals include plans to build black institutions at local, national and international levels and "to help eliminate oppression of black people everywhere." Chairman of Coordinating Committee is Haywood Henry of Harvard University.

Appendix IV

Leading Black Elected Officials by State, as of June 1970

ALABAMA

Johnnie Gay, Mayor of Allport
Moses Johnson, Mayor of Reed
Charles Kelley, Mayor of Dumas
Frank Smith, Mayor of Menifee

ALASKA

Joshua J. Wright, School Board Member, Anchorage

ARIZONA

Cloves Campbell, State Senator
Ethel Maynard, State Representative
Leon Thompson, State Representative

ARKANSAS

Clyde Foster, Mayor of Madison
Fred Grey, State Representative
Edgar Lawrence, Mayor of Attalla
Freddie C. Rogers, Mayor of Roosevelt City
J. R. Striplin, Mayor of Anniston (Hobson City)

CALIFORNIA

Yvonne Brathwaite, State Assemblywoman
Willie L. Brown, State Assemblyman
Ronald Dellums, U.S. Congressman
Douglas Dollarhide, Mayor of Compton
Mervin M. Dymally, State Senator

Bill Greene, State Assemblyman
Ben Gross, Vice-Mayor and Councilman of Milpitas
Augustus F. Hawkins, U.S. Congressman (see Hawkins entry)
George Livingston, Mayor of Richmond
John J. Miller, State Assemblyman
Leon Ralph, State Assemblyman
Herbert White, Mayor of Pittsburg

COLORADO

George Brown, State Senator
Paul L. Hamilton, State Representative
Jerome C. Rose, State Representative

CONNECTICUT

Boce W. Barlow, Jr., State Senator
Otha Nathaniel Brown, Jr., State Representative and Majority Leader
Leonard G. Frazier, State Representative
Gerald A. Lamb, State Treasurer
Lorenzo Morgan, State Representative
Bruce L. Morris, State Representative

DELAWARE

Charles E. Butcher, State Representative
Oliver Fonville, State Representative
Herman Holloway, Sr., State Senator

DISTRICT OF COLUMBIA

Anita Ford Allen, President of School Board

FLORIDA

Joe Lan Kershaw, State Representative
E. Hilton Knowles, Vice-Mayor of Deerfield Beach
Nathaniel Vereen, Mayor of Eatonville

GEORGIA

William H. Alexander, State Representative

Julian Bond, State Representative (see Bond entry)
Benjamin D. Brown, State Representative
Julius C. Daugherty, State Representative
James E. Dean, State Representative
Richard A. Dent, State Representative
Clarence G. Ezzard, State Representative
Grace T. Hamilton, State Representative
Bobby L. Hill, State Representative
John Hood, State Representative
Maynard Jackson, Vice-Mayor of Atlanta (see Maynard Jackson entry)
Leroy Johnson, State Senator
E. J. Shepherd, State Representative
Albert W. Thompson, State Representative
Horace T. Ward, State Senator

HAWAII

Charles M. Campbell, Councilman-at-Large in Honolulu

ILLINOIS

Lewis A. Caldwell, State Representative
James Y. Carter, State Representative
Charles Chew, Jr., State Senator
Otis G. Collins, State Representative
Corneal A. Davis, State Representative
William Dawson, U.S. Congressman (see Dawson entry)
Raymond W. Ewell, State Representative
J. Horace Gardner, State Representative
Elwood Graham, State Representative
Kenneth Hall, State Representative
James E. McLendon, State Representative
Richard H. Newhouse, State Senator
Cecil A. Partee, State Senator
Isaac R. Sims, State Representative
Fred J. Smith, State Senator
Marian F. Smith, Mayor of Robbins

James C. Taylor, State Representative
Robert L. Thompson, State Representative
Genoa Washington, State Representative
Harold Washington, State Representative

INDIANA

Harriet B. Conn, State Representative
Ray P. Crowe, State Representative
Choice Edward, State Representative
Richard C. Hatcher, Mayor of Gary
(*see* Hatcher entry)

IOWA

A. June Franklin, State Representative

KANSAS

James P. Davis, State Representative
Clarence C. Love, State Representative
Billy Q. McCray, State Representative
A. Price Woodward, Mayor of Wichita

KENTUCKY

Georgia M. Davis, State Senator
Mae Street Kidd, State Representative
Hughes E. McGill, State Representative
Luska J. Twyman, Mayor of Glasgow

LOUISIANA

John Bobb, Jr., Mayor of Grand Coteau
Harry Minns, Mayor of East Hodge
Ernest N. Morial, State Representative
B. T. Woodward, Mayor of Grambling

MARYLAND

Floyd B. Adams, State Delegate
Aris T. Allen, State Delegate
Troy Brailey, State Delegate

Lawrence Brooks, Mayor of Fairmount Heights
Joseph A. Chester, State Delegate
Isaiah Dixon, Jr., State Delegate
Calvin A. Douglas, State Delegate
Bessie H. Johnson, Mayor of Highland Beach
Arthur King, State Delegate
Lena K. Lee, State Delegate
Charles McGee, Mayor of Seat Pleasant
Clarence Mitchell, III, State Senator
(*see* Mitchell entry)
Lloyal Randolph, State Delegate
Decatur Trotter, Jr., Mayor of Glenarden
Verda F. Welcome, State Senator

MASSACHUSETTS

Edward Brooke, U.S. Senator (*see* Brooke entry)
Franklin W. Holgate, State Representative
George A. Johnson, State Representative

MICHIGAN

Robert B. Blackwell, Mayor of Highland Park
James Bradley, State Representative
Basil Brown, State Senator
Arthur Cartwright, State Senator
John Conyers, U.S. Congressman (*see* Conyers entry)
James Del Rio, State Representative
Charles Diggs, Jr., U.S. Congressman (*see* Diggs entry)
George H. Edwards, State Representative
Daisy Elliott, State Representative
Rosetta Ferguson, State Representative
David S. Holmes, Jr., State Representative
Raymond W. Hood, State Representative
Matthew McNeeley, State Representative

Clarence B. Sabbath, Mayor Pro Tem of River Rouge

Nelis J. Saunders, State Representative

Jackie Vaughn, II, State Representative

Coleman A. Young, State Senator

MINNESOTA

Stephen Maxwell, District Court Judge, St. Paul

MISSISSIPPI

Robert G. Clark, State Representative

Charles Evers, Mayor of Fayette (*see* Evers entry)

Moses Lewis, Sr., Mayor of Winstonville

Earl Lucas, Mayor of Mound Bayou

MISSOURI

Johnny S. Aikens, State Representative

J. B. Banks, State Representative

Deverne L. Calloway, State Representative

William L. Clay, U.S. Congressman (*see* Clay entry)

Russell Goward, State Representative

Harold L. Holliday, State Representative

Raymond Howard, State Senator

Travis B. Howard, Mayor of Howardville

Herman A. Johnson, State Representative

Leon J. Jordan, State Representative

Theodore D. McNeal, State Senator

Leroy Malcolm, State Representative

Robert Metcalf, Mayor of Kinloch

Franklin Payne, State Representative

Nathaniel J. Rivers, State Representative

Henry C. Ross, State Representative

James T. Troupe, State Representative

Fred Williams, State Representative

NEBRASKA

Damion Lacroix, School Board Member, Omaha

E. T. Streeter, School Board Member, Omaha

NEVADA

Woodrow Wilson, State Assemblyman

NEW JERSEY

Matthew G. Carter, Mayor of Montclair

Frank Cornwall, State Assemblyman

Kennth A. Gibson, Mayor of Newark (*see* Gibson entry)

William S. Hart, Mayor of East Orange

Hilliard R. Moore, Mayor of Lawnside

Ronald Owens, State Assemblyman

George C. Richardson, State Assemblyman

S. Howard Woodson, Jr., State Assemblyman

NEW MEXICO

Lenton Malry, State Representative

NEW YORK

Betram L. Baker, State Assemblyman

Guy Brewer, State Assemblyman

Shirley Chisholm, U.S. Congresswoman (*see* Chisholm entry)

Edward R. Dudley, State Supreme Court Judge

Arthur O. Eve, State Assemblyman

Thomas R. Fortune, State Assemblyman

Basil A. Paterson, State Senator (*see* Paterson entry)

Adam Clayton Powell, U.S. Congressman (*see* Powell entry)

Charles Rangel, State Assemblyman (*see* Rangell entry)

Mark T. Southall, State Assemblyman

Waldaba Stewart, State Senator

Percy Sutton, Manhattan Borough President (*see* Sutton entry)

Samuel D. Wright, State Assemblyman

NORTH CAROLINA

Alex Brown, Mayor of Greenevers

Felton J. Capel, Mayor Pro Tem and Treasurer of Southern Pince

Henry E. Frye, State Representative

Theboud Jeffers, Mayor Pro Tem of Gastonia

Howard Lee, Mayor of Chapel Hill

W. Raymond Mallewson, Mayor of Tarboro

OHIO

David D. Albritton, State Representative

John W. E. Bowen, State Senator

William F. Bowen, State Representative

Phillip M. DeLaine, State Representative

Phale D. Hale, State Representative

James T. Henry, Sr., Mayor of Xenia

Thomas E. Hill, State Representative

M. Morris Jackson, State Senator

Troy Lee James, State Representative

Calvin C. Johnson, State Senator

Casey Jones, State Representative

James Howell McGee, Mayor of Dayton

C. J. McLin, Jr., State Representative

William Mallory, State Representative

Samuel S. Perry, Mayor of Woodmere Village (Cleveland)

Larry G. Smith, State Representative

Carl B. Stokes, Mayor of Cleveland (*see* Carl B. Stokes entry)

Louis Stokes, U.S. Congressman (*see* Louis Stokes entry)

Penn Zeigler, Mayor of Lincoln Heights

OKLAHOMA

Hannah D. Atkins, State Representative

Duncan Carl, Mayor of Taft

Archibald B. Hill, Jr., State Representative

Ben H. Hill, State Representative

A. Visanio Johnson, State Representative

E. Melvin Porter, State Senator

Sam Wilcot, Mayor of Boley

PENNSYLVANIA

Sarah A. Anderson, State Representative

Herbert Arlene, State Senator

James D. Barber, State Representative

Freeman Hawkins, State Senator

K. Leroy Irvis, State Representative and Majority Leader

Joel M. Johnson, State Representative

Theodore Johnson, State Representative

Paul M. Lawson, State Representative

Mitchell W. Melton, State Representative

Robert N. C. Nix, U.S. Congressman (*see* Nix entry)

Ulysses Shelton, State Representative

Earl Vann, State Representative

RHODE ISLAND

Peter J. Coelho, State Representative

SOUTH CAROLINA

Charles H. Ross, Mayor of Summerville

Mildren Rucker, Mayor of Windy Hill Beach

TENNESSEE

M. G. Blakemore, State Representative

Robert J. Booker, State Representative

Alvin King, State Representative

Harold M. Love, State Representative

Ira H. Murphy, State Representative

J. O. Patterson, Jr., State Senator

James I. Taylor, State Representative

Avon N. Williams, Jr., State Senator

TEXAS

Curtis M. Graves, State Representative
Zan Wesley Holmes, Jr., State Representative
Alfred Jones, Mayor of Easton
Barbara Jordan, State Senator

VIRGINIA

William Ferguson Reid, State Delegate
Arthur Robinson, Jr., State Delegate
William Robinson, State Delegate
Lawrence D. Wilder, State Senator

WASHINGTON

George Fleming, State Representative

WEST VIRGINIA

S. J. Baskerville, School Board Member, Charleston

WISCONSIN

Lloyd Barbee, State Assemblyman

WYOMING

Rogers Wise, School Board Member, Cheyenne

Black Elected Officials in United States

	TOTAL	U.S. CONGRESS	STATE SENATORS	STATE REPRESENTATIVES	STATE OTHERS	COUNTY COMMISSIONERS, SUPERVISORS	COUNTY ELECTION COMMISSIONERS	COUNTY OTHERS	CITY MAYORS	CITY COUNCILMEN ALDERMEN	CITY OTHERS	LAW JUDGES, MAGISTRATES	LAW CONSTABLES MARSHALS	LAW JUSTICES OF PEACE	LAW OTHERS	SCHOOL BOARD
ALABAMA	89			1		4		4	4	38	2		9	19		8
ALASKA	1															1
ARIZONA	7		1	2												4
ARKANSAS	56								4	9	1			4		38
CALIFORNIA	109	2	1	5		1			3	27	1	14				55
COLORADO	7		1	2						2		1				1
CONNECTICUT	46		1	4						23	1		5			11
DELAWARE	9		1	2		1				4						1
DISTRICT OF COLUMBIA	8															8
FLORIDA	38			1		1			2	30	1		2			1
GEORGIA	39		2	12		3			1	14		1				6
HAWAII	1									1						
ILLINOIS	77	1	4	14					1	21	2	9				25
INDIANA	31			3		2		1	1	8	2	2		1		11
IOWA	5			1								2				2
KANSAS	6			3		1			1							1
KENTUCKY	41		1	2		1			1	22		4	4			6
LOUISIANA	66			1		5			3	29			13	7		8
MARYLAND	44		2	9					5	24		4				
MASSACHUSETTS	8	1*		2						2						3
MICHIGAN	110	2	3	10		25		2	2	22		11	1			32
MINNESOTA	8			1								1	2			4
MISSISSIPPI	84			1		4	16	1	3	33			8	10	1	5
MISSOURI	65	1	2	13					2	23	4	5	1		1	13
NEBRASKA	2															2
NEVADA	3			1						1		1				
NEW JERSEY	79			4		3		1	4	38	1					20
NEW MEXICO	3			1						2						
NEW YORK	121	2	3	9		4				10	2	20				71
NORTH CAROLINA	68			1		1			5	47		1				13
OHIO	89	1	3	10		1			4	40	3	11	1			15
OKLAHOMA	36		1	4					2	10						19
PENNSYLVANIA	57	1	2	9				1		13	1	17	4			9
RHODE ISLAND	2			1						1						
SOUTH CAROLINA	42					2			2	29	1	4				4
TENNESSEE	39		2	6						9		12	3	1	2	4
TEXAS	30		1	2					1	15						11
VIRGINIA	45		1	2		4		1		31				6		
WASHINGTON	4			1						1		2				
WEST VIRGINIA	1															1
WISCONSIN	10			1		2				6						1
WYOMING	1															1
TOTALS	1581	11	32	141	0	65	16	11	51	585	23	123	47	57	4	423

*U.S. Senator

June 19, 1970

Note: Nine states have no black elected officials: Idaho, Maine, Montana, New Hampshire, North Dakota, Oregon, South Dakota, Utah and Vermont.

The MARC Corporation   1819 H St., N.W.   Washington, D.C. 20006

*Bibliography &
Index*

Bibliography

NOTE: The following is a selection of books thought by the editors to be of particular importance in gaining a wider understanding of the struggle for equal rights by minority groups, especially over the last fifteen years.

Allport, Gordon W., *The Nature of Prejudice*. Reading, Mass., Addison-Wesley, 1954.

Altshuler, Alan A., *Community Control*. New York, Pegasus, 1970.

Anthony, Earl, *Picking Up the Gun: A Report on the Black Panthers*. New York, Dial Press, 1970.

Banfield, Edward, *The Unheavenly City*. Boston, Little, Brown & Co., 1970.

Baldwin, James, *The Fire Next Time*. New York, Dial Press, 1963.

Barbour, Floyd B., ed., *The Black Power Revolt*. New York, Collier Books, 1969.

Bayley, David H., and Mendelsohn, Harold, *Minorities and the Police*. New York, Free Press, 1969.

Bennett, Lerone, Jr., *Confrontation: Black and White*. Chicago, Johnson Publishing Co., 1965.

Berry, Brewton, *Almost White*. New York, Macmillan Co., 1969.

Berube, Maurice, and Gittell, Marilyn, eds., *Confrontation at Ocean Hill Brownsville: The New York School Strikes of 1968*. New York, Praeger, 1969.

Blaustein, Albert P., and Zangrando, Robert, eds., *Civil Rights and the American Negro*. New York, Washington Square Press, 1968.

Bosmajian, Haig A., and Hamida, *The Rhetoric of the Civil Rights Movement*. New York, Random House, 1969.

Boulware, Marcus H., *The Oratory of Negro Leaders: 1900–1968*. Westport, Conn., Negro Univ. Press, 1969.

Bracey, John H., Jr., et al., eds., *Black Nationalism in America*. Indianapolis, Bobbs-Merrill Co., 1970.

Brazier, Arthur M., *Black Self-Determination: The Story of the Woodlawn Organization*. Grand Rapids, Mich., William B. Eerdmans Publishing Co., 1969.

Broderick, Francis L., and Meier, August, eds., *Negro Protest Thought in the Twentieth Century*. Indianapolis, Bobbs-Merrill Co., 1966.

Brown, H. Rap, *Die Nigger Die*. New York, Dial Press, 1969.

Bullock, Paul, ed., *Watts: The Aftermath*. New York, Grove Press, 1970.

Cahn, E. S., ed., *Our Brother's Keeper: The Indian in White America*. Cleveland, World Publishing Co., 1969.

Carmichael, Stokely, and Hamilton, Charles V., *Black Power: The Politics of Liberation in America*. New York, Random House, 1967.

Carson, Josephine, *Silent Voices: The Southern Negro Woman Today*. New York, Delacorte Press, 1969.

Chase, William M., and Collier, Peter, eds., *Justice Denied: The Black Man in White America*. New York, Harcourt, Brace & World, 1970.

Clark, Kenneth B., *Dark Ghetto*. New York, Harper & Row, 1965.

Clark, John Hendrik, *Malcolm X: The Man and His Time*. New York, Macmillan, 1969.

Cleaver, Eldridge, *Post-Prison Writings and Speeches*. New York, Random House, 1969.

Cleaver, Eldridge, *Soul on Ice*. New York, McGraw-Hill, 1968.

Connery, Robert H., ed., *Urban Riots: Violence and Social Change*. New York, Random House, 1969.

Cruse, Harold, *Rebellion or Revolution?* New York, Apollo Editions, 1969.

Cruse, Harold, *The Crisis of the Negro Intellectual*. New York, Apollo Editions, 1968.

Daniels, Roger, *The Politics of Prejudice*. New York, Atheneum, 1969.

Daniels, Roger, and Kitano, Harry H., *American Racism*. Englewood Cliffs, N.J., Prentice-Hall, 1970.

Deloria, Vine, Jr., *Custer Died for Your Sins: An Indian Manifesto*. New York, Macmillan Co., 1969.

Drake, St. Clair, and Cayton, Horace R., *Black Metropolis: A Study of Negro Life in a Northern City*. New York, Harcourt, Brace & World, 1970.

Dunne, John G., *Delano: The Story of the California Grape Strike*. New York, Farrar, Straus & Giroux, 1967.

Edwards, Henry, *The Revolt of the Black Athlete*. New York, Free Press, 1969.

Eichelberger, William L., *Reality in Black and White*. Philadelphia, Westminster, 1969.

Essien-Udom, Essien Udosen, *Black Nationalism: A Search for Identity in America*. Chicago, Univ. of Chicago Press, 1962.

Fager, Charles, *Uncertain Resurrection: The Poor People's Washington Campaign*. Grand Rapids, Mich., William B. Eerdmans Publishing Co., 1969.

Fager, Charles, *White Reflections on Black Power*. Grand Rapids, Mich., William B. Eerdmans Publishing Co., 1967.

Fanon, Frantz, *Black Skin, White Masks*. New York, Grove Press, 1967.

Fanon, Frantz, *The Wretched of the Earth*. New York, Grove Press, 1965.

Fisher, Sethard, ed., *Power and the Black Community*. New York, Random House, 1970.

Franklin, John Hope, *Color and Race*. Boston, Beacon Press, 1969.

Franklin, John Hope, and Starr, Isidore, eds., *The Negro in Twentieth Century America: A Reader on the Struggle for Civil Rights*. New York, Random House, 1967.

Ginzberg, Eli, *The Troublesome Presence*. New York, Free Press, 1964.

Glock, Charles Y., and Siegleman, Ellen, eds., *Prejudice, U.S.A.* New York, Praeger, 1969.

Good, Paul, *The American Serfs.* New York, Ballantine, 1969.

Goro, Herb, *The Block.* New York, Random House, 1970.

Grant, Joan, *Black Protest.* New York, St. Martin's Press, 1970.

Hale, Frank W., ed., *The Cry for Freedom.* Cranbury, N.J., A. S. Barnes, 1970.

Hayden, Thomas, *Rebellion in Newark: Official Violence and Ghetto Response.* New York, Random House, 1967.

Herndon, James, *The Way It Spozed to Be.* New York, Simon & Schuster, 1968.

Hilton, Bruce, *The Delta Ministry.* New York, Macmillan Co., 1969.

Hines, Paul D., *A Guide to Human Rights Education.* Washington, D.C., Natl. Council for the Social Studies, 1969.

Holloway, Harry, *The Politics of the Southern Negro.* New York, Random House, 1969.

Hosokawa, Bill, *Nisei: The Quiet Americans.* New York, Morrow, 1969.

Howell, Leon, *Freedom City: The Substance of Things Hoped For.* Richmond, John Knox Press, 1969.

Jordan, Winthrop D., ed., *The Negro Versus Equality.* Chicago, Rand McNally Co., 1969.

Keech, William R., *The Impact of Negro Voting.* Chicago, Rand McNally Co., 1970.

Killens, John O., *Black Man's Burden.* New York, Simon & Schuster, 1970.

Killian, Lewis M., *The Impossible Revolution?* New York, Random House, 1968.

King, Coretta Scott, *My Life with Martin Luther King, Jr.* New York, Holt, Rinehart & Winston, 1969.

King, Martin Luther, Jr., *Where Do We Go from Here: Chaos or Community?* New York, Harper & Row, 1967.

Knowles, Louis L., and Prewitt, Kenneth, eds., *Institutional Racism in America.* Englewood Cliffs, N.J., Prentice-Hall, 1970.

Kohl, Herbert R., *Thirty-Six Children.* New York, New American Library, 1968.

Kozol, Jonathan, *Death at an Early Age.* Boston, Houghton Mifflin Co., 1967.

Kvaraceus, William C., et al., *Negro Self-Concept: Implications for Schools and Citizenship.* New York, McGraw-Hill Book Co., 1965.

Leinwand, Gerard, ed., *Civil Rights and Civil Liberties.* New York, Washington Square Press, 1969.

Leinwand, Gerard, ed., *The Negro in the City.* New York, Washington Square Press, 1969.

Lester, Julius, *Look Out Whitey! Black Power's Gon' Get Your Momma!* New York, Dial Press, 1968.

Lipsky, Michael, *Protest in City Politics: Rent Strikes, Housing, and the Power of the Poor.* Chicago, Rand McNally Co., 1970.

Lomax, Louis, *The Negro Revolt.* New York, Harper & Row, 1962.

Mack, R., *Race, Class, and Power.* New York, American Book Co., 1968.

Malcolm X, *The Speeches of Malcolm X at Harvard.* New York, William Morrow Co., 1968.

Malcolm X, and Haley, Alex, *The Autobiography of Malcolm X.* New York, Grove Press, 1966.

Marden, Charles F., and Meyer, Gladys, *Minorities in American Society.* New York, American Book Co., 1968.

Marx, Gary T., *Protest and Prejudice.* New York, Harper & Row, 1969.

Matthiessen, Peter, *Sal Si Puedes: Cesar Chavez and the New American Revolution.* New York, Random House, 1969.

McClellan, Grand S., *Civil Rights.* New York, H. W. Wilson Co., 1964.

McCord, John H., ed., *With All Deliberate Speed: Civil Rights Theory and Reality.* Urbana, Ill., Univ. of Illinois Press, 1969.

McKissick, Floyd, *Three-Fifths of a Man.* New York, Macmillan Co., 1969.

McWilliams, Carey, *North from Mexico.* Westport, Conn., Greenwood Press, 1967.

Meier, August, and Rudwick, Elliott, eds., *The Making of Black America.* New York, Atheneum, 1969.

Muse, Benjamin, *The American Negro Revolution.* New York, Citadel Press, 1970.

Nabokov, Peter, *Tijerina and the Courthouse Raid.* Albuquerque, Univ. of New Mexico Press, 1969.

Oppenheimer, Martin, *The Urban Guerrilla.* Chicago, Quadrangle Books, 1969.

Osofsky, Gilbert, *Harlem: The Making of a Ghetto.* New York, Harper & Row, 1966.

Robinson, Armstead L., et al., eds., *Black Studies in the University.* New York, Bantam, 1969.

Rose, Peter I., *They and We: Racial and Ethnic Relations in the United States.* New York, Random House, 1964.

Samora, Julian, ed., *La Raza: Forgotten Americans.* Notre Dame, Ind., Univ. of Notre Dame Press, 1966.

Schuchter, Arnold, *White Power; Black Freedom.* Boston, Beacon Press, 1968.

Scott, Benjamin, *The Coming of the Black Man.* Boston, Beacon Press, 1969.

Scott, Robert L., and Brockriede, Wayne, *The Rhetoric of Black Power.* New York, Harper & Row, 1969.

Seale, Bobby, *Seize the Time.* New York, Random House, 1970.

Silberman, Charles E., *Crisis in Black and White.* New York, Random House, 1964.

Skolnick, Jerome H., et al., eds., *The Politics of Protest.* New York, Simon & Schuster, 1969.

Steiner, Gilbert Y., *Social Insecurity: The Politics of Welfare.* Chicago, Rand McNally Co., 1970.

Steiner, Stanley, *The New Indians.* New York, Dell Publishing Co., 1969.

Storing, Herbert J., ed., *What Country Have I? Political Writings by Black Americans.* New York, St. Martin's Press, 1970.

Sugarman, Tracy, *Stranger at the Gates: A Summer in Mississippi.* New York, Hill & Wang, 1967.

Szwed, John F., *Black America.* New York, Basic Books, 1970.

Vivian, C. T., *Black Power and the American Myth.* Philadelphia, Fortress Press, 1970.

Wagstaff, Thomas, ed., *Black Power: The Radical Response to White America.* Beverly Hills, Calif., Glencoe Press, 1969.

Watters, Pat, *The South and the Nation.* New York, Pantheon, 1969.

Watters, Pat, and Cleghorn, Resse, *Climbing Jacob's Ladder: The Arrival of Negroes in Southern Politics.* New York, Harcourt, Brace & World, 1970.

Weinstein, Allen, and Gatell, Frank O., eds., *The Segregation Era, 1863-1954: A Modern Reader.* New York, Oxford Univ. Press, 1970.

Woodward, C. Vann, *The Strange Career of Jim Crow.* New York, Oxford Univ. Press, 1966.

Wright, Nathan, *Black Power and Urban Unrest.* New York, Hawthorn Books, 1967.

Young, Whitney M., Jr., *Beyond Racism.* New York, McGraw-Hill, 1969.

Index

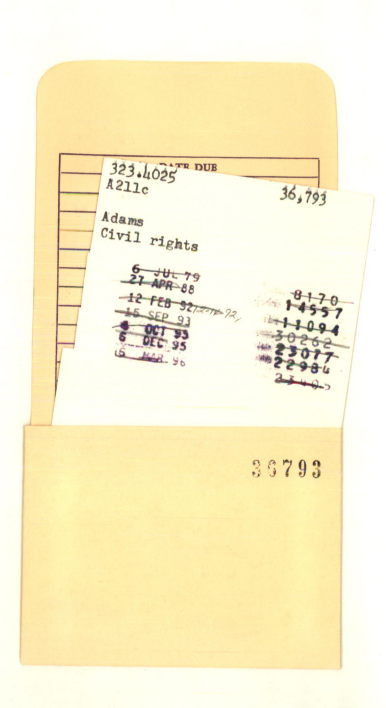